a STRONG HEART

— AN AUTOBIOGRAPHY IN PROGRESS —

SAKIB AWAN

LONGUEVILLE
MEDIA

LONGUEVILLE
MEDIA

First published 2021 for Sakib Awan
by
Longueville Media Pty Ltd
PO Box 205 Haberfield NSW 2045
www.longmedia.com.au
info@longmedia.com.au

Copyright © Sakib Awan 2021

All rights reserved. No part of this publication may be reproduced or transmitted in any form or by any means, electronic or mechanical, including photocopying, recording or by any information storage and retrieval system, without the prior permission in writing from the author and copyright holders.

Cover design: nina nielsen

Print ISBN: 978-0-6486978-7-9
eBook ISBN: 978-0-6486978-8-6
POD ISBN: 978-0-6486978-1-7

A catalogue record for this book is available from the National Library of Australia

To Neelo, Zeenat, Saba, and Ismat

Acknowledgements

There are a great many people I wish to thank for their help while I wrote the story of my life, but none more so than my ever-loving, ever-patient wife, Neelo. Thank you. We have been through many years and adventures together in life, business, and family. And we have survived and thrived as we embarked on each of those adventures. Thank you also to Zeenat, Saba, and Ismat, my daughters, for your assistance and for the time you have given to remind me of stories and anecdotes – and to learn about new aspects of your father's life you never knew! I hope this book will stand as a record of our family for you, your children – my grandchildren – and future generations of our family, wherever they might settle.

Mrs Norma Grant, you have been a rock to our family over the many years since we first met in Darwin. Your invaluable suggestions on this manuscript lent an important perspective to our lives and I thank you from the bottom of my heart for your input. To my publisher at Longueville Media, David Longfield, thank you for your patience, guidance, assistance in editing, and your in-depth research to ensure nothing fell through the cracks. It has been an enormous pleasure working with you on this project. There will be many more stories.

To our East Timor Trading Group family in Timor-Leste: a key intention of writing my story was that it might inspire others who have the opportunity to build lives, whether in new countries as Neelo and I have, or in a developing nation like Timor-Leste. You are a dedicated and talented group of men and women who have great opportunities in a still-young country. I have no doubt many of you will seize those opportunities and become leaders in your communities, in business, or in both. Although I am no longer with you in Díli, I watch with great anticipation.

To Shane Stone, you recognised potential in Neelo and me in the early days of our business life in Australia, at a time when others did not.

Thank you for your vision and decades of support during our formative business days in Darwin and beyond.

To Dr José Ramos-Horta and Xanana Gusmão, thank you for the encouragement and support you gave us when we arrived in Timor-Leste and during our time there. It is an honour to have contributions from you in my book. And to Mari Alkatiri, I must also give thanks for the support and guidance you provided over the years. From difficult and humble beginnings, the tireless and dedicated leadership from such leaders as you has created the conditions and infrastructure that allowed your country to step onto the world stage, as well as for businesses like East Timor Trading Group to be established. I am privileged to have such eminent and inspiring friends from a country that has given my family so much. Thank you for two decades of wonderful memories.

Contents

Acknowledgements v

Forewords

    H.E. José Ramos-Horta ix

    The Hon. Shane Stone xiii

Preface xix

Part 1: Family 1

Part 2: Business 163

    H.E. Xanana Gusmão 164

Part 3: Home 195

Appendices

    Family & friends 225

    East Timor Trading Group, selected staff 226

    Staff Stories 227

Foreword

His Excellency,
Dr José Ramos-Horta AC GCollH GCL

The story of Timor-Leste includes people from many cultures. The Awan family, originally from Pakistan, came to Timor-Leste via Australia, where they made a new home for their young family more than 30 years ago. The Awans are one of the millions of immigrant families who help build economies while enriching the ethnic, cultural, and religious landscapes of their adopted countries.

My country's freedom is due to people of resilience, conviction, and faith who, alongside the Timorese, worked hard to prove that a bright future is possible. It is also due to an extraordinary movement of people across the world coalescing around shared ideals of justice and solidarity.

Sakib and Neelo Awan thrived in Timor-Leste because they have the heart and tenacity of the Timorese people. Together they have built the East Timor Trading Group into a model, socially responsible family business.

The Awans were no strangers to frontier towns. Their first business, Transglobal Marketing, began in Darwin in the early 1990s. This was an export business that won three export awards in a period of two years.

Sakib is a man of principle. He is hard working and visionary. He was one of the few enthusiastic supporters of Timor-Leste from before its first day of independence. In those uncertain days, he was brave enough to plant his flag firmly in our soil when others departed in fear, seeing only risk.

Despite all odds, and in the face of this risk, Sakib dug in deeper and committed to Timor-Leste with all his energy and heart. He has been rewarded with remarkable achievements to which many aspire but only few deliver.

While I may talk of Sakib, my words of admiration and gratitude extend wholeheartedly to his wife, Neelo, and the rest of his family, all of whom are great citizens of the world. Timor-Leste has been fortunate enough to have a cohort of dedicated, serious, and successful entrepreneurs like the Awans, who chose to bet on our future when most doubted it.

Since Sakib began his business in East Timor in 1999, the company's success has depended on maintaining a constant supply of important products for local market needs, which, given our country's instability then, was no easy task. And yet, the Awans remained in Díli, serving and distributing food in those dark days.

Yet, the distribution of goods is only part of the story. Sakib is full of courage and innovative ideas. The company employs around 300 full-time staff and contractors. It sets a benchmark in the service industry and operates a thriving wholesale food and beverage distribution network covering the whole country.

Sakib was the first entrepreneur to acquire international franchises to operate in Timor-Leste: Gloria Jean's Coffee opened in 2012, followed by Burger King a year later. There are now three Gloria Jean's outlets in Díli and four Burger King restaurants. Within two years of the first Burger King opening at Timor Plaza, the company was awarded the regional Burger King Asia-Pacific Operator of the Year award. East Timor Trading Group has also established a chain of Cheers retail outlets, as well as Makanan and Il Gelato outlets at the Timor Plaza Food Court.

Perhaps dearest to Sakib's heart, he also owns the Discovery Inn and Diya Restaurant. The hotel has held the top rating for Timor-Leste hotels on TripAdvisor for more than five years. As for the restaurant, I have had the opportunity to dine in some of the best restaurants around the world, and I am proud to say that one of the finest is Diya: a place of discovery and delight; a place that will defy your expectations. Since opening its doors in 2007, its innovative and tantalising menu has led the way in Díli's cosmopolitan dining scene. My office has frequently relied on Diya's chef to provide catering at official banquets and functions attended by numerous foreign dignitaries and heads of state, and he has always surpassed our guests' expectations. The service has been above par and the cuisine exceptional.

Sakib and Neelo are acutely aware that, over the long term, the opportunities they provide the Timorese people lead to better lives not only for their immediate employees but for their families and future generations of Timorese people. The experience and training given to the staff of the East Timor Trading Group have been exceptional, and have provided tangible benefits to immediate staff and to the future of Timor-Leste.

Foreign media are often quick to criticise my country. Perhaps this is because, from a distance, it may not be easy to see just how far Timor-Leste has come in the 20 years since independence. I know that Sakib has shared my confidence in my country from the day he arrived.

It is vital that the world now look at Timor-Leste as the success story it is and in the context of other countries that have become independent nations. Many fall in their early years of independence. In contrast, despite a brief period of violent civil unrest in 2006–2007, it is amazing what Timor-Leste has achieved with relative peace. This success must be recognised by the international community because that, along with the goodwill it engenders, will assist the country as it continues its stable, democratic growth in the region.

During my five-year presidency I honoured many individuals – Timorese and non-Timorese – teachers, doctors, police, military personnel, and entrepreneurs. In May 2012, I awarded Sakib Awan the Order of Timor-Leste for his outstanding services to our country. Sakib may have now left Díli due to his ill-health, but I hope that he and Neelo continue to think of Timor-Leste as home.

Sakib, Neelo, Zeenat, Saba, and Ismat Awan – you have brought so much joy to so many people in Timor-Leste. I will be eternally grateful to the adorable, loving, hard-working family that I consider a privilege to know. You have done immense good for our country and we must all feel indebted to you.

Now that your business is in the capable hands of your son-in-law, Sam, nd your daughter, Zeenat, I hope that they and future generations of your family will continue to carry on your legacy in the world, particularly in Timor-Leste.

I commend the story of Sakib Awan's life to readers and hope that his success will inspire others to follow in his footsteps.

Foreword

The Honourable Shane L. Stone AC QC

I first met Sakib Awan when I was the Northern Territory's Minister for Industry. In those days, I would visit companies, have a cup of coffee with the staff, and say, 'Tell me about your business'. We also held functions at the Sheraton Hotel on Mitchell Street, Darwin, where Sakib was working at the time.

It wasn't until he had left the Sheraton Hotel, and was trying his hand at exporting trepang, sea cucumber, and other seafood, that I got to know Sakib properly. This was the early 1990s, and the Northern Territory government had set up what we called the Trade Development Zone (TDZ). The aim was to give a *hand up* to enterprising businesses, not a *handout*. That was the big difference. The companies there did it all themselves, and it was a unique set-up in Australia. In the Northern Territory our start point was always 'what's right with this project', not what's wrong.

Sakib was a perfect fit to be offered a TDZ facility for his new business. He wasn't from our part of the world, but few are unless they are Indigenous. We're part of the region to the North more than we are to the South in many ways. And this was where Sakib had the edge. He recognised that there was a market for sea cucumber.

Sakib, a new bloke, saw the opportunity and away he went with the unqualified support of his wife, Neelo. He underwent enormous sacrifices, reminding me a lot of those soldier settlers who came back after World War II and established a new existence for themselves. Sakib, too, had that spirit about him. When he arrived in Darwin he had good street instinct, but he wasn't at all a big businessman. No one is. He learnt the lessons of life and profited from them.

I believe that Sakib's business instinct really began to develop when he was in the Territory because he was in the company of a number of local businesspeople who were in a similar situation. You can be anything you want in the Territory; no one asks you what school you went to - they won't even ask you if you went to school. It is the last frontier. It is quintessentially Australian and, while I know I sound like the leader of the cheer squad, that's the reality. The average age is about 28-29 and the young people always have two jobs. Most appreciate that the Territory is a frontier and they can make a go of it. You just need to roll up your sleeves and get on with it. Sakib found himself in that environment, surrounded by Australians, Chinese, Indonesians, and Indians who were all in it together and who all learnt from one another. Darwin is a very cosmopolitan, culturally diverse city.

Sakib came to me one day when I was Chief Minister and said, 'We've never had an Order of Australia award in the Darwin Muslim community'.

My response was, 'You can nominate someone you think should be considered'.

He was thinking about Mohammed Huq, who was about 90 years of age at that time. He'd been a meat inspector at the early meat works in the Top End and in Katherine, and was then President of the Islamic Society. He'd made a huge contribution to the community in the Territory. Sakib drove the application submission, and Mohammed Huq was awarded the Medal of the Order of Australia in 2000. He was a very proud Australian and man of faith.

Sakib was making the point that people from all parts of society need to be recognised as valuable members of the community. Darwin probably has the most honoured ethnic community in Australia. It is interesting when you go to Government House in Darwin because a lot of these people attend, very proudly wearing their medals. You can look at the sea of faces and think, this is unique; you don't see this diversity in Sydney or Melbourne.

The fact is that Sakib made his own luck in Darwin, that he succeeded through his and Neelo's hard work and endeavour. And again, when he set up business in East Timor, he made his own success. In my professional roles, I travelled to East Timor extensively before its independence, and I could see how difficult it was there. Sakib had to work in a new environment, but he brought a lot of skills that he'd learnt in Darwin and around the region, which prepared him well for what was ahead. In the face of multiple difficulties, he persisted. He worked hard. He got the brands. I really admire the way he has captured the world's biggest names, many of which are Fortune 500 brands. He put those deals together.

What Timor-Leste has in Sakib is someone who applies himself for the benefit of the local economy and for the employment of locals. I know they recognise what they have in him. The national award bestowed by Timor-Leste is well deserved. Sakib built his alliances and friendships with great skill, and has been a central part of that country's growth. He's been what we would call a good corporate citizen to Timor-Leste, as he has been in Australia.

I've known Sakib for decades, and yet, until this book, I hadn't known his full story, because there is always so much to discuss when we see each other. For all his confidence, Sakib also has the South Asian reserved quality. He is not brash and ostentatious; we other Aussies have a different way of presenting ourselves. Only recently, when I found out he was one of 11 children, I said to him, 'So, you would be the most successful'.

'Oh no, no', he said, 'this brother does this, and this brother does that ...' It was then that I realised they are an incredibly high-achieving family.

And, of course, there is Neelo. This is as much her story as it is Sakib's because without Neelo, there is no story. I saw Sakib in the depths of despair when the world was closing in on him during the Asian financial crisis in 1997. He was losing his business and the banks wouldn't give an inch. You didn't need the royal commission to work out how hard and uncompromising they could be, even then. But Neelo kept him going. As we say in public life, 'You get two for the price of one, and no one man or no one woman can be the star without the other person standing beside them.' It's that simple, and this was very true of Neelo.

Of course, Sakib is also challenged by his three daughters, who are all high achievers. He's a big, tough, Pakistani Australian man who is surrounded by formidable women.

When Sakib retired, I was national chairman of the Duke of Edinburgh's International Award, which is a youth organisation across 181 countries. It teaches young people the concept of civic responsibility and making a difference, as well as how important volunteering is across a range of activities. At any one time there are 25,000 Australians doing any one of the bronze, silver, or gold awards.

I recommended to Sakib and Neelo that they become involved in this internationally recognised youth awards program. I sat them down with some very high-profile award ambassadors in Sydney, who shared with them the nature of their contributions. That's when they decided they would become ambassadors. The beauty of the award is that the ambassador's program money goes direct to the participants.

In Sydney, the award is very focused on helping the poorer socio-economic parts of town. When Carmel Tebbutt was deputy premier of New South Wales, she told me that it was the single most effective program they had in connection with juvenile justice in prisons, something she also told Prince Edward when he visited. The chance to participate gives those in jail a sense of purpose, becoming involved in the program and learning life skills. Once you hear the success stories, you immediately see the benefits. It's such an important program, and having people like Sakib and Neelo on board is vital to its ongoing success.

Sakib is a micro-story all of his own in Darwin. He is very social; he's very good company. There have been others who have come from Pakistan, but he has been the most prominent in the community. Now that he has retired, I'm pleased to know that he's not divorced from the Territory; he still has his house in Darwin, which means he can continue to contribute to Darwin and its community in his retirement.

I'd also like to see him assist others wherever they might be, so they can benefit from his enormous experience. Sakib has a lot to offer and a wealth of lived experience to share. When you look at people who receive acknowledgement in this country, 90 per cent of them are those who have grown up within the country, be they Chinese, Greek, Italian, or another heritage. Sakib is someone who has come from the other side of the world and has achieved what so many people haven't.

When he arrived in Darwin, Sakib was proficient in English, but he didn't understand the cultural nuances that he would have to navigate, particularly those unique to the Territory. I remember asking him once, 'What did you find most challenging?'

'The way Australians insult each other as a term of endearment,' he replied.

'What do you mean?'

'Well, when someone says, "How are you doing, you old bastard?"'

Sakib took some time to come to terms with these strictly Australian expressions. No one just rolls into that. It's only now, with all that water under the bridge, that I can say: 'Sakib, you old bastard, what a success you have made of your life in Australia and in Timor-Leste! What a great contribution you and Neelo have made to both of your adopted countries. Yours is a wonderful story that I know will inspire others. Your retirement is now your time to share what you have built, and this book is a wonderful first step.'

Preface

As with every life, mine has been an adventure of the expected, punctuated by the unexpected. One road took me from Karachi to Montréal, Dubai, Islamabad, Sydney, and Darwin, following a career in international hotels. Another road led me to start my own business, which in turn offered me the privilege of experiencing the birth of the nation of Timor-Leste.

In this emerging nation, my wife, Neelo, and I established a distribution and retail business, East Timor Trading Group, which is based in Díli. Along the way I also found myself owning a boutique hotel, the Discovery Inn, Díli, something I would never have imagined had you asked the younger me working at the Intercontinental Hotel in Karachi. We employ more than 300 staff across our three arms of distribution, retail, and hospitality.

With a business of this size comes great responsibility and stress, because so many people's lives depend upon the decisions you make and the actions you take each day. This stress has taken its toll on my health, specifically my heart. As a result, in December 2016, at 60 years of age, I retired from the day-to-day running of the business and became chairman.

Now, living in Sydney, I find I have somewhat more time on my hands. I have never kept a personal diary, although my father was an avid diarist and a poet, and he filled two or three dozen journals. Through his work, he knew various figures around the Karachi literary world. One of those he respected and admired was the television personality, author, and poet Anwar Maqsood. Father's plan was that one day he would ask Mr Maqsood to compile his life's poems and writings into a book, so it could be published.

A significant regret in my life is that, after Father's death in 1987, almost all of this was lost. I look back now and wish that instead of ensuring I had a copy of the family tree, I had concentrated on publishing his journals. The wondrous thoughts that this complex, great man put down on paper throughout his life are now lost to our family and future generations – along with much of our family history.

As a result, I was determined to preserve what was left. One of my many retirement plans was to document my life story for the wider family, my children, and grandchildren. The result is this book: part memoir, part business history, and part reflections on life as I look back over my now 63 years. Looking forward, I hope that stories of my future philanthropic activities will allow me to contribute many more stories.

You will notice that this book contains few details of my immediate family – my children and grandchildren. We have always been a private family. While this is inherently problematic when writing one's autobiography, what it means is that as a family we have drawn a line in the sand. I have therefore chosen to reveal enough details of my personal, family, and business lives to provide a context and meaning to the story. The more personal family anecdotes and stories remain our private memories, as we all desire them to be.

My hope is that my story will provide a record for my family and inspiration for others to record their stories, because each of us has a story to pass down to future generations. I also hope that elements of the story relating to starting our business might be of practical assistance to aspiring businesspeople, wherever they might be around the world.

I believe it was George Orwell who said, 'Autobiography is only to be trusted when it tells something disgraceful'. As do we all, I have some regrets, some things I wish had turned out differently, many things of which I am immeasurably proud, but, I'm afraid, nothing too disgraceful.

I married Neelo, the love of my life. We have shared the good times and the tough across several countries, but all that we have, and all that we are, we built together. We have three wonderful, intelligent and well-rounded daughters, just as I hoped they would be, who fill us with pride. We also have a growing number of beautiful grandchildren, whose arrivals have left me overcome with emotions I never knew I possessed.

I have always been driven by a passion to achieve and to do things well. I have worked long hours. When I look back over the years, the one thing that has become clear to me is that life is short. The years pass swiftly. It is our responsibility, and ours alone, to make the most of each hour, each day, each week, and each year. We all face different opportunities and obstacles, and with each comes the choice of how to deal with them.

Part 1

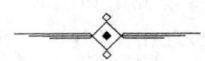

Family

I was born on 2 October 1956, the third son in a family of eleven. I have five older sisters, two older brothers, and three younger brothers:

- Safia Zakir, sister, born 1939
- Sabiha Jamil, sister, born 1941, died 2019
- Asif Un Nabi Khan, brother, born 1943
- Waris Un Nabi Awan, brother, born 1948
- Sarwat Awan, sister, born 1949
- Talat Nawab, sister, born 1951
- Mussarat Khan, sister, born 1955
- **Saqib Abbas Awan**, also spelt **Sakib**, yours truly, born 1956
- Ahsan Awan, brother, born 1958
- Nazar (Shaan) Abbas Awan, brother, born 1960
- Anwar Awan, brother, born 1966

Like most children, I was completely unaware of the challenges that my parents, older siblings, and people from a similar vintage had faced in coming to Pakistan. My mother was my father's fourth wife: my two older sisters and eldest brother are from a previous marriage. I can't imagine what they went through.

The name *Abbas* features in my name, and those of two of my siblings, and originates from the female doctor who attended the births of these three. I believe she told my father that he was blessed to have so many children, to which he replied, 'I'll give some of our children Abbas as their middle name.'

We all have our parents' distinct sense of right and wrong. I have my mother's warm, nurturing side and my father's fire-in-the-belly entrepreneurship – although increasingly less so his rigid toughness. Yet, in many ways I am not like any of my siblings, because I have always had a cheeky and irreverent sense of humour, which is not the norm in Pakistan at all. Pakistanis do not mock themselves. This sense of humour found its place in Australia, so perhaps my destiny was already mapped out for me.

I didn't know that my three oldest siblings were half-siblings until I was in high school, when a neighbour's son came up to me in the playground, wanting to get to me.

'They're not even your real sisters and brother.'

'What the hell do you know!'

I pushed him away and came home very upset. I told Mother what this boy had said.

'Calm down, we'll talk later. Have some water. Have some lunch.'

And then she said, very calmly, 'Well, this is the story: your father was married before, but there's no difference between any of your brothers and sisters, so I don't know why the neighbour's son is saying this. You know there's no difference, because we all live together and you have not known it until today.'

That was my mother. That was her acceptance and love. My eldest two sisters and brother, from my father's previous marriage, were as close to her as the rest of the family. However, it was quite something to find out as a teenager.

It was a little like the first time I learnt about how I came into this world. A kid at school described how it happens. Again, I got extremely upset. I beat the hell out of him.

'No! My parents would never do that!' I yelled. And again, I ran to my mother to ask, 'Is it true?'

Pause.

'I'll let your father explain that.'

In the end she did explain it to me.

In the 1950s, Pakistan was still finding its feet after the great upheaval of Partition, the process that resulted in the separation of Pakistan from India.

Pre-1947, the British had occupied India with its predominately Hindu and Muslim populations, but there were strong calls for independence after World War II. Britain's proposal was that India would remain under a centralised government, but divided into provinces: two predominantly Muslim and one predominantly Hindu.

While the overwhelming desire for independence had its origins many years earlier, in 1946 an election in essence decided whether Indian Muslims wanted a unified Indian state or to become an independent territory. The latter choice prevailed and that new homeland would eventually be called Pakistan. After further elections, leadership tussles, and some violent uprisings, in early 1947 the British government finally announced that it would leave India by 30 June that year, a decision that left the way open for India to split.

The area that became Pakistan was predominately Muslim, so it was decreed that Muslims should move to the region that would become Pakistan, and the Hindus there should relocate to what would remain India. While this was not comprehensively enforced, on the whole people complied and the Dominion of Pakistan was declared on 14 August 1947. Muhammad Ali Jinnah was sworn in as its first governor-general.

This was an incredibly unstable period, and yet there was also enormous opportunity for those with vision to seize the potential that this new nation would provide. My father was one of those with vision.

Just about every Muslim or Hindu family that chose or was forced to move experienced terrible trauma. There was looting, burning, killing, raping, and outbreaks of cholera. Fourteen million people travelled in one direction or the other across the new India-Pakistan border, as Hindus and Muslims moved to their new countries. There was an enormous number of deaths. My grandmother and my father's younger sister were forced to complete part of the journey on foot. Both died before reaching their destination.

Family tree

Our family tree document was drawn up some time in 1939 and printed in Lahore. This document allowed my father to make his land claim. It goes back seven generations, beginning in the late 16th century and ending with my father's generation.

The tree begins with the title *Kwaaj Bakhsh Pathan Awan*, where *Pathan Awan* is my family's caste and *Kwaaj Bakhsh* is the clan. Around 100 names are recorded on this document, although not one of them is female. Only the male line is recorded, because the majority of wealth and property is passed down through the male members of the family. According to cultural tradition, when a girl marries she receives some wealth by way of dowry, jewellery, and household gifts. Family trees were essentially practical documents that recorded property ownership to protect it over time.

We were fortunate enough to be able to identify a family land claim dating back to the late 16th century in Gurgaon, about 30 kilometres south-west of Delhi. The Partition agreement between the Pakistan and Indian governments, for those moving between countries, was that if you had documented proof through historical paperwork of entitlement to a particular parcel of land, you would be given a parcel of land of similar quality and size in Pakistan.

Our land in Gurgaon was prime agricultural land; thus, we received prime agricultural land in Lyallpur, now called Faisalabad, Pakistan. Interestingly, that original tract of land has now been developed and is worth hundreds of millions of dollars. The entire area is part of the Gurgaon–Delhi–Meerut Industrial Region, a major financial and industrial hub with the third-highest per capita income in India.

My parents

My mother, Ismat Jehan Awan, or 'Ammie', was born in the northern Indian Urdu-speaking town of Shahjahanpur, in Uttar Pradesh, in 1923. She was loving, peaceful, caring, non-controversial, and strong of will, the polar opposite of my father with his short temper and hot head.

After I moved to Australia and started a business, Ammie would call from time to time.

'Sakib, I need a few thousand dollars.'

'Why do you need so much money?'

'It's not for you to know. It's for a good cause. That's the end of it.'

Knowing there would be no argument and that it would indeed be for a good cause, I would always dutifully work out a way to provide the money. Money was tight in those early days, but we sent what we could. On reflection, fulfilling these requests from Ammie gave us a great deal of pleasure. The attitude of working hard and giving to the less fortunate was ingrained in us all from a young age by our parents. My brothers also provided what they could, when they were called upon.

Ammie knew the exchange rates for many countries around the world, so she knew exactly how much she needed from any of her children, wherever they lived. She was a non-government organisation in her own right!

When she died in Pakistan in 2010, there were almost 500 people at her Soyum (the wake, or the third day of the funeral). We were already due to travel to Pakistan for my nephew's wedding but, when we learnt of her death, we changed our plans and left a few days earlier. I arrived 24 hours after Ammie had passed away.

At her Soyum, I met so many people whom I did not know, although they had heard all about me and my brothers and sisters. They told me stories of their experiences of my mother.

She got my three daughters married.

She sent my five children to school.

She built a house for me.

The stories of Ammie's good deeds and financial support to those in need seemed endless. Because of her, I try to do a good deed every day. I hope that I have the time left to do more of the kinds of things my mother did for others. At the moment, I'm still here to do whatever it is that may come my way and to make the most of opportunities. I see this same attitude in all of my siblings. The many recipients of their generosity can thank my parents for the way they instilled in us a strong philanthropic heart.

All my siblings work hard at various philanthropic and social ventures on top of their own work or businesses, however, my brother Asif has taken it upon himself to step into Ammie's shoes full time. He travels around some of the most dangerous areas of Karachi by public transport, at great risk to his personal safety, to deliver much-needed help. When I expressed my concern over his use of public transport, he said it was far safer to enter these areas on a bus rather than by private car.

My father, Nabi Dad Khan Awan, or 'Abba Jee' as we called him, was born in 1909. He was a lightly built, healthy, modern-minded, principled man – creative and idealistic, resilient and practical, serious and tough. Very tough. He kept me on track and, due to his love of English and writing, was my English teacher as well.

'Learn an English word every day,' he would say.

We had several daily newspapers delivered to the house: *Dawn*, which is still published today; the *Morning News*, the oldest paper in Pakistan; the Urdu paper *Jang*; and the *Daily News*, an English-language afternoon newspaper. These, with *The Times*, *Newsweek*, *Reader's Digest*, and *Fortune*, meant there was a great deal of reading matter, both in English and Urdu, around our house.

My daily task was to pick a word that I could spell and use it in a sentence. But not just in one sentence; I had to use it in a sentence in the present and past tenses, and as a past participle. Not only did this benefit me, but while I was learning, I was also teaching my friends. Every evening the neighbourhood kids gathered.

'What's the word today?'

They learnt with me.

Abba Jee's expectations of himself were extremely high, and it was important to him that his whole family maintained similarly high standards. He followed a strict daily routine, was fit, and always careful of his diet.

Abba Jee had three children with his first wife before she died. He then had two more wives, both of whom died, before he met my mother. She was to be his fourth wife, and she told him she refused to continue his bad luck. They did, however, lose two of their children. He experienced a great deal of death and perhaps that was why he grew to be tough and resilient. He needed to cope with that level of loss in his life. At home, Father maintained the same tight regime of discipline, honesty, and integrity that he demonstrated at work.

If I were to look around at my childhood friends – we were all middle-class families – we always had a generous variety and quantity of food in the house. Every week a fruit vendor – *fruit wallaa* – would visit with a huge basket of seasonal fruits, weighing at least 25 kilograms, on his head. We always had three meals a day. We always had a comfortable way of life, and I have my father's hard work and vision to thank for that.

Abba Jee saw a golden opportunity to buy land in prime locations around the young city of Karachi. As a capital city, it was only 13 years old then; it was under-developed, and so land was relatively cheap. From this base, in 1960, Abba Jee began a real estate business, Awan House and Estate. This business made him financially comfortable, although not a tycoon by any means. He raised 11 children, magnified his investments, and left enough property in his estate to give his sons some advantage in their lives. The lesson I took from his life was that property equals financial security. I learnt that early.

Before starting the business, my father worked as a public servant in Karachi. My memory is that he didn't take a particular interest in the work, and was disillusioned because everything moved so slowly due to institutionalised corruption. For an honest public servant to provide for a family of 11 children was not an easy task.

Our family farmland was leased out to *mazaras*, tenants who worked the land. At the end of the year, they paid my father either a share of the profit or a fixed amount, whichever was agreed upon. I don't know exactly the details of my father's agreement with his mazaras, but I do know that every year, when he went to collect the money, he recognised that he did not enjoy the lifestyle that they did, these men who ploughed *his* land.

They were clearly prosperous and led healthy outdoor lives, and it dawned on him that he needed to do more. His salaried job provided a regular, secure income, but the additional income from the land provided a greater level of financial freedom. This realisation was a turning point.

Around 1960, Abba Jee took early retirement to pursue his own business idea: he would sell his agricultural land and invest in real estate in the city of Karachi. He had the capital, the foresight, and the confidence to see that if you had the opportunity to purchase land at this time, it would provide long-term income.

He acquired a great deal of prime, under-developed land in the new capital. His business model was to build one house each year and sell it for a healthy profit. That provided his income for the year. He wanted to be in control of his destiny. He built to his own standards and operated with independence. He knew in this way he could pay for his children's education and their weddings. None of these things he could have done as a public servant.

After many years with no control, he now held a tight rein on his new business. However, inevitably, as it grew, he came to see that he needed somebody to help. While he did not let go of the reins, in the mid-1960s, he did allow my elder brother Waris, who later joined the army, to work for him. At that time, Waris had a Hercules push bike, which I loved. I hoped that one day I would have one of my own. Sometimes I would ride it in the afternoons. However, I was so young that I couldn't even get onto it properly. I could only reach the pedals by undertaking a difficult contortion, twisting my legs inside the bike frame, leaving me looking somewhat like a circus clown. There is a classic Indian tradition of children riding bikes that are too big for them!

As the business grew, rather than selling all of the houses, my father decided to keep some and rent them out to provide an additional regular income stream.

Abba Jee loved to write in his journal each day, including writing poems in English and Urdu. He found solace and inspiration in the works of Ghalib and Allama Iqbal. As a migrant family, now spread across several countries, we didn't have one repository for our family history and now much of it has been lost. Diversity is wonderful, but it makes it difficult for future generations to understand where we came from, where they come from. As I have said, it is this loss that has driven me to write my story – for my children, my grandchildren, and their future children.

His journal is gone; the only item I still have of my father's was given to me by my mother.

'This is one of your father's cherished possessions,' she said to me.

She gave me an English-language Quran published in the 1930s, consisting of 30 beautifully bound *Siparahs* (volumes), which I willingly accepted, and still have with me in Australia. It was the only personal item I inherited from my father.

Money is different. We have been fortunate that the money from his estate helped us tremendously at a time when we needed it most, just after we started our business in 1991. I'm so grateful to have been born to parents who were tremendously caring and loving yet still strictly disciplined me to keep me in line!

Abba Jee's ethics have been passed on to me to a large degree. I was raised on the proverb that ignorance of the law is no excuse, and that you must always tell the truth, no matter how difficult it is. In business, that can create difficult situations. Sometimes people ask you a very direct question. To answer honestly while also demonstrating consideration for them, for other parties in the deal, each person's reputation, and the finer financial points of a business arrangement, can be extremely difficult. It is usually a matter of treading a fine line – providing an honest answer without compromising any party's integrity, or disclosing confidential information.

In my young years, I did so many things that gave Abba Jee cause to doubt that I would make something of myself one day. I would push him to the limits whenever I could. I was thrashed often because I was prone to disobedience.

'You will have a rude awakening one day soon, and you'll not be living the way you live now', he would warn me, repeatedly. 'You won't have a roof over your head and you won't even get a labourer's job.'

In 1987, Abba Jee had a massive heart attack and died without warning at the age of 78. I was doing quite well in the early years of my hotel career, but he never had the chance to see the success I have had in business. His death came just after Neelo and I arrived in Australia.

With a new job and two young children, we could not afford to return to Karachi for his funeral which, by Islamic tradition, must occur on the same day as the death. His death seems unfair to me now. He had no vices and lived well. Abba Jee should have lived much longer.

I hope he at least gained some satisfaction that I was heading in the right direction, although I wish he had lived long enough to see how successful I have been in both my family and business lives. My mother did get to witness this, and I hope that when they were reunited in heaven, she related all of our family stories to him.

Our family dynamic was that the elder children looked after the younger, because we were a family with a wide spread of ages. There was a great deal of respect given to elder siblings, and lots of support given to younger siblings. In particular, I hold my brother Waris in high esteem, as the wise elder in the family. He holds this position well, perhaps even more so today in the absence of our parents.

When the first of our siblings died in mid-2019, Waris's response was, 'First wicket down'.

We are a tight family and most of us love cricket, so I see this as a sign of affection. When I think that Waris will be 78 in only five years, I just can't comprehend that he'll be the same age as my father when he passed away, and that my generation is now reaching that age.

School

My education began at the Sherwood School. It was very British, although nestled in a lush green forest of England it was not. Instead, it was in Karachi. It was a relic of colonial days in which the English system of education was important. It was modelled on a typical English public school, like a private school in Australia. I remained there only until year 3. When the fees increased, our father moved my younger brother and me to the local public school where we remained.

I am essentially the product of two sides of the Pakistan school system, the private and public, the school of hard knocks if you wish. In Pakistan, year 10 is matriculation, while year 12 is intermediate. This is more or less the same as in Australia, with the School Certificate in year 10, followed by the Higher School Certificate in year 12.

I was stubborn. I never took an interest in my studies. I consistently failed to hand in my homework, and I remember on one occasion my punishment was to stand outside the classroom for several hours.

I still didn't learn.

'Bring your father to meet with us,' the principal demanded on one occasion.

Of course, that was the last thing I wanted to do. I went to my friend Zafar to ask his father, with whom I had a great relationship, if he would help me out. He was a gentle, loving and helpful person, who passed away in 2020 in his mid-90s. He agreed to meet the school principal as my 'uncle'. My father was conveniently travelling, or at least that was how I spun the story anyway. This happened twice. The second time, Zafar's girlfriend pretended to be my elder sister.

As an upside to my behaviour, I realised early that the greatest challenge in life was the ability to negotiate with people. I developed powers of persuasion and negotiation in relation to academic work. If only the education system had recognised those skills!

I don't know why I never applied myself. I was cocky. Perhaps I believed I could do the work easily, so I didn't bother. I also had a carefree, laid-back, 'she'll be right' attitude. I could identify the US, England, and Australia on a map. Did I need to learn more about these countries at school? No. All I needed to learn at school was a language and maths. I realised early that there was limited opportunity in Pakistan once school was over. My interest in education was limited to those subjects that would afford me a better life – elsewhere.

While I might not have applied myself to my schoolwork, I did apply myself to sport. In fact, I loved any kind of sport: cricket, soccer, hockey, flying kites – dogfights with kites, that is. However, cricket has always been foremost in my heart. I was captain of my school cricket team, which gave me status and recognition among my peers. I have continued to play cricket for much of my adult life. Since those early days, it has always been a time I give to myself. The meditation of cricket allowed me to step away from the stresses of business, to find my centre, to focus and to relax.

In those teenage years, many boys from the neighbourhood drifted into delinquency because they had no one to guide them. What helped to keep me in check were my position as cricket captain and my father, whom I both respected and feared.

If it were not for his discipline, I don't think I would be where I am today.

In 1976, without excelling, I completed school. It was a great relief to myself and even greater relief to my long-suffering parents. However, my parents' relief was soon replaced by concern that I was drifting into a life of nothing. In the days that followed school I was frustrated, lost, and at a loose end. I had time, was hanging out with friends, ambling around the city with them, and getting regularly thrashed by Abba Jee. I had not yet found any direction in life.

One night, I was sitting by a reasonably busy suburban arterial road with four friends. We had just been watching a cricket match played in England, during which a streaker had bolted across the field. It ended in the usual fashion with police rushing over with a coat to cover him and usher him off. We were in the mood to do something silly. Why don't we do that here? Let's streak! We decided that we would wait until the next car approached, and when it was about 20 metres away, we would streak across in front of it. One of my friends lived just across the road, so we knew we could head directly into his house and to safety. We took our clothes off as we saw the headlights of an approaching car. We calculated how fast it was going, leapt out, and ran as fast as we could, passing just in front of it. It wasn't travelling fast, but we did cut it fine! It gave us such a thrill. Was it disgraceful? My daughters cringe and laugh. Abba Jee would no doubt have had a different view, had he known about such behaviour.

Our other antics were riskier.

My mother became perplexed by my eating habits.

'Why don't you eat dinner, Sakib? Surely you are hungry. You've eaten nothing tonight, or other nights last week. What's going on?'

My friends and I always dressed well to go out. We had worked out that being dressed well, we could go to places and no one questioned us because we looked as though we were meant to be there. We dressed well because we had taken to crashing weddings and we had to look the part. Pakistani weddings are huge chaotic affairs, unlike the controlled seated events in Australia. Most of those we crashed were at the InterContinental Hotel. This was where I had completed my internship so I knew the lay of the land. I knew in which rooms weddings were held, how to access those rooms and how to blend in. And because of the event boards, we always knew the names of key members of the wedding party.

Using my inside knowledge, we perfected the approach and then began crashing larger weddings in the neighbourhood. Not just the odd one. No, no. We crashed many, many weddings and got ourselves dinners each night. We ate like kings. In time, Ammie found out what was going on and I was suitably chastised.

I knew I was pushing the boundaries, but I *could* see what was right and wrong. My parents had drummed that into me from a young age. That was what saved me: I could see a future and knew our antics had no place in the long term. Not all my friends saw this. My perspective gave me great confidence in my abilities because it also gave me a safety net. On top of this, I was the cricket captain, and so people in my community respected me. In return I also held that position in esteem and did not wish to jeopardise it.

All this youthful rebellion was great fun until, one night, I stepped too far over the line.

'What the hell have I done?'

I lay staring at the ceiling most of the night, repeating those words. I had pushed my exasperated father to his limit.

'Get out of this house,' he had said, dismissing me with a wave of his hand.

I had gone too far. I don't recall exactly what I had done this time, but I remember lying in the dark at my friend Edgar Saxby's house, praying that my mother would work out where I had landed after fleeing from home.

It was early 1976. I had just completed my year 12 studies. I was finally free, inspired to explore, and filled with romantic notions of where my post-school life would take me. Possibilities were everywhere, but I had no direction. I was cheeky, disobedient, difficult. I was a source of trouble for my parents but never, in my mind, disrespectful, although I did not always acquiesce to their demands.

At around 4 pm the next day there was a knock at the Saxbys' door. It was my mother, the kind and loving foil to my father's strict and rigid hand. 'Your father wants to see you,' she said. 'He has a proposition, if you'll come home and talk with him.'

'I'm not going home,' I said dramatically. I was 19 years old and standing my ground. After some discussion, I finally agreed to go. We arrived home as the sky was darkening. Father saw me, but played it very cool.

'Gullu,' he said, calling me by my family nickname. 'You're here now. Good.'

'Yes, I am,' I said, tail between my legs.

'We'll talk tonight after dinner.'

There was a famous poet from the subcontinent in the mid-1800s, around the time the British Raj arrived in India, called Mirza Ghalib. After dinner Father asked me to go with him and Ammie to the courtyard and he put on his most loved record, a selection of Ghalib's verses, sung by two voices.

'Come, sit next to me here', he said, and patted the seat. 'I want you to work for me.'

I wasn't interested. I stood my ground, the stubborn adolescent not wanting to give in to the injustice, whatever that might have been.

'If you do everything I ask you to do Monday to Friday, from 8am to 5pm, I will buy you a motorcycle.'

Bing!

One sentence and there it was. He understood what was in my heart more than I had expected, and he knew exactly what would get my full attention.

For anyone my age in those days to have their own motorcycle was a big deal. None of my friends had one. I didn't know anyone who did, but we all fantasised about what type we would buy, given the opportunity.

King of the road

Abba Jee looked at me. He knew I was finding it difficult to contain my excitement.

'How much would a motorcycle cost?' he asked.

In the back of everyone's mind is a constellation of cells dedicated to recording detailed facts about our innermost dreams. Those cells leapt into action. My mind flashed to the most expensive motorcycle I could think of.

'It's 11,000 rupees.'

Back then, around 10 Pakistani rupees equalled an Australian dollar, so 11,000 rupees was a considerable amount of money. But in my mind, there was only one bike, the bike every young Pakistani man coveted.

I never expected him to agree.

'OK. I'll draw up an agreement. You go to the civil court tomorrow. Get a stamped paper.'

He was referring to a British colonial document, originally introduced to regulate trade to some degree, and required for any contract above a certain value. It had to be purchased from lawyers' offices or courts for 10 or 20 rupees. My mind began to process the prospects ahead of me.

'And after work? May I use the bike after five o'clock?'

'Yes, of course.'

And my pride? Where was the natural injustice felt by young people at being told what to do by their parents? I agreed in an instant. This wasn't the time to stand my ground. Abba Jee handed me the money to buy the stamped paper. He was serious.

I could hardly sleep that night as all sorts of thoughts raced through my head.

I had given my father the price for a Honda CD175, otherwise known as King of the Road. As the advertisement said, this was the 'great new all-rounder, at home around town or putting the highway behind you'. It featured a 360-degree crankshaft, wasted spark ignition, single carburettor, parallel twin high-revving engine, 16-inch wheels, and a 100-mph speedometer. It had a push-button start. You were not allowed to own a larger or faster bike in Pakistan. Anything more powerful was reserved for the police, because they had to be able to catch offenders.

The next day, I arose at 7am to ensure I would arrive at the courts the moment they opened. I secured the stamped paper and rushed to the office, ready for work.

My father had a strict, if somewhat unusual routine. At breakfast time, he preferred to eat his lunch, while listening to the BBC, and to eat breakfast at lunchtime. His evening meal was indeed dinner, during which he would again listen to the BBC.

By the time Abba Jee arrived at the office at 9am, it was spick-and-span and I was seated, ready for work. I set up his typewriter with plain and carbon paper, ready for him to type. He walked in the door and looked at me, surprised.

'Oh. You haven't gone already?'

I sensed disappointment at my perceived lack of enthusiasm.

'No, no, I've been.' I showed him the paper.

Abba Jee smiled. 'That's very efficient.'

My father had an exceptional command of British English and owned a classic Royal typewriter from the 1960s, the Honda CD175 of typewriters. It was on a Royal that Ian Fleming created Bond, and Ernest Hemingway penned stories of war and bullfights. And it was on a Royal that Abba Jee would meticulously type out both poems and business contracts.

He typed my job description, listing my tasks clearly, in a series of bullet points. He added details of the motorcycle, noting that he would pay for fuel, maintenance, and servicing. I would have the use of the motorcycle from 5pm to 8pm every day and all day on Sunday. Yet, there was no mention of any actual remuneration for the work I would do. No wages. However, I recognised that this was not the time to deal with that issue.

We each signed the agreement and, in his careful handwriting, he wrote me a cash cheque for 11,000 rupees.

I found it difficult to contain my excitement. I first needed to cash the cheque. The bank was less than 100 metres from the office. I collected my younger brother, Ahsan, or 'Guddu' as we all called him, and went to the bank to cash the cheque immediately. We then took a bus to the main motorcycle market in Karachi, Akbar Road. The salesperson, being slightly more streetwise than us and seeing two young kids turn up with a wad of cash, jumped the price up by 250 rupees. We were short – a gaping hole opened up between me and my motorcycle. My brother and I returned home, despondent, to find my father had already turned in for his afternoon rest.

'Where is the motorcycle?' asked Ammie. When I told her the story, she said, 'If your father finds out that you haven't got the motorcycle yet, he might well change his mind. I don't want this to be a big disappointment. Go, run quick to Safia.' She was my eldest, married sister, who lived maybe two kilometres away. Another two kilometres!

'Run. Run now, Sakib. I'll call her and ask her to give you 250 rupees and I'll pay her when I see her next.'

Ammie could see what was going on for me. She could see I had potential. *He's disillusioned, he's not interested in much right now. This bike will harness his potential. God, give him guidance to the right path.*

Exhausted, but with the crisis averted, Guddu and I returned to the motorcycle shop.

The bike was only ever released in blue and red, so there was no decision to make. It had to be red – a beautiful dark red Honda CD175. It was a dream come true.

How do I explain it? For a young person like me, to go from not even having a pushbike to owning the best motorcycle available instantly made me very cool. Everybody recognised me. Suddenly, I was on the radar of all the young ladies who had never noticed me before. That bike transformed my life overnight.

Yet, I had no actual income, no money, to go out on all these dates that were so clearly coming my way.

The next day my father took me to the office to explain how his real estate business worked. He showed me the properties, took me through the process of buying and selling, and talked about the paperwork. He often dealt with many government departments and registry offices. I soon understood the process, and the cost of each step he undertook in selling or buying a property.

While our primary business income was from property sales, over time my father had also become an expert in conveyancing, which provided an additional revenue stream.

Karachi bureaucracy was very slow, so if you wanted something done, you had to pay speed money – an under-the-counter payment. Otherwise, you might have to wait for weeks. This was just the way the system worked, and it still does in many countries. The result of the extra payment was that instead of waiting for five hours, you got your paperwork dealt with there and then. My father always paid.

After several days, Abba Jee started asking me to visit the government offices to process the paperwork for property transactions. I soon realised that, in comparison to others, we paid much more.

I needed spending money. I couldn't ask my father for it because he'd given me the motorcycle instead of a salary. I knew I had to figure out a way to fund the activities available to me now that I could get out and about on the bike. It was time to get creative. My father might have been tough, but he was also fair and liked people to show initiative.

'Do you mind if I renegotiate our costs and keep the difference?' I asked him.

'As long as the efficiency of our transactions is not affected', he replied, 'I'll still give you the same amount of money. If you can negotiate the cost down, the difference is yours to keep.'

I found out how much other people paid and negotiated with every department and registry. Soon I was paying a mere third of what my father had previously paid. In no time, I was averaging nearly 3500 rupees per month, about AU$350 – serious money in the mid-1970s. I had no outgoings because I lived at home. My brother, Waris, who was a captain in the army, had a cash salary of around 900 rupees a month. Now, not only did I have the best motorcycle available but I had become the richest kid in the neighbourhood. I was awash with money and new-found confidence, and I developed a taste for the good life. Girls called me, rather than me calling them. Home telephones were not common then, with some people waiting as long as 20 years to get a line installed, and we were fortunate to have not just one but two telephones at home.

So, I befriended a lot of young ladies.

Whatever tasks my father gave me I performed at supersonic speed, faster than he expected. I negotiated our costs down and the balance went into my pocket. Having that motorcycle demolished every obstacle in my path and transformed my life on so many levels. Without it, I might not have got to where I am today. The deals I secured gave me confidence that I was in control of my own destiny. I knew I had learnt how to manage the system. I had simply seen an opening and taken it. The confidence that knowledge like that gives a 20-year-old is enormous.

However, there was one transaction of which I was particularly proud.

My sister Mussarat, who now lives in Canada, was soon to be married. Abba Jee needed money to pay for the wedding. All of my father's money was invested in properties – while he was asset rich he wasn't very liquid. He didn't really want to sell a property at that time to pay for the wedding because it was not the right time to sell. Instead, he decided to mortgage one of his houses.

This was a task and a half because a loan had already been taken out once against the property. This first loan had been paid off, but the bank still held a lien over the property and the original documents until the paperwork could be processed. The new loan could not be drawn up because the papers were held elsewhere. Firstly, we had to go to the House Building Finance Corporation to release the documents, then to the court to re-mortgage the property to another bank. This whole process, my father said, could not be done in less than three months. We've all experienced how long banks can take, and in those days it was more difficult in Pakistan. He didn't know where to turn. We were stuck.

I decided this was an opportunity for me. With some fast negotiations, calling on contacts, and generally schmoozing all concerned, I got it done in a fortnight. Abba Jee was overjoyed and astonished by what I had achieved. Admittedly, I even surprised myself.

The speed with which I approached these early business experiences felt completely natural to me. I was bursting with confidence. I dealt with professionals in the only way I knew how, and without fully realising it at the time, I had found my niche. While my understanding of business originally came from exposure to my father's business practices and dealing with the public on his behalf, I have always enjoyed dealing with people. Over the years I have learnt more skills and developed an understanding of how to interact with people in any walk of life.

I was definitely shrewd, even at that age, and very aggressive in my approach. I was not rude, but assertive in the sense that I had a thick skin and didn't take no for an answer. I knew things could be done. I knew other people were getting them done, so why shouldn't I? Back then, I approached every hurdle in life with this attitude and it served me well.

I had a desire to make things happen, a sense of urgency. I had a drive to achieve and to be focused. These traits I have carried with me throughout life and they are now immortalised in posters around my company's office, with sayings such as: 'Do tomorrow's work today'. Likewise, I didn't shy away from asking questions. I came to realise that if you don't ask questions, you don't get answers. Asking questions means that you gather the information you need to act immediately.

In Pakistan, and even in Australia, if you have connections, you simply make a phone call and things happen for you. Abba Jee knew a great number of people, but he refused to use those connections. He had seen enough of that world in operation as a public servant and he no longer wanted it - in his own business, he could work exactly the way he desired.

I worked hard each day. I worked extremely hard. I was driven by the opportunities provided by the money I earned and in the 1970s Karachi was a party city that provided an abundance of opportunities to spend my spoils. So I did!

Karachi: But not as you know it

Each day I would return home from work shortly after 5pm, jubilant that my free time had arrived and I could ride my beloved Honda for pleasure. I was performing beyond Abba Jee's expectations at work, so I was allowed to stay out late.

As the number of female friends in my circle grew, so ended the crashing of weddings. It was clear that they would not find that kind of activity amusing. Instead, we would go out in a group. Some of these female friends briefly became girlfriends.

It has always been important to me to dress well. I like to wear fashionable clothes that have style and I like to look after my clothes. Trousers, shirt, socks, belt, shoes, suits, handkerchief – whatever it is – all must work together. It not only makes you feel good to be dressed well but it shows that you have respect for those around you. It says: *'I have put in the effort to look good for you'*. I soon realised dressing well also impressed others around me.

As I became more popular with girls, the venues I was interested in also changed. Girls weren't permitted in parks or sports venues, but I was now old enough to get into discotheques.

The 1970s were Pakistan's years of peak tourism, because it found itself on the famous Hippie Trail. In the late 1960s, young men and women from Europe and the US, rebelling against the soullessness of Western capitalist society, embarked on what they saw as an overland journey to find freedom and enlightenment. Hippies went to India and Nepal via eastern Europe, Turkey, Iran, Afghanistan, and Pakistan. They went in buses, trains, falling-apart cars, or by hitchhiking. They came to Karachi for its beaches, nightlife, and hashish, which was freely available.

Pakistan was a modern society then, and no one questioned your faith when you visited nightclubs. Into the mid-1970s, disco was still an international phenomenon and Karachi was the envy of Pakistan – a vibrant city with its residents primed to enjoy a good night out.

Pakistan International Airlines was the face of the country and seen as one of the world's most progressive airlines. The uniform was designed by Pierre Cardin, so it was extremely fashionable. In addition, Pakistan's GDP was higher than that of Indonesia, Thailand, Malaysia, and the Philippines put together. It has been said that if ever Karachi's diverse ethnic, religious, and sectarian groups could find a way to work in harmony, Karachi had the potential to be a thriving cosmopolitan city like New York. Back then, such success might well have spread throughout the country. However, that outcome is now highly unlikely.

In those days, the hotels had fully stocked bars, sold imported and local brews, and catered to the wide variety of locals and tourists who regularly enjoyed themselves until the early hours of the morning.

The Horseshoe was a popular hangout, where we would often go to see the Underground 4 play. We also went to the Nasreen Room at the InterContinental Hotel, the Three Aces, the Beach Luxury Hotel, and the famous Metropole Hotel's Samar nightclub. Artists were flown in from Turkey, Lebanon, Australia, Egypt, Europe, and the US to perform at these nightclubs.

The Metropole Hotel was the largest in Karachi and covered a whole block in the city centre. Its nightclub, Samar, which opened in 1968, was the first disco in Karachi, and was famous for its live music performed by local or overseas bands. Dizzy Gillespie played there in the mid-1950s, and the garden accommodated 4000 people. It was a world-class venue.

The hotels always tried to outdo each other with elaborate and sensational advertising claims about their artists and events, and the InterContinental and Metropole led the way. Some acts were billed as 'Europe's most popular orchestra'. I suspect few people in Europe had heard of these artists, but no one was concerned about verifying claims of fame; all the hype was designed to add to the allure and mystique of an evening.

We regularly visited all these clubs and, of course, with new female friends came a new set of friends. Together, we would move from nightclub to nightclub to see bands such as the Talisman Set.

The curtains began to draw on this life of freedom when Zulfikar Ali Bhutto's populist government introduced prohibition in April 1977. Life in Karachi was never quite the same again. Martial law was declared, and all bars, nightclubs, and forms of entertainment in the city were closed. Dancing and places where men and women gathered together were shut down due to strict new laws relating to segregation of the sexes. In some cities there now were even male and female sections at bus stops. Virtually overnight, Pakistan became a different country. Looking back at it now, I find it difficult to imagine that my old Karachi ever existed.

Originally, the change was designed to be a temporary measure to win over the supporters of an alliance of right-wing religious parties and other anti-Bhutto voices in the country. Bhutto hoped for a second five-year term by winning enough right-wing votes to be returned to power. He said he would then gradually reverse prohibition. But his plan was thwarted when, three months later, in July 1977, his government was toppled in a military coup led by General Muhammad Zia-ul-Haq.

A new direction

It was 1978. I had been friends with a particular girl for long enough that one day her mother asked me what I did for a job.

'I work for my father,' I said proudly.

'No, I mean what do *you* do?'

What more could I say? That's all I had. She told me to come back and be more serious about her daughter when I had a job of my own – when I became somebody. If I wanted to be taken seriously as a potential husband, I clearly needed to find a career. This simple conversation prompted a discussion with Abba Jee about what form my future career would take.

As well as working for Abba Jee, I had completed some short courses at the Tourism and Hotel Training Institute of Pakistan. I had also engaged in some practical training in stewardship and front desk clerking at the InterContinental Hotel Karachi, as well as internships at two other hotels.

During one of these internships I met Naveed Malik, the resident manager of the InterContinental. Our family friends were successful professionals and I respected all of them, but in Mr Malik I saw another life that one could have, a giant leap from my day-to-day existence. This experience helped me to clarify a vision for my future. I joined the dots. I loved dealing with people. I loved order. I had my father's sense of high standards. However, I wanted a wider world, and I knew what could be achieved with the right connections. I decided the world of international hotels would deliver the life I wanted.

'I want to study hotel management,' I told my father.

International hotels are glamorous, inspiring places. They are pristine and ordered. Every day everything is in its place, tiptop, and as shiny as the day you get married. They are places where most people know how to behave well, where powerful people stay, and where deals are done.

The other appeal was that, regardless of your seniority, you have the chance to interact with people from around the world. Whether you talk for 15 seconds or 15 minutes, you can build a rapport with people from all walks of life. You can find yourself at the centre of a world of the famous and the infamous, celebrities, heads of state, dignitaries, and the wealthy and powerful from all corners of the globe. You can interact with people with different experiences, expectations, anxieties, and desires. And you can learn the whole time. By initiating conversations with strangers, you can break down barriers that are inherent in many social situations. When I held senior management roles, I was hardly ever in my office. I entertained and I visited people, and it was this that I found I loved so much. In life, there are always goals to meet and objectives required to achieve your projected income, but the way you do this in the hotel industry is totally different from a normal desk job. I have always been a people person, so what could be more satisfying than to feel like you are partying while you work?

'OK,' said my father, 'and where would you do that?'

'Anywhere.' I racked my brains about where I would like to go. 'North America.'

'Right. Well, let's apply.'

I was clearly my father's son. I had observed his disillusionment with the system and had some personal experience of it myself from working in his business. I realised a life restricted by bureaucracy and underhand payments was not for me. I also wanted to get out of Pakistan. The country was riddled with corruption; you could hardly move without paying someone. To achieve something completely legal, such as getting a visa, you needed a family contact who could get you inside the system to push the paperwork through. I realised I didn't want to live a life overshadowed by this.

So I searched for courses. I did not know how to apply, or even when the courses began; I just fired off applications left, right, and centre. The only problem was that it was the wrong time of year. However, my father was by now adequately impressed that I could do whatever I set my mind to, and completely supported my decision.

Research indicated that the important thing was to get a place at a university. Once you had that, you could move around wherever you liked. In those days, researching international colleges was not as easy as today because there was no internet. To find courses, I spoke to various people, and wrote to the American and Canadian embassies to request details of various universities. I created a shortlist of those institutions at which I felt I would have a chance of acceptance, and applied.

Under Zia-ul-Haq's martial law, troops were stationed in and around every corner of Karachi. My elder brother Waris had been appointed as Captain (G3 Brigade). He looked after security in the SITE industrial areas of Karachi's main business district. It was a terrible time in Pakistan, but Waris's position meant he could provide me with the contacts I needed to get my foreign exchange approved a little more quickly than normal. I completed the necessary paperwork to obtain a student visa for my move to Canada, and Waris arranged to have it approved by the State Bank of Pakistan. A short time later, in June 1978, I was accepted by Concordia University in Montréal. Success! I was accepted to study graphic design.

Graphic design? That was my way in. Concordia University didn't have a hotel management program so I decided I would go to Canada and sort things out when I arrived. I couldn't draw to save myself, but if all went to plan, I wouldn't have to.

Dhobi

On the whole, Karachi is a classic mild, tropical city of lazy warm days and nights. It gets a little cool in winter, down to 12-14 degrees Celsius, and up to the mid-30s in summer, with a monsoon season from July to September.

I arrived in Montréal in early September. I knew it got cold, but I was unprepared for the -20 degrees Celsius that hit me, with a wind chill factor that took it down to -40. It was so cold that another layer of skin grew on my nails. There was even an early snowfall that year. On the first day of that snowfall, I had an interview with the department head of a hotel called Château Champlain, now the Montréal Marriott Château Champlain. It was my first experience of snow and, as I crossed the road - right in the middle of one of the city's main streets - my feet went out from under me and I crashed down onto the ice. I simply wasn't able to cope with the cold. During my early weeks, I would take taxis even for short trips to avoid it. A couple of times the drivers didn't even charge me a fare. They said they didn't want to see me freeze on the street. I don't know why I didn't realise how cold it could get there.

I was alone and frozen in a foreign city for the first time in my life and my horizons expanded overnight. I learnt to cook, to be self-sufficient, and to work independently. Most importantly, I learnt about freedom.

I didn't attend even one day of the design course at Concordia. I simply turned up on the first day, selected my subjects, then spent the rest of my time looking for institutes that offered hotel management. That's how I found LaSalle College.

With an excess of youthful confidence and a good dose of naivety, I walked in the front door and said, 'I am here. I want to study hotel management. I don't have any money because the money I had was paid to Concordia University and it will take two or three weeks to get it back. Please don't remind me about it before the three weeks are up.'

Despite my father's prescriptive tuition in English, my spoken English was not all that good at the time. In addition, the lady in the office didn't like my asking not to be chased for the fees.

How could I explain that I was concerned that if they reminded me it would be upsetting, and I still wouldn't have any money to pay them?

I was accepted into LaSalle, although it turned out that that college was a lot like school for me. I didn't pay attention or take my studies seriously. Had I applied myself fully, I'm sure I would have achieved much more academically. I understood what they were trying to teach me – the floor was to be cleaned a certain way. But that was it. I didn't see why I needed to know the science behind how to clean a floor and then remember all of it. I knew how to clean it and I thought, now let me go and do it. I love to learn, but it was practice that motivated me, not theory. I knew I could survive. I knew I could do better, given the opportunity. I just had to make it through the course and get a job. My attitude was *'so please just let me do it'*.

Yet, it wasn't actually the college that was holding me back. It was me. Every night I partied, forgetting that I was there to study. The next day I would be too tired to function properly. Those early days of partying were mostly due to the culture shock of finding myself completely free and independent. I had been exposed to a Western way of life in Pakistan because of my friends and the places where we hung out, so the social life I experienced in Montréal wasn't a complete surprise, but it was a huge step up.

In Montréal, everyone was free. Everyone could do as they wished. What surprised me most was that everybody still tried to do the right thing. They were honest. They were forthright. They were upright citizens. They were good people. The Canadians did everything for themselves. They were themselves, rather than pretending to be someone else, which had not been the norm in Pakistan. They did not try to impress people by having staff to cook and clean, unlike Pakistan, where it was a sign of status. In Montréal, I did everything for myself, just like everyone else.

Montréal is a very friendly, safe place. In those days, it was considered one of the safest and best cities in which to live. In New York, for example, there was rampant killing and gang warfare. I knew I had made the right decision in coming to Canada.

After three months, I received my first report from the course. It was not awash with firsts, nor even seconds. I was failing. I knew then that I would have to pull myself together. I also did not have enough money to continue living the way I had been. I had blown my budget. I had to get back on track. I had had enough fun, and it was now time to start thinking, '*Why am I here?*' My lifestyle was not sustainable, and I knew it was time to finish what I had come to do.

A focus on study was all very well, but there was also the immediate issue of a shortage of money. I would have to solve that problem or I would have no food and no bed.

Foreign students weren't allowed to work, even in part-time jobs, as they are now. Somehow, after paying rent and partying, we were expected to survive with no income. I found I was not the only international student in this predicament. We all had to find jobs on the quiet that would provide enough money to pay for food and other living expenses. This meant taking jobs that locals passed over – jobs with poor employers who did not pay the correct wages and had us working in terrible conditions. As foreign students, we had few options and no bargaining power, so we made the most of what we could find. I met three other guys in the same situation and one of them introduced me to a man who leased a nearby industrial laundry for night operations. During the day, somebody else ran the laundry, but at night it was all his.

This guy had contracts with jeans manufacturers and other garment makers in the city. All garments had to be washed and ironed before sale, so he said to the manufacturers, 'If you deliver the completed clothes, I'll wash, iron, and hang them, and deliver them to you first thing the next morning, ready to be sold.'

My job was to load 10 washing machines with the newly manufactured clothes. It was that simple. Just put them in the washer and close the door; the rest was automatic. When the cycle was complete, the machine would beep, and I would move them to the dryer and begin another load. It was monotonous work. From night until morning, I washed and dried jeans and other garments, and transferred them via an elevator or a ramp to where eight or nine heavy-duty clothes presses did the job of ironing them, ready for sale. Upstairs was where the real money was made. The mostly Pakistanis or West Indians would make US$100 a night because they were paid by the number of garments they pressed. My aspiration, of course, was to move upstairs. The guys up there often made such good money that they could give up their studies and marry French-Canadian girls.

I made some good friends in the laundry: Himayath Hussein from India, and Adil Awan (no relation) from Pakistan. They invited me to share their apartment. In fact, it is amazing that they let me stay more than one night, given the volume of my snoring in those days. But this gesture turned out to be a true measure of their warmth and generosity, and we remain friends to this day.

I was overjoyed with the amount of money I was paid so soon after starting, something like CAD$144 for three days' work. What a success I was! I had landed on my feet! I could now afford to continue my studies without financial support from home.

Overjoyed, I called Abba Jee after I got my first pay packet.

'I've got a job. I'm able to support myself!'

'So where are you working?'

'In a laundry.'

My father's interpretation of the situation differed from mine. Perhaps I had not explained to him why I was so excited by the income. I never had any intention of giving up on my studies, but before I could explain this further he interjected ...

'You bloody fool. Did I send you to Montréal to become a *dhobi*?' A *dhobi* was a washerman or washerwoman.

He hung up.

I later found out he feared that I would give up my studies and continue to work in the laundry. I was confused. What did he expect me to do? Become governor of Quebec? Take over from René Lévesque as premier? He hadn't provided me with an income. When I was leaving Karachi he had called me to his office to offer a few words of wisdom, and said, 'Go make it happen. Live your dream.' He bought me a one-way ticket, paid for the first semester's tuition fees, and gave me three months' allowance.

Living the dream was what I was doing.

As a parent, I now look back at those days and I can understand his concern. He saw what a lot of other kids who left our neighbourhood were getting up to – doing odd jobs and not doing what they were supposed to do, which was to study and make something of themselves. I recognise that now.

The LaSalle course was a three-year diploma in hotel management, but because I also attended the summer school, I completed the course early, graduating in 1980.

My one stumbling block was the bartending course, which I failed twice. For the final exam, the teacher put the names of 40 or 50 cocktails in a bowl and we were required to pull one out and prepare it. Many were recipes that I still don't know by heart even today. I couldn't find the ingredients, even if they were in front of me. The teacher was intimidating and I was nervous. One of the easiest cocktails is a Bloody Mary and, although the ingredients were right in front of me, I couldn't find them because of the pressure. To make a Zombie or a Singapore Sling, I had to pull out the correct glass and recite the recipe out loud, in the correct sequence. It was beyond me: 'Highball glass, crushed ice, quarter ounce each of apple juice, pineapple juice, garnish with ...,' etc. I found it incredibly difficult, and worse, I didn't actually care. (I did later learn how to make these cocktails on the job.) Because I flunked that class twice, I couldn't graduate with my peers, and had to repeat the same course elsewhere.

During the final two semesters, we were also required to have practical training. The catch was that this required a work permit, which I knew was not easily obtainable, and by then it was too late for me to acquire one in time. Luckily, the person looking after placements introduced me to an Indian-French gourmet restaurant called *Pique Assiette*. It was later renamed the *Bombay Palace*. It was owned by a famous billionaire Indian restaurateur who now lives in New York and runs his local luxury hotel, Chakwal, as well as owning an international chain of restaurants. They were willing to give me a job, even without a visa, because they knew I needed the experience.

As the restaurant was so small, I got a decent position and began working as the maître d'. I was soon promoted to restaurant manager, and I stayed in that role for seven or eight months. One day - luckily, my day off - the immigration department raided the restaurant; it must have been tipped off. The owner became worried after this and gave me a letter to apply for an official permit. However, while I awaited the approval, the restaurant employed another manager. But this was OK because I was leaving in a few months anyway.

My time there provided me with wonderful experience. It was where I learnt my barista skills. We used to turn over CAD$3000 a day, excluding tips. The wait staff made $80-$100 a night in tips, on top of their wages; however, as manager, I didn't enjoy those benefits. At the time, I didn't see that I needed more. In retrospect, this was an odd choice. If I had accepted the tips, I would most likely have been able to afford my airfare home.

I graduated just three months after my fellow classmates. With my diploma of hotel management proudly in hand, it was time for me to leave Canada. The problem was that, although I had worked hard, I was flat broke. There was no way I could afford my ticket home. After some calls and negotiations, I ended up working out an international arrangement with a distant relative, whose daughter lived in Virginia. The daughter sent me the money, and repayment was organised from Karachi.

I flew out of Mirabel Airport in December 1980 on my way home, stopping first at New York's JFK. I turned up at the counter there with 50 kilograms of excess luggage. There was no way I was leaving my textbooks behind! I was directed to the manager, told him my story, and he let me pass, with a good luck wish. This was an early lesson in both the art and pleasure I found in negotiation. I boarded Pakistan International Airlines' (PIA) last flight of the day to Karachi.

The country was in flux. Prohibition was scheduled to begin the next day and my PIA flight was the last one to serve alcohol. There was a stopover in Frankfurt. Twenty-four hours later, I was in Karachi, where Waris met me at the airport.

Graduation

Waris was a little agitated and anxious, which was unlike him.

'Look, Abba Jee is in a bad state. He's just come out of hospital and is at home now. He's expecting to see you right away.'

Abba Jee was quite sick; he had a problem with his prostate.

I walked in the front door and my father's first words were, 'All your paperwork is in order? You've graduated?'

'Yes.'

'Show it to me,' he said, motioning from his sickbed. 'Waris, have a look. Is it all good?'

It wasn't that he didn't trust me. He just wanted to see my diploma for himself because it gave him great pleasure to see that I had fulfilled my promise and succeeded, that I had returned with honour and dignity.

I wish he were alive today to see how far I've come, how well all of us have done. He would have been a very happy and proud man. Still, I'm sure that he is watching over all of us.

That diploma was my last formal college-based study. After that would come various professional development courses with Sheraton on specific areas of hotel management. In particular, its sales negotiations course would change my life. It was like the motorcycle all over again. But that experience was still a few years down the track.

But enough of study, the heart was now my focus. I had remained in touch with a girl I had become friends with before leaving for Canada. I had now returned home with prospects for a good career. I was somebody. After some communication between our parents, Ammie sent my marriage proposal to the girl's mother, whom I felt was sure to be impressed with me now. Meanwhile, my mother left Karachi for five weeks to visit my sister, who was having a baby. However, in the background other things were happening and I was left out. By the time Ammie returned, the girl was committed to another suitor.

Some time later I became close to another girl. She was intelligent and accomplished. She went to good schools, and topped English at Karachi University. Ammie knew her, however, and she was deemed unsuitable. As a young man, I had no say in this matter. It was important to us that our families bless our relationship. We both respected our parents and decided we would not go against their wishes. In my first relationship, I was the victim; now the tables had turned and this time it was *my* family who challenged *my* choice.

I knew then, and I still believe now, that such conservatism, and particularly the more rigorous standards that applied to girls, was not right. With three daughters and a granddaughter, I would be horrified to think they might face such sexism today, and that their choice of a husband might be dictated by myself and Neelo.

Our hearts were broken, but that relationship wasn't meant to be. I truly hope that that girl has since found the happiness in her life that I have found in mine.

In seeking to recover from this setback of the heart, I turned my attention to work.

During my first year in Canada, Abba Jee had retired from his business, having grown it from nothing to becoming a sizeable company. He also undertook civic work at this time, including being a councillor for the Pakistan Employees Cooperative Housing Society (PECHS).

PECHS is one of the leading residential areas in Karachi, and my father was deeply involved from its early days for many, many years. Similar to a local council, the society administers two hospitals, a school, and the PECHS College – a tertiary education college with an undergraduate program of around 2500 students. My father ran the college until a principal was appointed; then he stepped aside.

Abba Jee was the college's largest donor. Waris has followed in his footsteps and held elected positions at various times over the past 25 years, including the position of secretary. He is currently chairman, which is the equivalent of mayor.

Abba Jee was a charitable man his whole life. At the college's groundbreaking ceremony, the minister for finance even exclaimed, 'You are donating such a large amount of money and I'm not giving a cent!'

My father had always been a powerhouse of energy but he had become elderly, unwell, and he struggled to manage the work himself. What the business needed was for someone younger to take over and grow it, so that it could expand and prosper, which is exactly what Waris did. Waris retired from his very successful military career as a captain in the Pakistan Army and took over Awan House and Estate. He had been an instructor at the army's School of Infantry and Tactics and was highly respected. Many people believe that, had he remained in the army and all had gone well, without doubt he would have reached the rank of general.

Waris proposed a very clear handover. If he were to manage the business, then father wouldn't have any say in it. He had contemporary views, a new style, and would run the business differently. This was not because he disagreed with father's management; it was far from that. If father had stayed on, he would have worried about details. Waris understood that if it were to be his business, he had to have ownership over all aspects. With fresh eyes, and being from a new generation, Waris had a wider perspective and new ideas to implement – he had his own vision, which he has achieved, and has grown the business immeasurably.

Waris and I have never discussed whether he regretted relinquishing what promised to be a successful military career, but he has been extremely successful with the business and is financially much better off because of it. Waris simply stepped in and took over like a leader. With his military training and discipline, he took the whole family in the right direction. We have all benefited from his natural leadership skills and business acumen. He has diversified and increased the size of the business 100-fold. It now develops multi-storey medium-sized buildings around Karachi, and contributes to many charitable and community works.

My generation is now reaching the next stage of our lives, and we are looking to retire. Waris is my dearest friend. He has grandchildren, and no doubt the next generation will soon take over and stamp their vision on the family business.

Early career

The Taj Mahal, 1981

Eager to embark on my career, I applied for a number of hotel jobs around Karachi. A couple of positions appeared quite quickly, one at the Taj Mahal Hotel, another at the Sheraton. This hotel was still under construction but was starting to hire. However, completion was several months off, so the decision was made for me – the Taj Mahal it was.

I had my interview and was appointed front office manager for the 200-room hotel. While the name may suggest that it was a part of the famous Taj Group of Hotels in India, it was not. Now called the Regent Plaza Hotel & Convention Centre, it is an imposing white 1970s building only 10 minutes from the city centre, with a grand atrium that extends the full height of its interior.

The hotel was fairly new, and my role was to establish the front office department. From my studies, I knew running this department would require 30 different forms, maybe more. This was the era before computers and we ran on the Whitney system, a cumbersome, custom-designed, document management system for hotels. I put a suite of forms in place, and made sure all staff were trained in their use. The system was running smoothly. Then I found myself challenged by my managing director about the number of documents we were using.

It turned out that what I expected of the role of front office manager was not at all the reality. At graduation from LaSalle College, the dean had said in his farewell speech, 'Boys and girls, go out and learn.' At the time, I thought: *'What the hell have I done for the past three academic years, other than that? I've learnt what I need to know about hotel management. I'm ready to become an efficient and knowledgeable departmental manager – at the very least.'*

Little did I know then that what we had learnt at college was bookish and based on broad principles and generic processes. What we would face upon leaving was the reality that each hotel, or chain of hotels, comes with its own set of guidelines as to how a task is to be performed. Everything is documented and delivered as per standard operating procedures for that hotel or chain.

The managing director was clearly out to cut costs. I was paid only 1800 rupees a month when, before I studied in Montréal, I made 3500 rupees a month. On these wages I couldn't even afford the quality of suits I was expected to wear. But what was I to do? I needed a job. I was a new graduate. Accordingly, I was cheap to employ.

I like to think that I set up the department and trained the staff well, due to my technical knowledge from the course and my earlier training at the InterContinental Hotel. But then it was time to look for jobs further afield. I quit on the spot and remained unemployed for a good few months until one of my closest friends, Zafar Amir, visited Karachi for a holiday.

'Come back with me to Dubai,' he suggested. 'I'll arrange for a seven-day visa and you can look for a job. Dubai is full of hotels.'

I had nothing to lose.

Abba Jee kindly paid for my ticket and I travelled with Zafar to Dubai, where, within days, I was offered a job at the Sharjah Continental Hotel. At this time, Dubai was somewhat of a backwater. Emirates Airlines would not exist for another five years; there was only Gulf Air. In fact, it was only around 2004 that the Dubai government realised that its prime location, halfway between Europe and Asia, afforded a golden opportunity to recreate the city as a centre of aviation's new Silk Road. In a momentous turnaround, it moved from an oil- and trade-reliant economy to an aviation and tourism centre. Since then, Dubai has become a major global transit hub.

Sharjah Continental Hotel, 1981–1984

In the relatively quiet city of Sharjah, the Sharjah Continental Hotel was *the* hospitality jewel. It was the most beautiful and luxurious hotel in the United Arab Emirates, owned by an extremely wealthy Kuwaiti businessman, Mubarak Al Hasawi. His wealth was such that he owned his own private Boeing 737.

Now called the Radisson Blu Resort Sharjah, the Continental was a massive, five-star luxury hotel with around 350 rooms. It had a private beach, cabanas, six or seven restaurants that offered various cuisines, and every sports facility you can imagine – tennis, squash, a spa, a bowling alley, and more.

As assistant front office manager, I was expected to speak Arabic. I couldn't, but I swiftly learnt the top hundred or so common words and phrases so I could communicate with guests.

I was well aware of how fortunate I was to be offered the job. I was in charge of all the elements of reservations which, in a hotel of its size, was another major learning curve. I began to understand what the dean had meant in his final speech when he said, 'Go out and learn'. When I look back, it was at the Continental where I learnt the most about the world of international hotels.

When I began the job, I had one assistant, had to deal with another time-consuming paper-based reservations system, and was also called on regularly to fill in for most front-of-house roles. As a result, three or four months into the job, I grew disillusioned. I had a piece of paper from Canada, which I believed should allow me to set the agenda and be noticed. I hoped for responsibility and to receive more recognition. In retrospect, these were clearly the wrong expectations. I still didn't quite fathom how the world worked.

One particular day, I had a trivial gripe about some issue that I felt should have been managed differently. I handed in my resignation and called my father to tell him. Of course, I knew not to expect sympathy from him. I think I just needed his chagrin to bring me back to my senses.

It was the Montréal laundry all over again.

'Take the letter back. This is not what you want, Sakib.'

I found myself once again in a not-unfamiliar position, my pride slightly tarnished and my tail between my legs. I went to visit the human resources manager, who was a very understanding English woman.

'If it's not too late, I'd like to withdraw my resignation.'

With a few words of support and some wise advice from an experienced hand, she tore up my letter. Crisis averted. How would I have faced my father if she had refused to accept my retraction?

Love of my life

In 1983, I had a good job at a more than reputable hotel and was on track with my career. I was also of the age where, it is fair to say, I was in the right position to marry. I had informed my now ex-girlfriend, by letter, that my family did not approve of our relationship. To be outcast from family was not an option for either of us. It was a few months after this that Ammie called.

'It is time for you to get married and to settle down with a family, Sakib. I have looked right, left, and centre for a girl. It's not easy with you being overseas. What are we going to do?'

Ammie clearly had her matchmaker eyes open and was intent on resolving this situation. She suggested several names. I accepted her suggestions gratefully, but made it clear that I wanted someone whom I knew would stand shoulder-to-shoulder with me. I wanted an equal. I knew the girls she suggested would not be that. Standing up to tradition was difficult, but this was my life and I wanted far more equality in marriage than was usual in Pakistan at that time. And I knew where girls with similar wishes and family experiences were likely to be living.

Our neighbour, Mrs Mirza (known as Auntie to us), had two daughters who had not long returned from almost 10 years of study in London, where they had completed their A-levels. Neelofer, or Neelo as she was affectionately known, had also completed a diploma of business administration at Westminster College, London.

Neelo was born in 1958, so we were of a similar age. Mrs Mirza and her daughters used to relax in the cool evenings on their balcony that overlooked our house and the street. Neelo was particularly funny and would provide her family with a detailed commentary as they watched my daily comings and goings below. I had noticed her from a distance when we met casually with the family and so was aware of her intelligence, humour, and beauty – qualities she still possesses, I might add.

'What about someone in the neighbourhood?' I suggested.

This got Ammie thinking. 'Perhaps, Mrs Mirza's daughter, Neelofer?' she suggested. 'Your brother Nadeem (Anwar) has already suggested her to me.'

My mother and Mrs Mirza were good friends, but this was a delicate topic.

Neelo's father, Dr Tajuddin Ahmed Mirza, had been a doctor in the British Army before Partition. He then served in both the Indian and Pakistan armies. By the time he retired, he held the rank of naval lieutenant commander. His military career meant the family had lived in various places, not all of which were conducive to raising children in a safe and stable environment, or with suitable educational facilities. Dr Mirza took an early retirement from the navy. After spending some time working in his own clinic, he got a job in Saudi Arabia. He and his wife then decided it would be best to send their two girls to England, where one of their sons was already studying, and where they would receive a good quality, stable education.

Dr Mirza passed away in 1981, soon after retiring from his medical career at 64. Neelo was 23 years old – so young to lose one's father. Even as a doctor, he didn't receive the appropriate medical treatment when it was needed. He had been admitted as an emergency patient and treated by the cardiologist on duty, not his own, which caused some confusion in the hospital administration. At the time, Neelo was working in Karachi, and this was the first death she had experienced in her immediate family. Distant relatives had died, but as Neelo has said, 'When somebody in your immediate family dies – your father – it's different. It's the end of your world as you know it.'

Dr Mirza saw four out of his five children married, but, sadly, not Neelo. However, as the youngest, and the only child not yet married, she was very close to her mother.

Neelo's elder sister would often bake cakes and send them over to my parents and, as was the custom in Pakistan, a plate should never be returned empty. This meant there was a perpetual exchange of food between our houses over the years that we were neighbours.

One afternoon Ammie rustled up the courage to knock on Mrs Mirza's door.

Mrs Mirza was a well-read, sophisticated lady who had the sensitivity and insight to immediately pick up on subtle signals. My mother wasn't a regular visitor, so when she turned up unannounced and without a plate, Mrs Mirza immediately knew the visit was for more than a casual chat over a cup of tea.

'Mrs Awan, why don't you stay and have lunch with us?' she asked.

Ammie stayed for lunch and, by all accounts, it was a stilted and awkward meal. My mother claims she was lost for words. She just didn't know how to broach the topic.

'Mrs Awan, come and lie down and rest for a little while. You really don't seem to be yourself today. I will make some tea for us.'

'Thank you, Mrs Mirza, I will be fine.'

Eventually, mother summoned the strength to raise the topic.

'Mrs Mirza, I'm actually here to speak about Neelo and Sakib. Sakib is now 26. He has a good job. It is really time that he married. Neelo has now returned to Karachi. She is a wonderful girl, and I would like to ask for her hand for Sakib.'

This revelation from my mother was no doubt met with a warm smile, which signalled tacit approval from Mrs Mirza.

'Well, they have known each other at a distance for so long, but haven't properly spoken before, so shall we let them decide?', Mrs Mirza suggested.

My mother agreed. 'He's had girlfriends, as young ones all do, but he is settled now. And once married, all my boys are very sincere and faithful to their wives.'

As Neelo had been in London since she was a young teenager, we had spoken only on rare occasions when she was home and the family had visited our house. She needed some convincing and this informal chat between our mothers and her sister, Nazo, was instrumental in her change of heart.

We had never before considered each other as a potential husband or wife, that is certain.

It was arranged that I would return from Dubai for a few days so that Neelo and I could meet properly.

Given that my trip home was brief, time was of the essence. Mrs Mirza invited me to their house, and Neelo and I sat on the verandah, had tea and cakes and chatted. The Mirzas' house sat slightly forward of ours on its block, and from that vantage point it suddenly struck me exactly how much they could see of our house. They had the potential to see all the goings-on in our property. They had a clear view of our garden, our driveway and, if they wished, they could look directly inside. What a perfect position for Neelo's narration of the life of Sakib! From our house, set further back, we could see nothing of the Mirzas' life.

Our meeting at home went well and we progressed to dinner alone together. I selected a suitably impressive restaurant and visited the Interflora shop at the InterContinental Hotel to buy flowers. Neelo wore a beautiful silk dress. Her mother, I later learnt, had argued against her original choice of outfit.

'What? You cannot go out like this! No, no,' Mrs Mirza had protested. 'You must not wear a cotton dress. You must wear silk!'

Over dinner, we talked about our lives, and a range of topics we can no longer recall, before broaching the core topic.

'So, our mothers are planning that we should marry. What do you think about that?' I asked.

We spoke more about our lives and hopes for the future. We both knew what was going on, as we had been *spoken for* by this stage. At the end of dinner, I presented Neelo with the flowers.

'Neelo, will you marry me?'

'I will, Sakib.'

And that was it. There was no courtship. That would come later. Ours was an arranged marriage of sorts, softly arranged one could say. Many marriages in Pakistan at that time were arranged with no involvement of the bride and groom.

However, my younger brothers noticed that once our marriage was certain, the flow of cakes between our houses stopped. Neelo's story is that her sister, who baked them, had children by that time and simply had less time to bake. I prefer to think that it had all been a family plan to lure me with cake to meet Neelo. If that were the case, it was a successful strategy.

I could not have married a better person. I would marry Neelo again any day of the week, day or night. I love her. She's a wonderful, caring, loving partner who stands shoulder-to-shoulder with me.

We worked hard together in those early years to establish our relationship. With Neelo, there is no shying away from anything. Over the years, this quality has become more and more apparent to me. I tend to focus on the big picture, I speak to people and pull plans together, and I worry. Neelo is a methodical, details person who effortlessly ties up the finer points. We are very well matched.

I cannot begin to imagine life without my wonderful Neelo. We can make each other smile, even when we are unhappy or stressed.

Shaadi

My parents' house at 6/50B1 PECHS has been in the family since 1955 and now belongs to one of my younger brothers, who bought out the other members of the family. It is a large house and was initially rented to the Italian ambassador, then to a famous belly dancer, and subsequently a mining magnate. It has seen a great deal of history and many famous Karachi residents have passed through its doors. It is currently rented out as a commercial building, because that area is now a business district. It is only 20 metres from the main road that connects the city to the airport, Shahrah-e-Faisal Road.

From the early 1960s until 1976, the house was rented to a school and Neelo's mother was the headmistress. Neelo attended the school when she was young, and the very classroom in which she had studied became our wedding suite. That same room is where our eldest daughter, Zeenat, was born two months prematurely, because there was not enough time to get to the hospital. The two grandmothers, Neelo's mother and Ammie, delivered her right there. Fortunately, Mrs Mirza, having been the wife of a doctor, had helped deliver babies before, so she had some knowledge of what to do. My elder brother Waris and his wife, Hameeda, and my younger brothers ran up and down the stairs providing hot towels and whatever else our mothers demanded. Zeenat was named by Abba Jee, who was reciting the Quran at the time and said the word Zeenat. It is a tradition for elders to name a child. I wanted the name Ismat, after my mother, but Abba Jee said no. He reasoned that when the child inevitably got into trouble for something while growing up, we would shout her name, and he felt that that would be inappropriate. Later, when my youngest daughter Ismat was born, after my father had passed away, my mother was delighted to have a granddaughter named after her.

Perhaps because it was such a momentous event – delivering a baby when you've never done it before – or perhaps because Zeenat was our first child, the two grandmothers decided they would bury the placenta in the garden. No doubt there are many superstitions around that, and it adds to the house's rich layers of history – and a greener garden!

The Pakistani *Shaadi*, or marriage, comprises five ceremonies – *Nikah, Mayun, Mehndi, Rukhsati,* and *Valima* – held over a period of weeks and variously attended by the bride and groom's family and friends. Ours was particularly extended because I was still working in the UAE and I explained to my parents that I didn't want to hold the final ceremony until Neelo's UAE visa was ready. In Pakistan, that can take three or four months, or even longer. Taking all the functions and ceremonies into account, there would have been more than 1000 people in attendance.

Because I am one of 11 children, many of whom already had families, *Nikah* was an enormous ceremony, the largest by far, attended by around 300 people. Following the ceremony, I returned to the UAE and waited for Neelo's visa to be approved. This took nearly seven months, at which point I returned home for the remaining ceremonies.

Mayun was held at Neelo's house and involved much song and dance. For one week, Neelo wore yellow, and with her close group of female friends and family, her hands and face were painted with a paste called *ubtan*. Made from turmeric, sandalwood powder, herbs and oils, this is a beautification process.

Mehndi, which takes its name from *mendhika*, the Sanskrit name for the henna plant, is the henna ceremony, and traditionally takes place just prior to the wedding. The *Mehndi* paste is made by drying the henna leaves in the sun before grinding and sieving them to obtain a fine, mossy green powder. The powder is combined with water, lemon juice, and drops of eucalyptus oil, mixed into a smooth paste, left overnight, and then poured into a slim, fine-pointed plastic cone so it can be applied with accuracy and delicacy, mainly to the bride's palms, back of her hands, and feet.

Our farewell, or *Rukhsati* in Urdu, where the bride is bid farewell by her family and heads off to her new life, was quite literal for us – within days we would leave Pakistan.

The final ceremony was *Valima*, the banquet, the official end to the wedding and our farewell to the many family and friends who attended.

We departed Karachi for the UAE with Neelo's henna still as bold as the day it was drawn.

To a non-*Desi*, this series of ceremonies might seem like an elaborate celebration for a young couple who really know little about each other. How could we possibly know which way our lives would turn? Would we enjoy each other's company? Would we annoy each other?

The reality is, how you choose to live your new life together is completely within your control. Leaving our single lives, we committed to *one* life, *together*. We committed ourselves to each other, to the adventures, the good days and the difficult days, whatever was to come our way. We were just like every other young couple who walks out of their wedding and says, 'It's our life now. Let's go and live it, together.'

I wanted Neelo to have a honeymoon and to relax and enjoy her new life – at least for a few months until her henna faded – but I did not get my way. Perhaps our life was not to be quite as I had dreamt. Within a week, she jumped headlong into our life together. She got a job because we could not enjoy a reasonable quality of life in Sharjah on only one salary. It was an expensive city in which to live and we were on our own. Half of our income went towards rent, but we also wanted to live in the fashion to which we had been accustomed. It was up to us to live our life the way we wanted, and that required two salaries.

'OK', Neelo said. 'We just got married. So what? I'll go and work. We do this together from now on.'

Neelo attended her first job interview at a law firm within a few days of our arrival, still with her henna and wearing 12 gold bangles.

'It seems I need a job more than you, with the amount of gold you're wearing,' said the woman who interviewed her.

'Oh, yes, the henna, the bangles. I just got married.'

Neelo's parents had paid the school and college fees as well as daily expenses for Neelo and her sister over the years, but during her diploma studies, Neelo had worked every Saturday at Marks & Spencer on Oxford Street, London, to earn extra money. On returning to Pakistan, she had worked for an advertising agency, and then in human resources and administration for Upjohn Pharmaceuticals. Both of these positions had given her great experience to bring to any position in the UAE. This was instantly recognised and the law firm employed her on the spot.

My mother had never worked, as was traditional for women in past generations. Now it is different. When we married, this cultural shift had not yet begun. Getting a job immediately was simply classic Neelo. She is a very special person: smart, charming, strong, gentle, and compassionate. She works hard at whatever she does, and leaps into life with a great sense of humour, which has helped us face some tough times together. I cannot imagine what my life would have been without her.

Abba Jee was inspired and wrote many poems about my feelings for Neelo upon our marriage. Only two of those poems remain vivid for me. One is a humorous piece of writing that I remember well because it was passed around the family often. His advice must be taken in the context of the time: it is on the role of a daughter or daughter-in-law as viewed by a man who was born in 1909. In the context of the 21st century, it's a wonderful snapshot of expectations from a 19th century Indian perspective. He gave this poem to each of his daughters and daughters-in-law at the time of their marriage:

Some Advice to a Daughter on Her Marriage

1. Your husband is your lifelong companion with no parallel; your behaviour towards each other should be loving and respectful enough to endure the span of your lives.
2. Forgo and forget the eccentricities of your spouse; rather, enjoy them.
3. Swallow the bitter pills that may come from those around you and respond to them tastefully.
4. Life, particularly conjugal life, is what you make of it, with the mixture of pleasures of your husband to give it a romantic flavour.
5. Keep in mind the dietary value of the food your family needs.
6. Live within your family budget; try to keep it in surplus.

7. You must save every month, even if it is only one rupee. The more you save, the better your prospects.
8. Carry out a weekly, fortnightly, or at least a monthly survey of things in your house to see if they need to be changed, repaired, replaced, or rejected.
9. Find the basic cause of your poverty; don't regret it, but try to fight it and cure it as a couple, with team spirit.
10. The act of sex should not be so excessive as to overly consume either the wife or husband. *[This from a man with 11 children!]*
11. Practising reciprocity will provide greater benefit in conjugal life than any other walk of your life.
12. Children are the joint concern of both wife and husband, and should be secured, reared, and brought up with joint effort and skill.
13. Cultivate a proper ability to love your spouse above all.
14. Family planning should be properly and strictly observed and followed according to your resources, income, and stamina in life. *[No doubt my father was a confident and fit man.]*
15. Contentment is the best source of happiness and should be adhered to as a habit.
16. The search for academic, scientific, general, and practical knowledge is the best hobby in life.
17. HEALTH IS WEALTH and should be given priority in all aspects of life.
18. Trust in God and do the right thing, at the right time, in the right direction, and with the right intention.
19. Try your best to avoid showing anger towards your spouse, however embarrassing the circumstances you may confront.
20. Be a willing and cooperative partner in life to make it happy, happier, and happiest.
21. Spouses should reflect on any idiotic feelings in relation to each other and try to get rid of them.

22. Do not accept harassment from your spouse or in-laws – have the courage to convert it into a humorous dialogue with all the calmness at your command.

N.D.K. Awan
Your Father's Blessings

Neelo had returned to Pakistan after her education in England fluent in English. As a man of linguistics, Abba Jee admired her for this. Added to that, she was a daughter of Dr and Mrs Mirza, whom he and the community greatly respected. What more could he want for one of his sons?

Overall, I was very well treated by Sharjah Continental Hotel and I gained a great deal of valuable experience. In truth, I didn't really have a legitimate issue with the way it was run. As with all hotels it was very disciplined and perhaps I was not 100 per cent ready for that. If staff stepped out of line there was zero tolerance.

International hotels set high professional standards and I worked 10-hour days, six days a week. For convenience, we chose to live in Sharjah, not too far from the hotel. With my schedule there was not much time for a social life, but on the occasions that we did go out into the city or to catch up with friends we had made, there was no escape from the formality and restrictions on life there.

Sharjah was essentially a satellite city of Dubai. Back in the 1980s, Dubai was not the size it is today; nevertheless, it was slightly more cosmopolitan and trade-focused than Sharjah. While you felt safe, because the laws were so strict, it was still a golden prison. You couldn't be yourself. If you want to do your own thing in any way, you cannot survive in the UAE – the environment ultimately wears you down. After several years, we realised that we had no desire to live like that forever. Professionally, it was not possible for me to advance my career, because in the UAE those of us from the subcontinent are still treated as second-class citizens. To be promoted, I had either to become fluent in Arabic and remain at the Sharjah Continental Hotel, or move on and look for other positions in different countries. There was no other option. The law in the UAE meant that if you left a job you could not work in another position there for 12 months.

The three and a half years in Sharjah provided me with a strong foundation in terms of experience and a detailed knowledge of how a major five-star hotel was run. I was ready to move up. With serendipitous timing, I came across an advertisement for a position that would provide us with an ideal opportunity to move closer to home.

Return to Pakistan

The advertisement was for a senior position in rooms division management at the Holiday Inn, Islamabad. I was invited for an interview. I took an extra day off work at the Continental, and while Neelo remained in Sharjah, I went to the airport after work to catch the two-hour flight to Karachi. I stayed with my parents overnight, and the next morning flew to Islamabad.

The person who greeted me that day, Zulfiqar Malik, would later become general manager of the hotel and is still general manager of one of the hotels in the Marriott chain. When I left Islamabad that afternoon, I had the job.

The Holiday Inn Islamabad on Agha Khan Road, now the Marriott Hotel, is an imposing building. In 1984, it was the only five-star hotel in the city and was regarded as *the* hotel at which to stay.

In my new role, everyone who was anyone in Pakistan wanted to be my friend. I held the keys to the rooms, and that power placed me in an interesting position. Five-star hotels aim to accommodate important guests, who sometimes turn up without a booking, and to satisfy whatever bizarre or difficult requests those guests have. This is not always possible, but the ace up my sleeve was that I knew our superior suites were often vacant, so a regular or important guest could be upsold to a suite.

Given the large number of people who passed through the hotel every day, it was imperative that reservations were tightly controlled. We would reconfirm all bookings one day before each guest's arrival, whether by telex or telephone, and double-check the correspondence. It was enormously time consuming, but with such a busy hotel, it was the only way to ensure the system ran smoothly. I would personally check every booking to ensure that each guest had confirmed, and reconfirmed, and that a payment was received for the booking.

One comically awkward situation I remember was when quite a senior businessman, who was a regular guest, took all the expensive coffee-table books from the room when he left. Housekeeping staff and the front desk cashier came to see me, feeling somewhat apprehensive.

'Housekeeping says that he's taken the books away,' the cashier told me.

Given who he was, it was unclear exactly how this would pan out. There are few situations more delicate than potentially embarrassing a guest publicly so it was decided that, as the most senior person available, I would ask him about it. Anyone more junior and he would have ignored them, or worse. We all knew him to be prickly at the best of times. With deference, I approached him in the lobby.

'I understand from housekeeping that you like the coffee-table books in your room, and that you may be interested in buying them. You were not to know, but there is a cost involved here. Would you like me to charge this to your hotel bill, or would you prefer to pay cash?'

'Oh, I'm so sorry. I didn't know I had to pay for them', he said.

He opened his suitcase then and there, in the lobby, took the books out, and gave them to me. Who knows what the truth was, but the problem was solved far more easily than I had expected.

Another time, there was a more sobering incident. A Pakistani feudal lord, a powerful landowner who considered himself the equivalent of British gentry, chased a European lady around the hotel. Various staff tried to stop him, but he knew that the order for him to be removed had come from me. He stormed into my office and physically attacked me. He yanked my hair and we went fist to fist, as I tried to hold him off. Hotel security was always on hand to protect guests and staff, but on rare occasions, outside help was required. This was one of those times. The police were called and he was apprehended and taken away. Two hours later, he was free and roaming around the lobby again as if he owned the place, and looking to attack me again.

It was horrific to be attacked in one's own office in a five-star luxury hotel. This did not conform with my idea of such hotels. They were meant to be civilised places where everyone knows how to behave. That's what I signed up for.

Our return to Pakistan proved to be the right decision because on 28 December 1984, our first child, Zeenat, was born. Raising one child, let alone future children, in Sharjah would have been extremely difficult, what with long work hours and no family support.

Although we were now closer to home, being in Islamabad with no family around us was still not what we wanted, particularly when Neelo became pregnant with our second child. My mother arrived to be with us for this birth, but when an urgent matter arose, she was called back to Karachi. That was when Neelo's mother flew in. At 10am on 21 December 1985, I dropped Neelo and her mum off at Islamabad Private Hospital. I remember it was a cold day and the hospital's reverse-cycle air-conditioner wasn't working as it should. Instead, it was blasting out cold air.

Neelo sent me home to collect something and, as I was out, I decided to take some flowers back with me. It was a public holiday, however, and everything was closed. Half an hour after I had dropped them off at the hospital, Saba was born, and I was nowhere to be found. I didn't expect the baby to come so quickly! The flowers were a nice idea, but as it turned out, not the cleverest one.

Neelo has had good fortune with the birthing of our children, all three of whom arrived promptly. She has been active for each, because her mum always said to her, 'This is a natural part of your life. Live and enjoy it.'

Turning back to work, my role meant that I would often receive phone calls from people who needed my help. On one of those occasions, a call came from the office of the then vice president of Sheraton South Asia, Dieter Janssen, who was based at the Karachi Sheraton. A friend of his, Mr Rosenthal, had arrived at the hotel only to find that there was no booking for him. He was a regular guest and worked for a large German power plant company.

We called Dieter Janssen's assistant, Behroze Edulji, to check the situation.

'Oh, look, I've screwed up,' she said. 'I didn't call. Is there any way you can find a room?'

'We will work something out, I'm sure', I reassured her. 'Don't worry about it.' And we did.

A few months later, I was having tea with Mr Rosenthal.

'Why is an enterprising guy like you in a dead city like Islamabad?', he asked.

Islamabad is a capital city like Canberra. If you want a more exciting life of concerts, restaurants, stage shows, and the like, you needed to be in Karachi.

'Ideally, I would love to be in Karachi, because that's where my family is.'

'Give me your CV. I'll see what I can do', he replied.

One thing I've always had at hand is an up-to-date CV, where only a few minor changes might be required. I gave him a copy before he left that Friday. On Monday morning I had a phone call from Behroze Edulji.

'Mr Rosenthal met with Dieter Janssen over the weekend. He spoke very highly of you and we have your CV here. Mr Janssen would like to meet. When could you come?'

'Tomorrow is my day off. I can come to Karachi in the morning.'

The next day I flew to Karachi, met with Dieter Janssen, and left the meeting with an employment contract in my hand. I returned to Islamabad, resigned, and gave notice to our landlord. One month later we were in Karachi, and I started my new job as sales manager at the Karachi Sheraton.

Go out and learn

I didn't know the first thing about sales. I was a process person. A people manager. Once again, the words of the dean at LaSalle College echoed in my ears. With each new role I secured, my respect for his wisdom grew.

This would be another steep learning curve. The Karachi Sheraton was the number one hotel in Pakistan at the time, and I was responsible for new business development. The ace up my sleeve now was that I was in my hometown, and if the key to sales is anything, it's contacts. Upon arrival, I made time to see as many of my old contacts around the city as possible. My co-workers were extremely helpful, and most helped me out with contacts and new business leads.

The position was not without its challenges, however. Fairly early on, the managing director of a large pharmaceutical company took me to task, claiming I had charged a higher room rate than the hotel down the road. The Sheraton did not sell on price, but at the time I lacked sufficient sales skills to address his complaint satisfactorily. I knew I shouldn't argue on price, but out of respect, I also couldn't say to him, 'These are the key reasons we are better'. I wasn't equipped to argue in that persuasive way. I floundered. After all, I was an operations man who had just gone into sales and marketing. Years later, sales negotiation training through Sheraton Australia would teach me persuasion skills, and enable me to identify the pros and cons of our offer versus the competition.

Shortly after I began, I had the opportunity to have us declared the official hotel for the ICC Cricket World Cup, which was to be held in India and Pakistan from 8 October to 8 November 1987. This was the first time the tournament would be held outside England. It was an important event for Pakistan, and an important contract for us, not only financially but also because of the profile we would receive, locally, and internationally.

A few months before, I had been a spectator at the One Day International in Rawalpindi. There I saw an old family friend, Tahir Memon. He was with the president of Pakistan, General Zia-ul-Haq, the man who led Pakistan through the Mujahideen days. The general was a powerful man, and everybody wanted to be in his circle.

Tahir *Bhai* (brother), as I called him, was a senior executive at a large business that organised sports tournaments such as the cricket Wills Cup; he had also purchased one of my father's houses and become a family friend. Importantly, at this time, he was also the honorary head of the ICC World Cup Organising Committee.

I had returned from Dubai with an assemblage of new gadgets not yet available in Pakistan. I was particularly fond of photography and my collection of gadgetry included a state-of-the-art camera. Towards the end of the match between Pakistan and the West Indies, the president decided, without warning, that he would go and greet the team. The most senior person with him was Tahir Bhai, so he accompanied the president down to the pitch.

As soon as I saw them together, I pulled out my camera and shadowed them from the pavilion right down to the pitch, shooting the whole time. The press must have been caught off-guard as I found myself the only one close to them with a camera. I took 17 or so shots of my 36-photo roll – this was in the days of film. Tahir Bhai was desperate to get hold of copies and sent his manager to collect them from me soon afterwards. He was extremely grateful.

'Whatever I can do for you, Sakib, let me know.'

A few months after that, I heard that the Pearl Continental Hotel chain had won the accommodation contract for the World Cup teams. It was an ideal time to contact Tahir Bhai about whether, when in Karachi, the World Cup teams could stay at the Sheraton.

'That's fine. Yes, I can organise that,' he promised.

When Dieter Janssen heard, he could not fathom how I had delivered such a prize deal for his hotel. He wanted to be sure, convinced that there must be some loose ends to tie up. Perhaps he didn't believe me. In any case, he sent the hotel's director of sales with me to meet with Tahir Bhai, who summarily dismissed his presence as unnecessary.

'I gave my word to Sakib. It's done. Please take his word as gospel.'

After that, I acquired a reputation for achieving successes that others could not. One of my other major successes was a revival of the entire pharmaceutical marketing sector, which included conferences, symposia, seminars, and the like. Securing the World Cup teams was a great success. Unfortunately, before the World Cup took place, I had already left the hotel, so I wasn't there to meet our guests.

Outside the safe world of my international hotel, Pakistan was still a dictatorship, ruled under martial law, as it had been since 1977 when Zia ul-Haq seized power. While there might have been a movement towards democracy with the return from exile of Benazir Bhutto, the country still had a long way to go. Hundreds of thousands of people peacefully rallied in the streets in 1986 in support of Bhutto, demanding that Zia ul-Haq be ousted.

'Zia out! Zia must go! Zia is a dog!', the crowds shouted. No one knew at the time which way it would go. There was pressure from outside the country too, with more than 120 Afghan-led terrorist attacks. The uncertainty and violence sat heavily in our hearts and permeated our lives. It seemed clear to me that, at that time, Pakistan provided little hope for a safe, prosperous future for Neelo's and my growing family.

Family & disillusionment

Karachi is such a large and varied city, it is more like a country. At the time of independence in 1947, the city's population was just under one million. When my father retired from the public service to begin his business, it had risen to 1.85 million. Forty years later, upon my departure for Australia in 1987, it had grown to seven million. In 2017, the national census suggested it was around 16 million; however, the true count is likely to be more than 20 million.

If you are wealthy, life there is much like life in any other major international city – to a degree. Wonderful food is available, and you can live in an expensive house with domestic staff. However, you will need to be protected by heavily armed personal security guards and have bars on your windows. You will have to haggle and negotiate on every purchase, your electricity supply will be irregular, and the traffic police will constantly stop you to collect their regular bribes.

For the less well-off, the city is a mass of traffic-clogged anarchic roads, the pollution is terrible, sewers overflow, fresh water is hard to come by, and you might not even have electricity.

These problems are not exclusive to Pakistan, of course; similar situations exist in many developing nations. However, there is always hope, and when a population or a government puts their minds to it, change can come swiftly. In 2014, Karachi was ranked as the sixth most dangerous city in the world; by 2018 it was 60th, with Darwin and Townsville ranked as more dangerous per head of population. That's a dramatic improvement over a brief period.

While there are frustrations that come with living in Pakistan, and I had lived with them for most of my younger life, it had not become easier for me. I had lived abroad and experienced how other countries operated; the freedom of Canada as well as the awkward mix of extravagance and restriction in the UAE had both shown me the possibilities the rest of the world offered. I know that while I still understand how to operate in a city like Karachi, if we went back to live in Pakistan, my children would not survive a day. They don't have the street smarts that are necessary to navigate that kind of world.

It is important to be realistic. Nepotism and corruption exist in every country; you have only to look at the deals and donations done both in business and politics around the world. However, on the whole, success is based on your own merits, learning the process and living the life you choose within your own moral boundaries. Australia is a small country of around 25 million people. Pakistan has a population of more than 200 million. With a population of that size comes complexity.

While my frustrations with Pakistan may be numerous, the country is still in my blood and I will always remain tied to the land and proud of my origins. After all, that land contains an incredible and proud history of human development. Largely within the borders of Pakistan, the Indus Valley was home to one of the three Old World civilisations, along with Egypt and Mesopotamia. This civilisation dates back to 3300BC. Its cities were home to up to 60,000 people, with grand public architecture, and an administrative system that built functional public structures such as dockyards, granaries, warehouses, protective city walls, and a Romeworthy drainage system. It was an urban civilisation, not unlike ours in some ways, that also developed one of the earliest systems of weights and measures. These people created art that we recognise today in the form of fine, elegant earthenware pottery decorated with ornate, coloured, geometric patterns, as well as figures of fish, birds, and bulls. While that is an incredible heritage, Indigenous history in Australia, which is fortunate to have a living connection with a culture that dates back 50,000 or more years, makes the Indus Valley civilisations look like yesterday.

An opportunity

The Sheraton Corporation celebrated its 50th anniversary in 1987 at an extravagant event held at one of the chain's best-known hotels, Hawaii's Waikiki Sheraton. General managers and directors of sales and marketing from around the world attended, and were presented with a vision of where the company was headed, including in Australia. The hospitality market in Australia was booming at that time, and the direction from head office was that Sheraton staff were to make the most of this opportunity. Around Australia, 150 four- and five-star hotels were already under construction by various chains. That number of new hotels meant there would be a major skills shortage in the sector.

This was the break Neelo and I had dreamt about. I sat, poker-faced, as our entire department was debriefed. That evening I relayed the details to Neelo. We decided this was an opportunity of a lifetime and we were perfectly placed to maximise it.

The office next to mine in the Karachi Sheraton was occupied by Dieter Janssen's executive assistant, the wonderful and powerful Behroze Edulji. With Behroze on your side, you could achieve anything in that hotel – and possibly whatever you dreamt of in other countries too.

There was no internet in 1987 and, to my knowledge, Behroze had the only commercial fax machine available to the public in Karachi. Back then, most international reservations, cancellations, and confirmations were processed by telex, so this was an important machine. It is also the reason that Neelo and I were able to move to Australia only two and a half months later instead of the seven to 12 months normally required for a transfer of that kind. We were on our way while others waited for letters to be sent to and from Australia. Fax machines were already common there then, but not in Pakistan.

Australia was our chance to start anew in a secure, financially strong – in fact, booming – country. Besides, while Pakistan hoped for more independence, Australia and the UK had passed the *Australia Act* the previous year, giving responsibility for all laws and the Constitution to the Australian government. In a civilised process, without unrest or protests from anyone, Australia became its own sovereign, completely independent, modern nation. We hoped soon to be citizens.

Neelo's sister, Shireen, lived in Papua New Guinea with her Pakistani-Australian geologist husband, who was a senior civil servant. She had been granted Australian citizenship because they had lived in Papua New Guinea since before 1975 when it was still an Australian territory. With serendipitous timing, they were in Pakistan for a holiday at that time. We called on her that very day to ask if she would sponsor us.

'Of course. Absolutely, no problem.'

I called the Australian High Commission in Islamabad the next morning. I had them fax the initial information pack to Behroze Edulji's fax machine and the complete application pack was sent by post. The forms arrived at the office right next door to mine. It took us quite some time to complete these detailed forms, as they required all sorts of paperwork that one doesn't typically have at hand.

We couriered the forms to the High Commission and I pursued their progress by phone. When I said a call was from the Karachi Sheraton Hotel, it usually cut through the red tape with the Pakistani staff, and I would be put straight through to the person with whom I wished to speak. In this case, it was First Secretary, Consular Affairs, Gregory Blake, who had been given the additional duties of migration interviews and processing. At this time, the Australian mission in Pakistan was small because it was considered a marginal country from a migration perspective. By 2019, there would be a fully fledged department, headed by a migration team.

I secured a date for the whole family to be interviewed so that our suitability as migrants could be assessed. Zeenat and Saba, aged two-and-a-half and one-and-a-half respectively, were with us and they toddled around Mr Blake's interview room, opening drawers and cupboards, while we talked.

'Don't worry about it; just leave them to their own devices,' he assured us. 'There's nothing that they can damage here. Neelo, your sister has sponsored you, but she lives in Papua New Guinea, so who will look after you when you arrive in Australia? Who will show you where to shop, and where the supermarkets are, and how to find accommodation?'

I was impressed that he had given thought to how we might find a supermarket, but it seemed trivial in the scheme of things. Neelo did her best to assuage his concerns.

'I studied and lived in London for almost 10 years, and Sakib has returned only recently from nearly three years of living and studying in Montréal. We've both lived and worked in the UAE, so we have a great deal of experience in other cities and countries. I don't see any reason why Australia should be radically different. I'm sure we can navigate the systems.'

The only niggling doubt in Neelo's mind about Australia then, but which couldn't possibly be mentioned, was that she had learnt about the White Australia Policy. This was a suite of policies built up over many years that were designed to stop people of non-European origin – especially those from Asia and the Pacific islands – emigrating to Australia. Any vestiges of the policy had been all but legislated out of existence by the Whitlam Government in 1975 with the *Racial Discrimination Act*, but the big question remained: can a population change such an attitude that quickly?

Regardless of her unspoken concerns, Neelo's response seemed to convince Mr Blake on the whole, but he remained concerned with the point that an Australian citizen was meant to be present to help newcomers to settle. Whether that was a rule or not, I didn't know, so I asked.

'Well, what is the law?'

'Your contact in Australia should arrange for your accommodation and an appropriate settlement.'

'Well, if you're concerned about accommodation, they own a house in Wentworthville in Sydney. It's currently rented, but they can arrange for it to be vacated so that we could move in on arrival. And they could meet us in Sydney.'

This response really upset him.

'You mean to say you would put an Australian family out on the street? That's not fair.'

I couldn't get a break!

'So, you have asked me to give you a solution and that is one solution. If this doesn't work for you, then I have another: I work for Sheraton Hotels. I can organise a room at the Sheraton Hotel in Sydney and we can stay there for whatever length of time is required to meet your condition. That's not an issue. I can organise that.'

But he was determined to hold on to this problem, trying every which way to see if I would break down, but I was not giving up.

Neither was he.

'Well, I would need you to get a job offer before you go.'

'The kind of job I have is not like a waiter or receptionist. It's senior management, and positions are not offered by way of letters and phone calls saying, "Give me a job". There would need to be a vacant management position and I would first need a visa to apply.'

We had another debate about that.

'I can't give you a short-term travel visa while another visa application is under way. It's against the normal rules.' He, too, was frustrated.

So, I could not even visit Australia to look for a job in the interim, which seemed to me to be the best possible solution. We appeared to be at a stalemate. Then it struck me.

'Normal rules,' I suggested, 'would give the applicant a fair chance. But you are saying they don't give me a fair chance to seek a job offer suitable for my qualifications and level of experience. Many people would go and get a job as a cook in a small hotel or Pakistani restaurant, but that's not my area. My skills are in management. I am sure you know that Australia is in a major tourism development phase right now, and the industry specifically needs people with my background. I will not be a burden. In fact, Australia needs me more than I need Australia.'

That's when it hit him. He suddenly understood my skills.

This negotiation had taken two and a half hours.

'OK, Sakib, I'll give you a tourist visa so you can visit Australia to search for a job. Once you have an offer, we'll provide a permanent residency visa for you and your family. OK?'

We shook hands. I knew how fortunate I was that the stalemate had been broken. It was highly unusual for an embassy to grant a visa of any other type when you were under consideration for a permanent residency visa. We flew back to Karachi from Islamabad and I booked a return ticket to Sydney for a 10-day visit.

Before I left for Sydney, I alerted a few Sheraton clients that I would be away for 10 days. One fellow, the late John Warman, who was then administration manager for Union Texas Petroleum in Karachi, represented one of my larger accounts. I always looked after him very well, and I didn't want to disappear without reassuring him that someone would take my place in my absence.

'I'd like to take you for lunch when you're free,' I said. 'I may be moving to Australia soon, but I'm visiting for 10 days first to look around. This is a heads-up for you that the moment my successor is appointed, I will introduce you.'

'Australia! That will be wonderful. I'd love to catch up for lunch and I'll bring my chief geologist, Tim Hargreaves. You'll find him fascinating – he's Australian, so he may enlighten and guide you about Down Under.'

Days later, John and Tim met me at the hotel's popular Lotus Court Chinese restaurant, where Tim suggested that before I left Karachi I should write to the Australian hotels where I intended to make in-person inquiries. I had not thought of that strategy. I had simply planned to turn up. My strategy was based purely on confidence that I would find a role, apply, and get the job there and then, as had often happened in the past, and my visa problem would be solved.

'No, no,' Tim insisted, 'it will be a much stronger proposition if you go prepared. I'm happy to draft the letter for you, so it's all in order before you leave.' I was grateful. While my English was good, I lacked the necessary confidence and skills to write professional letters, particularly when so much was resting on them.

Tim and I met a couple of days later. At that time, he had the only computer in his company. Not even the Union Texas Petroleum head office had such a machine. I presented him with a list of all the major hotels in Sydney in the *World Hotels Directory*, the industry bible at the time. On his cutting-edge 256K computer, using early word-processing software, he drafted eloquent letters to hotels in Sydney that essentially said, all in the correct Australian lingo, 'This is what I am looking for; here is my CV; I will arrive in Sydney on this date. I will call to make an appointment to discuss any opportunities that may be open at your hotel.'

Ten days or so before my departure for Australia, I mailed the letters. I had done all I could from Karachi. Our future was now in the hands of Pakistan Post. What could possibly go wrong?

A 'Stirling' result

I flew to Sydney on my scouting trip in late April 1987, feeling a reasonable amount of pressure to find a job, and desperately hoping that my letters had arrived safely. I knew that demand was high – and on the rise – in the hospitality industry, so I reasoned it shouldn't be too difficult a task. In theory, at least.

It is easy to like Sydney and its people. I found it lively and beautiful – really, really beautiful – and very clean. It was quite different from the tropical climate of Karachi. The people were down-to-earth, friendly, and happy. They didn't seem to care about much; the classic 'She'll be right, mate' ruled.

My first priority was to find somewhere to stay, before starting my search for this all-important job. I checked in to the Sebel Town House in Elizabeth Bay, near Kings Cross, known as the unofficial residence for domestic and international musicians. I came across it at the Sydney airport tourist desk because it had a special room rate on offer. It was expensive, but I was only staying until I tracked down my childhood friend, Cajie De Sousa, who lived in Sydney with his wife, June, and daughter, Jackie. Immediately after arriving at the hotel, I called a few contacts who might know his whereabouts. After several calls, I located him in Doonside, an hour out of Sydney's central business district. While waiting for him to arrive, I figured I might as well make the most of the room I was paying for and managed to sleep for a few hours.

The next day I made calls to the hotels to which I had sent letters and arranged appointments for that day with two, the Sheraton Wentworth and the Hyde Park Hotel, both of which drew blanks. I spent the rest of the day walking around the city looking to acquaint myself with some of its other hotels. On the second day, my first call was to the Cambridge Inn on Riley Street in Surry Hills.

'We received your letter, and we would like to meet you.'

I walked the short distance from the train station to the hotel to meet the general manager. I explained my situation and he gave me a job on the spot. We discussed the time frame: I would return to Pakistan, resign from my current position, obtain the visa we needed, and the family would pack up and move to Sydney. I would begin work within a few weeks.

The Cambridge Inn was a small hotel of 120 rooms and I was to work as night manager to start with, because that was the only position open. But as time went by, the general manager assured me, I would move into other, more senior positions, as I had the requisite experience.

I called Neelo to let her know the good news. However, our old adversary in the Pakistan migration office demanded further paperwork, and that the original documents be posted directly to him. When would this end, I wondered.

I now had a job, I reminded myself, so I simply needed to follow the process to its conclusion. I went to the immigration office in Sydney to collect the form that my new employer had to sign. I was impressed by how simple it all was in Australia. There was no need for a stamp, and I didn't have to pay anyone. The only additional work required was to satisfy the Australian High Commission in Pakistan that our paperwork was in order. I diligently completed every detail to the letter. In Pakistan, things could be held up or cancelled without rhyme or reason; success or failure could depend on how an admin person felt on the day he saw you – at least, this is how it was perceived by many. As much as humanly possible, I left nothing to chance.

I had learnt that the consulting firm of PricewaterhouseCoopers (PwC) had a migration partnership at 50 Bridge Street in Sydney, so while I was in the city one day, I decided to see if it could expedite our visa. I met with the head of the section, the powerfully named Stirling Henry – surely he could help, I thought. Stirling had retired from his role as New South Wales State Director of the Department of Immigration and Ethnic Affairs, and was one of the founders of the Migration Institute of Australia when he began his own migration business in conjunction with PwC. He was the first migration adviser in Australia to become an official Registered Migration Agent, and so was issued the registered licence number 001. I waited in his office, going crazy with my camera, taking countless pictures, because a tiny portion of his window afforded an incredible view of the Harbour Bridge. We briefly discussed my situation and conversations with the High Commission in Pakistan, and then he examined my paperwork.

'You don't need your sister-in-law to sponsor you. You are sponsored in your own right. I've just done the calculation and you score 70. You only need 60 to qualify on a skills transfer basis. I'll draft a telex to the Pakistan office to articulate the case. It's all very clear cut.'

I was there for an hour. He charged me $150, which I happily paid. The telex he sent to Pakistan pointed out that all the conditions had now been met and the final paperwork was now to be signed off. It was not a demand, but in essence said, 'Hey come on, I've done what you requested. Your country needs people with the skills and experience I have, so you're not doing me a favour; I will be contributing to Australia.'

I returned to Karachi earlier than expected, with the quiet stress we had lived with for some months slightly abated — we were to live in Australia.

While waiting for our visa paperwork to be processed by immigration, I received a call from my ex-boss, the general manager of the Holiday Inn Islamabad.

'I've got a brilliant offer for you, Sakib. It's a very senior position, and I think you would do a great job. Maybe you could visit and we can discuss it?'

I was intrigued. From the way he spoke, without disclosing any details, it had to be a very senior position. We agreed to meet at the end of the week.

The position turned out to be the rooms division manager, covering the entire front office, cashiers, lobby manager, housekeeping, engineering, security, and more. It was essentially the second-in-charge of the hotel and several levels above my previous position.

I was torn. On one hand, my head said this was a wonderful opportunity – offers of such senior positions are not made lightly. On the other hand, my heart was drawn to this new land of unknown opportunity.

That evening, I spoke to Abba Jee, who was on his way upstairs to listen to his beloved BBC report.

'Wonderful job, congratulations! Pakistan is not the place for you. You've worked hard to get permanent residency in Australia. They need people like you. Go!'

I knew in my heart that Abba Jee was right. Neelo also had her heart set on Australia.

Days later, our visas arrived. I handed in my resignation to the Sheraton Karachi and, three weeks later, in July 1987, we arrived in Sydney.

'No, no, you don't need to bring anything, not even a pram,' I said confidently to Neelo as we packed our baggage.

All we brought with us were our clothes. I don't know why I said that we wouldn't even need a pram when we left for Australia: we had two children under three. Perhaps I imagined that life here would be so easy and inspiring that our children would instantly take to their feet to experience the culture and life of this amazing new country! Who knows what I was thinking?

We arrived in the middle of winter so it was quite cold – not Montréal cold, of course, but chilly. We had no car, and I soon very much wished we had brought our prams. Neelo still tells this story and I suspect will never let me forget this small misstep.

Australia: First impressions

We arrived one year before Australia celebrated its 1988 bicentenary. The country was certainly living life to the full: it was awash with excitement and money.

We knew from Sheraton Hotels that Australia was in the midst of a tourism boom that had begun with Paul Hogan's classic 'shrimp on the barbie' ad campaign. Australia was sold to tourists with the clichés: 'fair dinkum', 'g'day', and 'mate'. None of it made any sense to us. In particular, the lack of formality when speaking to people felt wrong to me. It was as though little respect was being given to someone you didn't know, or someone who was your elder.

Then there was the isolation. Australia was isolated. Even though there had been various waves of migrants for decades, many of those cultures did not seem to have meshed, integrated, or done anything within the mainstream white culture. And while tourists might have been coming for many years, the country hadn't yet caught up with cultural trends from around the world. Take food, for instance. Thirty years ago, Australia was dominated by typical English-inspired foods: steak and vegetables, bangers and mash, pies and sausage rolls, fish and chips. And then there was the distinctive Australian version of Chinese food as served in the Chinese restaurants dotted around the cities and found in every country town, a hangover from the 19th century goldrush days.

Travellers to Canada or the US 40 years earlier were exposed to cuisines from around the world – I had worked at Pique Assiette, the Indian-French restaurant in Montréal back in 1980. Such a restaurant was unheard of in Sydney in 1987. Every day Pique Assiette was packed, not with Indians or other south Asians, but by locals who couldn't get enough of this fusion cuisine. The same happened in Montréal with Thai, Mexican, and Chinese restaurants. In Australia, world cuisine would take another decade or more to evolve. These days you can find anything you desire; indeed, we pride ourselves on what we call Modern Australian, a diverse mix of many culinary influences from around the world.

The changes in Australian culture have been predominately led by waves of migrants from various countries. Upon arrival, each suffered their own discrimination and were labelled outsiders. When we arrived from Pakistan, Australian attention was focused on the Vietnamese 'boat people'. Before that, and for many decades, it had been Greeks, Maltese, and Italians, many of whom migrated on the promise of jobs on major infrastructure projects, such as roads and the Snowy Mountains Hydroelectric Scheme. They subsequently helped to establish Australia's building industry and its strong Italian food culture. Before that, it was the Lebanese, who established the Australian haberdashery trade. More recently, Indian students and Muslims have established themselves in their new nation. While it has taken decades for some of these groups to overcome racism and secure their place in Australia, each, in their distinct way, has contributed to the rich and dynamic culture we see today. Together they have made us, on the whole, an incredible multicultural success story, something we should embrace.

I have experienced the odd instance of racism but, overall, I feel that the country embraced me from day one. Although I had some difficulties settling, these were simply because the culture was so foreign to me. It remains my hope that white Australia's attitude towards migrants will improve to match their enthusiasm for international cuisine. Accordingly, I was elated to see Malala Yousafzai speak when she was in Sydney in 2018. As the father of three girls, it was inspiring to see this young Pakistani Muslim woman speak with such intelligence, strength, truth, and courage about promoting the education of women around the world. She is extremely confident for her age, articulate, and even included some humour about India beating Australia at cricket:

'How could you lose to India?'

An awkward chuckle rippled across the room.

Seated in the 7600-seat Sydney Convention Centre, among an audience that was 99 per cent white Australian, I was thrilled to see her reception from such an adoring crowd. It also reassured me that perhaps Pakistan would soon be one of those countries moving beyond the troubles brought on by the actions of a minority of extremists; that the world would see it as the peaceful nation that it is, and Islam as the peaceful religion that it is. After all, Pakistan is a nation of diverse people, just like Australia. In fact, in 2019, Pakistan was named by the influential *Condé Nast Traveller* as the world's 'ultimate adventure travel destination'.[1]

I have enormous respect for all religions. Even though I was born into Islam, I am a humanist and I believe that all people are born equal. I admire any person who pursues their own beliefs with passion, as long as it supports and upholds fundamental human values and human rights.

Overall, I know that white Australians have good intentions towards migrants, although our most recent disturbing trend has been the government's heartless offshore processing and detention centres for asylum seekers. These fly in the face of Australia's fundamental ethos of equality. While we appear to be on the right track for these detention centres to come to an end, I fear that this offshore strategy will not disappear permanently. Added to that, we have to face up to the worst part of Australia's 230-year white history: the treatment of our First Nations people, who have faced terrible hardships. Sadly, that is an ongoing tragedy. Very little has improved for our Indigenous communities although their terrible treatment has been highlighted for generations, now. Neither of these situations makes sense to me

---

1   Lizzie Pook and Tabitha Joyce, 'The Best Holiday Destinations for 2020', *Condé Nast Traveller*: https://www.cntraveller.com/gallery/best-holiday-destinations-2020.

in today's world, particularly since Australia is a signatory to so many international human rights treaties.

Ideally, we need our leaders to be role models. In 2018, I listened to an impressive speech by Mehreen Faruqi, a new Australian senator of Pakistani heritage, who took her oath in federal parliament. While I do not agree with all her party's politics, I admire her. The undercurrent of racism in Australia means that for a migrant to attain such a position, you have to be 10 times more careful and vigilant, and put in 110 per cent effort, because the smallest misstep will be used against you.

As a member of a minority in any country, it is important to stand up for yourself, and others in a similar position. I believe that the election of Mehreen Faruqi demonstrates that if you strive to be the best and reach the stars, you can – that power is within you. Faruqi is a wonderful new role model. Those who would stop you will give up after one, two, maybe three attempts. You just have to keep moving forward, keep at it, and put in that 110 per cent. While it makes me sad that this is necessary, I am also a pragmatist. I have faith in Australia and its people, and Neelo and I have never, not even for one minute, regretted our decision to move here. When I think of other countries in which to live, there are few I would seriously consider.

The Cambridge Inn was, and still is, a four-star hotel and, having opened in 1979, was still quite new. Somewhat tucked away in Surry Hills, it was famous as the home of Cyrano's, Sydney's first five-star restaurant. It was the first to offer the fashionable nouvelle cuisine, a style of French cooking that Australia had not experienced before, and a style that would later dominate any restaurant that saw itself as cutting edge.

In a small alley behind the hotel was a little flat that the manager was kind enough to give us to live in until we settled in our own place. The flat had not been used for some time, so it was in a far from liveable condition. While it was a generous offer, which we thought would be suitable for a while, it proved not to be. It was dark and damp. Shortly after we moved in, Neelo came face to face with a rat that ran across the living room floor.

'I want to be out of here. We need to be out of here now!'

In addition, a week or two after I started work, I realised that this wasn't a hotel at which I could use my skills. While it was a well-run independent establishment, its small team offered limited services and lacked the scope for promotion that I had hoped for. Within a month, I was already applying for jobs at larger hotels.

It wasn't long before I found an advertisement for the night manager position at the Holiday Inn Menzies, on top of Wynyard Station. As a result of my time at the Holiday Inn Islamabad, I secured an interview immediately. I arrived at the hotel in good time on the day of my interview, and while walking through the lobby, suddenly felt a tap on my shoulder. I turned and found myself face to face with Rolf Bauer, the general manager of the Holiday Inn Karachi, sister hotel to the Holiday Inn Islamabad.

'Sakib! What are you doing here?'

'We've moved to Australia. I live here.'

'But what are you doing here, now, at the hotel?'

'I have an interview for the night manager position.'

'It's so good to see you. Let me take you to the office. It's down in the basement and not easy to find.'

We wound along several corridors beneath the hotel and past back entrances, chatting about the hotel and my reasons for leaving Pakistan. Then he delivered me into the hands of the human resources director.

'Sakib's a great guy', Rolf said, by way of introduction. 'I worked with him in Pakistan. We need him here.' After the interview, I was offered the job.

We moved out of the Cambridge Inn, content to leave our damp little apartment to the rats and to look for a place of our own.

Bondi Beach. Our first home in Australia. What better place to settle?

We had come with a few references, knowing we would need them to find a decent rental property, which we soon did: a recently refurbished two-bedroom apartment with a sunroom at 6 Hastings Parade, Bondi Beach.

The sound of the waves that rolled ceaselessly onto this famous beach became the beautiful background to our new life. I worked night shifts and Neelo secured a paralegal position at Minter Ellison, one of the largest law firms in Sydney. This meant that the free time we had to explore the area and its beaches was, unfortunately, limited. However, knowing that the little apartment close to the beach would not always be ours, we tried to make the most of the area while it was on our doorstep. We also took the children to the city's other attractions, such as Taronga Zoo, as much as possible.

Zeenat and Saba were too young to go to childcare, so we found a nanny, an elderly Pakistani lady who could speak English and broken Urdu, which the kids understood. At this age, they did not converse a great deal in Urdu, or English for that matter, but they knew key words and we wanted them to become familiar with English. The nanny remained with us for about eight months.

Like many young couples, it was a struggle in those early days. Financially, it was tough at times; one month we could buy only one transport ticket. We didn't put either of our names on it, so I'd come back from work and get off at Bondi Beach where Neelo was waiting. While we embraced, I would slip the monthly pass into her pocket and then off she'd go. Of course, that didn't last. I got stuck once or twice finishing late at work, which meant Neelo was stranded at the bus stop without a pass.

'We only save 14 dollars,' said Neelo. 'It's not worth the trouble we are making for ourselves.'

Every now and then, I would come home in the early hours of the morning after a night shift and look after the kids, feed them, and then sleep while Neelo prepared to leave for work. It was an exhausting period and very tough because we had virtually no time when we were not too exhausted to simply talk to each other.

One day after a night shift, I was sitting on one of our few pieces of furniture watching television. An advertisement for a new Logan Homes housing development came on the screen. In the 1970s and 1980s, Logan Homes was a well-known builder of modular kit homes in Sydney's western suburbs such as Blacktown, Doonside, Toongabbie, and so on. The idea of a brand-new home in our new country sparked my interest. However, I tucked this thought away for another time as I knew that, right then, it was not possible.

Not long after we had settled, a good friend of mine, Raj Chawla, and his wife, Azarmeen, came to visit us from Pakistan, although we still lacked sufficient furniture to accommodate everyone.

'Raj,' I suggested, on my day off, 'let's go for a day trip. I saw an advertisement for new homes in the suburbs and I'd like to go and have a look. You'll see more of Sydney, too.'

Neelo, Azarmeen, and our two children stayed at the Bondi Beach flat while Raj and I headed off to the Logan Homes office in Toongabbie. The well-dressed agent took us to nearby Doonside. Standing with map in hand, he pointed to a display home in front of us.

'This is the house we can build for you, here and here', he said, pointing to various spots on the map, 'on this, this, or this block. We also have a few other styles.' He directed our attention down the street. 'Which one do you like, and which block do you want?'

His brashness and the Australian lack of formality caught me off guard. It was something I would find disconcerting for many years.

'Well, I very much like this particular design,' I said, pointing to the house that appealed most to me, 'and I like this block.'

'Right. Forty-nine Rosenthal Street, Doonside, it is,' he declared. As this was a newly developed area, there were few trees along the streets and the houses were mostly new, single storey, on quite large 700-square-metre or so blocks. The house featured a crisp white brick veneer, with a small entrance porch, a family room, bathroom, garage, and three bedrooms (one for Zeenat and Saba to share, the master bedroom, and one guest room). An open field sat opposite. The salesman drove us back to his office. 'If you give me a deposit today, it's yours.'

'Oh no, I'm sorry, I've not come prepared to give you a deposit.' I work fast as a rule, but buying a house that very day had not entered my mind.

'Doesn't matter how much, mate. Have you got $20 with you?'

'Yes, I've got $20. But what if my wife says no?'

'Well then, you've lost 20 bucks.'

He was a good salesman.

'OK, here it is.' I handed over the cash on the spot.

The company committed to arrange finance, and we had to pay a deposit of five per cent in six months, once the house was built and ready for settlement. The cost was $62,000, which meant we had to find $3100, plus conveyancing. The problem was we had no money except for the $1000 that Neelo's mother had given to her when we left Pakistan. How would we find $3100? And how would we furnish the house on top of that? We had just started new jobs. It would take 18 to 24 months to save the money. We would need the five per cent in six months.

However, Neelo was used to my speed in making decisions, and she, too, liked the idea. So, I went to the local ANZ bank branch at Bondi Beach and sat down with a young man who listened to what I wanted. I had decided that the only way we would be able to pay the deposit was by credit card, but we had no credit history on which any institution would issue us with a card. It was as I expected.

'You've just arrived and it's not doable unless you have a credit history in this country.'

'That's why I wish to start developing a history.'

The young man thought a moment.

'Well, there's one way I can suggest. How much money do you have now?'

'$1000.'

'OK, great. I'll issue you two credit cards.'

One of these was a Visa card, which I still have. The other one was an ANZ Bankcard. Each would have a limit of $500, he said. He instructed me to spend up to that limit on each, pay off the card, and then apply for a credit limit increase. This was 1987 and there was a lot of easy money around. We got the cards, started to spend, and paid them off.

We used this system to our full advantage and paid our deposit. Neelo's sister Shireen lent us $1000 to buy furniture. By the time our house was ready to move into, we had acquired four more credit cards, which gave us access to the money we needed to pay the five per cent deposit and furnish the house.

The Top End

Early in 1988, I received a call from Sheraton Hotels in Sydney.

'We have a sales manager position based in Darwin, looking after conferences and conventions. Would you be interested?'

When we arrived in Australia 18 months before, Sheraton Hotels was one of the companies at which I had applied, but at that time it had nothing available.

'Absolutely,' I replied, without hesitation, and without even considering that it was in Darwin. After all, it was still Australia.

It was also a promotion from my position at the Menzies, where I had moved from night manager to duty manager, and then to senior duty manager. However, these positions required me to work afternoon shifts, which I didn't particularly like because by the time I finished work late at night, the buses and trains had often stopped running.

We had moved into our home at Doonside about 10 months before, and even though the hotel often gave me a Cabcharge voucher to get home, it was an extremely long day – the night manager would take over from the duty manager at 11pm or midnight. Things usually occurred on my duty manager shift for which I had to write incident reports, adding another two to three hours to my shift. I would often not arrive home until the early hours of the morning, which in my mind was just not sustainable for us to have a decent life. Neelo was still working in the city, so I hardly saw her.

A promotion also meant more money, and as we had recently bought a second-hand car, we had heavy financial commitments. To get through this establishment period took hard work, focus, and the tenacity to stick to the plan that we had made for ourselves.

I had immediately noticed a difference in attitude among people employed in the hospitality industry in Australia in the 1980s when compared to those in the UAE and Pakistan. Hospitality in Australia was not as service orientated as it is today, especially in the hotels in which I worked. Most of the front desk staff were white, and ethnic minorities worked only with the concierge as doormen or in similar jobs. I was a bit taken aback with the attitude of staff when dealing with guests, which seemed to be: 'This guy doesn't pay my salary. I'm an Australian, and so I get paid, no matter how I do my job.' I was used to staff whose attitude was: 'I will give every customer the best service I can and get them to rave about me.' There was very much a mentality of entitlement, one of getting rather than giving, an attitude completely different from the way I had always operated. (Note: over the past 35 years, Australia has evolved to meet higher customer expectations and now observes international-level standards of customer service.)

My first interview for the Darwin position was with Bill Edwards, vice president of marketing for Australia and the Pacific for Sheraton Corporation, based in Sydney. Interestingly, when I looked at all the five-star hotels in Sydney, I found no general managers from my cultural background or similar, leaving me to wonder whether my career progression would be limited in Australia.

At the end of the interview, Bill Edwards mentioned Art Lopez, the general manager in Darwin.

'He's a tough man from the Philippines, but if you know your stuff, you'll survive, and he will love you.'

Perhaps, I thought, Darwin would prove to be more multicultural and provide more senior opportunities for me than Sydney.

I proceeded to the next interview and received a ticket to fly to Darwin to meet Art Lopez. The interview was a casual chat for about an hour on Australian and world politics, my background, and other topics, before he took me to lunch. I suspect he wanted to see first hand my dining etiquette.

At the end of lunch he said, 'The job is yours if you want it'. I extended my hand. Without consulting Neelo, I accepted. I knew I'd be able to sell it to her and, besides, Sheraton would not have flown me to

Darwin unless it was serious. In our minds, we were already preparing for the move.

We put our house on the market as soon as possible because we wanted to buy a house in Darwin. Never having sold a house in Australia, we were unaware of the conventions of what is included in the sale and what you are supposed to take with you. We took our curtains with us and we wanted to give our washing line to our neighbour, an Afghan lady who did not have one and with whom we had become friends. All of this left the estate agent slightly perplexed.

House prices over the previous 10 months had increased almost daily, and the house that had cost us $62,000 sold for $135,000. The timing couldn't have been more fortuitous because this was about two months before Black Monday, the international financial market crash of 19 October 1987. By the end of October, the Australian stock market had fallen almost 42 per cent and house prices were crashing.

Darwin in 1988 would be part two of our life in Australia, and before leaving Sydney we prepared young Zeenat by teaching her to say 'G'day'.

Upon our arrival in the Top End, we rented an apartment in Houston Street, Darwin, on the edge of the Gardens Park Golf Course. Here we remained for six months while we searched for a family home. We finally settled on 14 Dripstone Road, a good-sized family home with a pool for the kids, not far from the university at Casuarina. Now clear of debt, the money we had in the bank allowed us to buy a new car.

Sheraton Hotels had three properties in the Northern Territory: Alice Springs, Ayers Rock and, of course, Darwin. The Darwin hotel (which has since become the Hilton Hotel) was on Mitchell Street, not far from the Northern Territory's Government House.

My primary role was to oversee sales for the Darwin property and to get to know anyone and everyone who could become a client for the hotel. As it was the major hotel in the city, I had access to a great variety of people. Where I saw the opportunity to secure a specific client, I would often include a night or two at one of our other properties in the Northern Territory, sometimes even a day or two in Bali, Brunei, Singapore, or Kuala Lumpur. Guests would come to one of our Territory properties and get the additional nights and travel free. It was so easy to set up through the conference and convention organisers, and people loved the one-price offer.

In August 1990, the charismatic prime minister Bob Hawke visited Darwin at the time of the Darwin Cup, one of the biggest events of the year. He stayed at the hotel, and I had the opportunity to greet him. That week, Neelo and I also took the family to the Cup at the Darwin Turf Club. Zeenat and Saba spotted Mr Hawke and ran up to take hold of his hand. When Neelo struggled to retrieve her camera in time to take a photo of the three, Mr Hawke waved to her and said, 'Don't worry, take your time. I'm not goin' anywhere.' A year later, the same thing happened at the Mindil Beach festival.

A couple of months after my arrival we organised an event for the hotel's fourth anniversary. I asked my general manager Art Lopez if I could invite a few useful contacts in the media and he agreed. Two of them were Nigel Adlam, the editor of the *Sunday Territorian*, a weekly edition of the *Northern Territory News*, and a subeditor, Warwick Sinclair.

'If you can give us some exposure, it would be great,' I said, and left it at that.

The party turned into a *Who's Who* of Darwin. We put on a huge spread: a range of cuisines, several bars, and someone carving an ice sculpture. The next Monday, Art Lopez called me into his office.

'Have you seen the paper today?' I shook my head. 'I know this was you', he said, laying the paper out on his desk to reveal a huge double-page spread with many photo captions written by Warwick Sinclair about the event. I was stunned. It was more publicity than we could ever have dreamt of receiving.

The Sheraton Darwin's part-time public relations consultant, David Nicholson, was on a retainer to take care of public relations activities and publicity, as well as being a regular contributor to the *NT News*. At this stage I had not yet met David, however, I knew of him. While my intention was not to show him up, I can see in retrospect that he might have been pretty angry, thinking I was trying to take his job.

'Who the bloody hell is this Sakib, and where did he blow in from?'

It was a less than ideal way to meet, but we soon became close friends. A great writer, he knew exactly how and where to place words to achieve the desired outcome.

Shortly after I arrived in Darwin, Ian Fergusson, the local Qantas manager and one of my clients, asked if I would be interested in joining the Rotary Club. I had heard much about Rotary over the years. He put me forward for membership and I began attending the weekly Thursday meetings.

Many Rotary Clubs in Australia struggle to maintain membership numbers, but not so Darwin. It is still one of the most successful Rotary Clubs in the country. As well as being the oldest community club in Darwin, it is the only one based in the city and still all male.

Virtually every decision maker whom I met as sales manager for Sheraton was a member. The heads of all the banks attended, the airlines, the oil companies, most large businesses – you name it, they all attended the Rotary Club of Darwin. Every Thursday night a great deal of business was done. I worked hard at the hotel and met a lot of good people. However, Rotary provided the opportunity for me to make lifelong friends: the Northern Territory Police Commissioner, Mick Palmer; Assistant Commissioner, the late Saus Grant; the late Lyle McIntosh, head of the Department of Asian Relations Trade and Industry; Hugh Bradley, who was at the time managing partner at Ward Keller, one of Darwin's leading law firms; Ambassador Brendan Doran and his wife, Debbie Chapman, director of DFAT's Northern Territory office. Many of the friendships I developed through the Rotary Club are still strong, even though we now live in Sydney again.

There was also a broad multicultural demographic among the members. I heard inspiring stories about people who had come to Darwin from Italy, China, or Greece, working as bricklayers or electricians, who now owned major businesses. Nick Paspaley snr, a club member, began as a pearl diver and built one of Australia's most successful companies, Paspaley Pearls. Every Thursday night there is now a Paspaley Shirt of the Night Award, where to win you have to wear a loud shirt in his honour.

Rotary has been incredibly important to my life in Australia. A small city like Darwin means that you live close to most of the people you meet, and you build bonds and trust. This does not happen so easily in large cities like Sydney.

Another legacy of Rotary is that I learnt of the Four-Way Test, Rotary's moral code that can be applied to all personal and business relationships and makes us aware of the things we think, the actions we take, and what we say.

1. Is it the truth?
2. Is it fair to all concerned?
3. Will it build goodwill and better friendships?
4. Will it be beneficial to all concerned?

This is a clear and simple test that fits well into the code of behaviour instilled into me by my parents, and it can be applied to any situation.

Not long after our arrival, while we were looking for a house to buy, we stopped to ask directions from a man who was working in his garden. I gave him the address and he began to explain how to get there.

'Wait a minute,' he said, putting down his tools. 'Just follow me.' He got into his car and promptly led us a kilometre away to the house we were trying to find. We were astonished by his kindness. We would soon learn that such behaviour was common in Darwin. I would say hello or nod to people on the street, say hello to a stranger in an elevator or in a shop, and always be met with a warm response.

In Sydney, people don't always know how to respond to a stranger who engages with them; sometimes there is fear and they may try to move away. Despite the potential reaction, I still stick with my Darwin self in Sydney and aim for at least one interaction with a stranger, or at least one act of kindness to someone, every day. Regardless of how big or small it is, when I can bring a little bit of Darwin to Sydney, I do it, despite the strange looks I sometimes receive.

Sales negotiation techniques

If my beautiful deep-red Honda CD175 motorcycle was the pivotal point of my youth, the ITT Sheraton sales negotiation techniques course was the first major turning point of my business life. It was the most influential short training course I undertook, and I applied it from then on throughout my career – in fact, throughout my life. Negotiation is not just about business; it is inherent in life. 'If you give me this, or if you let me play with that for half an hour,' my grandchildren will inevitably say, I'll go and do this for you.' Negotiation occurs between us all every day, so it is important to learn to do it well.

In business, there are many ways to look at the same deal, and if you can identify these, you will negotiate much more effectively. The sales negotiation techniques course was developed specifically by the ITT Sheraton Corporation in Boston and delivered to senior managers throughout the company. The bottom line is that no matter how far behind you are, there is always a way to capture the transaction you are after.

I had street-smart ways but I realised early on that I was out of my depth when negotiating with potential clients – or existing clients, for that matter – about the hotel and travel deals that we offered. What the course did was to provide me with a structure to follow, a formalised roadmap of how to approach each transaction, and it fundamentally changed the way I do business. The beauty of it was that it boiled down to commonsense.

How does it work? In negotiation, most of us have one simple fear: that the other party will find a better deal elsewhere. How do you deal with that fear? The most important thing is to undertake deep, detailed research. I'll preface this by pointing out that it is easy to overvalue your own offering; most of us overvalue our possessions. For example, during a student research project, the Nobel Laureate Daniel Kahneman famously found that students selling plain, nondescript coffee mugs usually set prices higher than their student buyers were willing to pay.[2] As a seller, it is easy to suffer from a loss of objectivity. Firstly, you must overcome this. One way is to look for outside help. Find an impartial contact and work through your product or offering with them.

When you enter a negotiation situation, there are three reassuring points to remember:
- Negotiation is a very human process, so try to find areas of synergy between you and your buyer and build a personal link, based on honesty and trust.
- Avoid negotiating on price alone – be creative.
- Everybody is open to negotiation – everyone.

The theory behind the Sheraton strategy is by no means unique. It is a well-documented one, and similar processes are presented in negotiation courses from universities and colleges around the world. With practice, you will develop your own style, but the basic strategy is:

1. **Undertake objective research**
   a. View your product objectively; that is, look at it for what it is, and not at how you sell it.
   b. Identify your competitor's product and what it lacks in comparison to your product. If you don't know your competitor's product and price, then devise ways to find out.

2. **Identify your true competition**
   Compare your findings logically, in a commonsense way to say, 'Here is my product, and here is my competitor's, but I'm asking $10 more. It's the same bed. It's the same breakfast.' How do you convince the customer that yours is worth more?

---

2   Daniel Kahneman, Jack L Knetsch, & Richard H Thaler, 'Anomalies: The Endowment Effect, Loss Aversion, and Status Quo Bias', *The Journal of Economic Perspectives*, 5(1), Winter 1991, pp 193–206.

3. **Describe your benefits and your competitor's weaknesses**
    a. Identify and list the benefits that you offer over your competitor; for example, access to a club lounge or a return airport transfer at checkout.
    b. Show that your product doesn't have the weaknesses that your competitor claims it does.

An example might be: 'My product comes with Sheraton Starwood Membership, or with frequent guest points, and we have 15,000 hotels around the world at which you can claim the benefits.' (A useful benefit of perks like this is that it is actually a negligible cost to the hotel.) What does my competitor have? Maybe 500 hotels around the world – or none? So, there is one of your benefits.

I am going to add a fourth item here, which was not included in the Sheraton course, but I believe is important:

4. **Know your buyer**
    Look at the deal from the other side: be clear on what your buyer is looking for in the deal *and* understand what type of person/company they are – anything professional or personal gives you an advantage. If you were the buyer, what competitors would you speak to? What events have occurred recently in their business world that might influence or drive their decision?

Following this trusted process will help you improve negotiation skills, whether at home or at work.

At Sheraton, it was my job to meet with conference and convention organisers and corporates that might send their staff or executives to Darwin. Why should they come to us, they would ask. I would reply that if they came to Darwin for a three-day conference, I would give them two nights free in Bali, including airfare and accommodation.

We had sharpened our pencils so as to attract guests to Darwin who would generate revenue, not only in the hotel, restaurants, bars, and shops but in the wider community and around the city. That meant I could co-opt local partners to be part of our deal.

In collaboration with a convention or event organiser we could offer our Bali hotel, because it was part of the Sheraton group. What they didn't know was that I also negotiated deals with the domestic airlines (Qantas or Ansett) and partnership deals with international airlines (Garuda, Merpati, Malaysian Airlines, or Singapore Airlines) to provide flights at very little extra cost. Sometimes there were also government tourism incentives that the international airlines would receive as part of the deal, so we could piggyback on those. The client had no idea how the deal was structured or its background workings; they simply paid their one price and got an extremely attractive package through the convention or event organiser.

Looking at deals in this way comes very naturally to me now, but it's all about how you conceive it, how you present it, how much background information you have gathered – and some good lateral thinking. These are strategies that I trained my staff to use. My management team members were all trained this way, and those managers passed their training and experience on to their staff to use daily.

So, not only was that single course that I attended in 1988 transformational throughout Sheraton Hotels but, more than that, the techniques I learnt there have now been passed on to future business leaders in Timor-Leste, providing them with stronger job prospects and enabling their families to live healthier and more prosperous lives. That's the power of education.

As my experience grew throughout my career and business life, I would sharpen and hone these skills – always on the lookout for ways to expand on and improve negotiation opportunities. Now, technology has advanced our business and personal lives far beyond the face-to-face world in which I grew up. Global companies such as Facebook, Google, and the like allow us to access hitherto unimaginable databanks of and about consumers. The age of *surveillance capitalism*, so named by Shoshana Zuboff,[3] allows us to communicate directly to customers that we never need to see or to speak to personally. As Zuboff points out, such business practices have inherent risks because of the power acquired by these companies as they collect more and more data about us as individuals; however, used respectfully and wisely, the technology allows us to expand our product offering in a targeted fashion. They allow us to make more complex and broader links that provide a new depth and breadth to our marketing and negotiation potential. These corporations allow small businesses to operate in a global market, so understanding and harnessing their power is vital to successful business this century.

Leaving Sheraton

I had learnt much. It was time now to apply my negotiation skills to my own life and to apply lateral thinking to my family life. This led me to the Sheraton Nusa Dua, in Bali, a five-star resort-style hotel nestled among seven hectares of lush tropical gardens and blue lagoons, all located on Nusa Dua's idyllic tropical beach.

My deepest desire at this time was to give Neelo the opportunity to be a lady of leisure. We had worked hard for many years. My plan was to work in this luxurious resort and live a charmed expat life, relaxing and taking our children to swim in tropical waters every weekend.

The general manager liked my CV and offered me the role of director of sales. I discussed my interest in transferring to Bali with Sheraton's personnel department and they promised that, given that the general manager in Nusa Dua was keen, they would organise the transfer. It was all done simply on goodwill. My dream was coming true.

We didn't want to be held up during the move so we put our house in Dripstone Road on the market. When that sold, we took out a short-term rental on a townhouse in Somerville Gardens, Parap, while we

---

3   Shoshana Zuboff, *The Age of Surveillance Capitalism: The Fight for the Future at the New Frontier of Power*, Profile Books, 2019.

waited for the process to be completed. All we had to do was wait for my manager in Darwin to sign off on the position and release me.

'I'm afraid I can't let you go, Sakib. There's too high a turnover in the sales and marketing department at the moment. Stay here for another six months, we'll settle the staff, and find you something else suitable.'

I had thought nothing of the lack of formality of this arrangement at the time, assuming that everyone would act in their usual honourable fashion. Several months later, the 'something else' turned out to be a position at the Sheraton Wentworth, in Sydney. It's a lovely hotel but returning to Sydney wasn't in my plans. People had made promises and I was unimpressed that they reneged on these promises with little or no concern for my wishes.

My dismay was compounded when I discovered that the business was restructuring because the hotel owner had decided to sell. My boss, who was a decent, professional woman, then uncharacteristically attacked me over a recent new business win. I had won a large and highly desirable oil and gas client, whom I had worked on for some time, from our competitor, the Beaufort Hotel. She accused me of unethical tactics by converting somebody else's key account into ours. It made no sense.

'What do you mean? My job is to acquire new business! They were clearly in the market for a new hotel because they were looking for alternatives. I offered the alternative and they moved over. This is unethical? It's my job! If I can't do my job, why do you need me?'

To say I was furious would be an understatement. I was also disgusted with the way I had been treated. If this was how they treated me after almost four years of service, then, I reasoned, it was their loss. I wrote my resignation letter, in which I highlighted several decisions that didn't make sense to me, and then called the director of human resources and the chief of security.

'I'm resigning. Please come and see what I've taken from my office.'

I left everything behind, including my business cards – I left everything except my own personal items.

Looking back, I know now that they were cutting staff ahead of the sale of the hotel. The behind-the-scenes politics was a tightly held secret.

I had refused to go to Sydney and so they had to find another way to get rid of me, because the new owner would not want any of the Sheraton management team. The new brand would have its own team. If you worked in the bar, the front office, housekeeping, or maintenance, for example, you could remain, but every brand of hotels brings in its own people at the senior management level. As I had learnt in my early days after college, each brand has its own rigid style of business, and it is easier and cheaper to transfer staff than to train new ones.

However, the upheavals in my life were soon rivalled by world events. It was now 1991, the year of the first Gulf War. The Australian economy had gone completely haywire and interest rates soared to 18 per cent. Jobs were hard to come by, and I had just left mine. What would I do now?

One decision was easy: Neelo and I had built a wonderful life for ourselves in Darwin, with numerous great family friends. I had made good business contacts while at the hotel and through the Rotary Club, so I felt well established in the city. I just had to work out what I would do professionally. We would also have to find another home. What we found was a modest house at 14 Tudawali Street, Ludmilla, further out of the city towards the airport. Neelo and I discussed work prospects and decided that I had no reason to remain in the hotel industry. While I had built a good career in hotels, perhaps it was time for a change.

Transglobal Marketing

For six months in 1991, I deployed all the research and negotiation skills I had learnt throughout my life to identify business opportunities in Darwin. One after the other, I identified markets, researched them, and rejected them.

I was open to ideas and advice to ensure we embarked on this venture correctly from the start. Around this time, an old family friend of 45 years, Saeed Ahmad was a high-flying executive for a watch company, and based in Singapore. A fellow Pakistani, he was the epitome of the success we hoped to achieve. Generous with his time and wisdom, Saeed and I talked in great detail about options for this planned business, right down to what it should be called. Neelo and I mulled over his ideas, and when it came to deciding on a name, he suggested the words 'global' and 'marketing' would be advantageous. After a brief discussion, we became *Transglobal Marketing*.

Saeed held my hand through the establishment of the business and with no agreed terms or fine print, he offered to provide much-needed seed funding. It was not a loan or for a share of the business. It was purely a friend offering to assist another friend to achieve their dreams. As with other valued friends in our lives, we have remained in close contact since those early days and I have done whatever I could over the years to repay his generosity and confidence in our ability to create a business from nothing.

Now with an opening which Saeed, and my gut instinct, told me was my future business, I revealed my vision to my Rotary contacts.

One of Darwin's wealthier businessmen and the local Rotary Club's Sergeant at Arms, Kerry Ambrose-Pearce, asked me to sit next to him at Rotary one evening. The way he interrogated me about my future, I suspected he was going to offer me a job. Instead, I explained my plan.

'You came here only six years ago as a sales manager for Holden,' I said, 'and now you own it and every car agency in town. Neelo and I won't leave Darwin. I want to be like you. I've just registered the business name Transglobal Marketing, and I plan to export anything Australia has to offer to the Asian market. In this club I see so many inspirational figures, and you are one of them.'

Word got around the club and I received a few friendly laughs. They all knew my background; I had never engaged in this type of business. In fact, I had never run any type of business, but I took note of the role models around me and was determined to emulate them.

Another notable guiding star for my business dream was Penny Tastula. Her business was closer to home for me. She began as a sales manager at the Darwin casino. She worked hard over decades and built many businesses and made a great success of her life in travel and tourism in the Northern Territory. Even today, in her 70s, she is driven to succeed.

Kerry, Penny, and others like them, opened my eyes to opportunity and gave me the confidence that, with the correct approach, I could achieve my dreams.

There is an economic co-operation initiative in South-East Asia entitled BIMP-EAGA. The acronym does not exactly roll off the tongue, but it stands for the Brunei Darussalam-Indonesia-Malaysia-Philippines East ASEAN Growth Area. The objective behind its 1994 creation was to accelerate economic development in the eastern part of these four countries, which previously lacked development. In Darwin, the contact for this initiative was the Australian Trade Commission, headed by Trade Commissioner Dennis Hooley. I paid him a visit.

'I would like to be able to export whatever Australia has to offer. I don't have any money,' I confessed, 'but I'm sure I can do it'. I received an amused look.

'How do you plan on doing this without any money?'

I had done my research.

'The buyer will open a letter of credit, I will request a transferable letter of credit in my name, and then transfer that to my supplier. The supplier won't know who my buyer is, and vice versa.'

In the Northern Territory, there is an attitude that one can do or try anything, but even for the Territory, Commissioner Hooley thought this was pretty airy-fairy stuff.

Next, I went to the Northern Territory Department of Trade and met with a facilitator, Michael Gallagher, who gave me much the same response.

It became clear I would need to jump in and do this myself, so I did the research, talking to anyone I felt could offer a product idea or advice about exporting. Then I spotted an article about an Adelaide-based business that dealt in shark fins. This piqued my interest.

Shark fins have been considered a delicacy in China for two millennia. As China began to open up in the 1980s, its middle class grew and demand for this delicacy increased dramatically, with the price doubling between 1991 and 1996. For us, the price of the rare high-quality fins that we would buy from licensed Australian fisherman would quadruple under such demand.

I looked into buyers, sellers, markets – anything I could find – followed by a visit to the wharves, where I checked who traded shark fins, and who didn't. It turned out the quantities available in Darwin were minuscule.

If I were to start exporting fins, I would need tonnes of them, but they were not available in such quantities at that time. Later those quantities would become available, but initially I had to look further afield, to Oman, Sri Lanka, the Maldives, and Pakistan for the amounts required to sell in the South-East Asia region.

From my conversations with fishermen around the wharf I found another lead: mud crabs. I discovered a fellow who had a fishing licence for mud crabs and bought some live crabs from him, all packaged and ready to transport and sell. There was no way I was going near those enormous claws! Imagine, I had come from a five-star hotel background and now I reeked of fish after my market visits. My kids wouldn't hug me until I had taken a shower and changed my clothes.

For several months we sold live Northern Territory mud crabs to De Costi Seafoods and Doyle's Restaurant, in Sydney, and to a range of other wholesalers and restaurants. We also supplied a well-known fine dining restaurant at The Rocks in Sydney. The chef was a Singaporean fellow who approached us and said, 'I want to buy from you, but you'll need to be able to supply to my specifications'.

He described his requirements and we delivered. On one of my visits to Sydney, he invited me to dinner and cooked some fresh barramundi. It melted in my mouth. It was obvious there was such a clear difference between the fresh and the standard frozen fish from the Northern Territory.

I also sampled his chilli crab dish, for which he gave me the recipe. I enjoy cooking but don't do it regularly. My usual dishes at that time were lamb mince and my mother's recipe for chicken korma. That mud crab recipe has now become my signature dish. I've cooked it on many occasions, and each time it's a great success with guests.

Our trade to the Sydney restaurants and others continued until, out of blue one day, we received an order for shark fins on a whole new scale.

Trade Development Zone, Darwin

That one order of shark fins came to more than my entire annual salary, which was about US$48,000 when I'd left the hotel industry. I purchased the fins in Oman, and had them shipped directly to Singapore. There the boxes were re-labelled with my branding, and dispatched to the buyer in China, via Hong Kong. We didn't even see the product before it arrived in Singapore. We just purchased it on faith that it was all good quality. I was not allowed to enter the bonded warehouse in Singapore, so their staff repackaged it for me. I orchestrated the whole deal from Darwin, completely hands off.

My eyes were opened. We had a business. My world had just changed.

The process was this: the buyer was in Hong Kong, so he opened a transferable letter of credit in my name, which I transferred to the company from which I purchased the shark fins in Oman, without the Hong Kong client knowing where the money was going. As far as he was concerned, I simply received the product in Singapore.

It was such a simple transaction, and that's how we started.

I hired a few experienced consultants who helped me to put the business processes and financial structure in order for this first deal. One of these was Bob Twomey, who wrote our business plan. Eighteen months later, in the second half of 1993, business was so good that Bob encouraged us to enter the Northern Territory's New Exporter Awards.

These were held annually at 'The Tank', a gymnasium at Darwin High School, the city's largest function venue, which held 600-700 people. We applied for the award, as suggested, and won. I dedicated it to Neelo for working so hard with me.

That evening, I ran into Michael Gallagher.

'What you've done can't be done!' he exclaimed. 'We don't understand. So many people have come to discuss business like yours with us.'

I held up my award.

'Well, you might say that, but look what I've got!'

Commissioner Hooley was also there, as well as the then trade minister Shane Stone and primary industry minister Mike Reid. They must have discussed our business and realised our potential. The next day I received a phone call from Shane Stone's office saying that he and Mike Reid would like to visit our premises.

'Of course they are welcome, but I have no premises.'

There was a pause.

'But how could you win the award if you don't have premises?'

'We use the Wyuna cold storage facility in Stuart Park. They have an Australian Quarantine and Inspection Service-approved processing room for export purposes. I rent it on an hourly or daily basis and hold products in cold storage to fulfil orders. It's that simple.'

At that time, I was a one-man band by day, with Neelo working with me after hours. Zeenat and Saba were old enough to send faxes after school and help run errands. They had a real sense of contribution, knowing they were helping their mum and dad to establish a business that was important to us as a family. They knew that to succeed, we needed to share the load, however small their share might be. Zeenat, who now helps run the businesses in Díli, tells people that she's been in the workforce since the age of eight or nine.

There was a moment of silence at the other end of the phone while the minister's staffer took this in. Still perplexed, he put a time in the diary for the two ministers to visit the Wyuna cold store.

They turned up and were fascinated. They'd never seen my business model before – or the product. I talked them through the process and the products and added, 'I'm also looking at sea cucumber'.

'Oh, you're going to do *trepang*?' asked Shane Stone.

They knew about the sea cucumber trade in the region, or *trepang*, as it's called in Indonesia. Sea cucumber breed prolifically in Northern Territory waters, so much so that in some places off the coast, you can't walk in the water without treading on them.

For centuries Makassan fisherman from Sulawesi, modern-day Indonesia, known as *trepangers*, have sailed down to the Australian coast to collect trepang. They would fill their sailing craft with rocks as ballast for the journey south, and dump them on the beach when they arrived. There are places on the Northern Territory coast where you can still see the ballast rocks that were left on the shore. After harvesting the trepang, they would string it up to dry in the sun, then load up their boats, and wait for a wind change to take them back to Sulawesi. Their ballast when returning home was their catch.

At the time I knew little of these stories, and had no knowledge of how I would actually do this, but I learnt as I went along.

As the ministers were leaving, Shane Stone stopped and turned to me.

'Why don't you move into proper premises? We've got plenty of space available in the TDZ, the Trade Development Zone. It's like a five-star factory zone exclusively for export-related businesses.'

It was, back then, the only facility of its type in Australia.

'Ah no, I can't afford that.'

'Don't worry about affordability. You can operate on a daily rental. Go and see Lyle McIntosh. He'll sort it out for you.' Lyle McIntosh was head of the Department of Asian Relations, Trade and Industry (DARTI), one of the most senior bureaucrats in the Territory and, as with many people who have played an influential role in my life, a member of the Rotary Club.

I hesitated. This didn't seem to be a direction I felt I could take at the time, but two days later I called him anyway.

'Shane called me and seems to think that you need proper premises,' Lyle said, 'and he wants to give you something. Come and see me.'

We met and he explained how the system worked. DARTI would assist with the establishment of factories and the TDZ would sell them to me under vendor finance. I was offered two factories, one for live exports of mud crabs and fish, and the other to house the cooking and drying facilities, chillers, and processing rooms. It was everything I needed and, by my calculation, a great deal.

The TDZ operated from 1985 until 2003, and was Australia's first attempt to create a special economic zone that would encourage businesses to come to the Top End and increase trade into Asia. These zones have been established in various other countries, with Singapore and Hong Kong in effect being special economic zones themselves. These trade enclaves share the following features:

- They inject foreign direct investment (FDI) and capital into the country.
- Products and services developed in these zones must be exported.
- They enjoy an exemption or reduction of duties.
- They employ and upskill the local population.
- They reduce the amount of red tape and bureaucratic procedures for those in the zone.
- They allow the free importation of raw materials, components, and equipment.

I had no experience preparing documents such as those required for government submissions, so we engaged a local business consultant, Peter Anderson, to write a business plan, work out projections, and estimate the fit-out cost for the facility. Peter had spent most of his life in the Territory and had run his own management consultancy since 1973. He became our trusted business adviser and has continued to be so, ever since. I never make a big decision about the business without his input and advice. He is one of several incredible people in my life who have enabled me to achieve what I have.

We received a grant from the Northern Territory Government to fund 50 per cent of Peter's costs, which would help us to chart the company's development. Our revised business plan was prepared and our world changed again.

We expanded. We borrowed. The overdraft went higher. We not only won the Northern Territory's New Exporter Award in 1993, but again in 1994. And we were selected as one of the finalists in the 1993-1994 Australian Exporter of the Year Awards, held in Canberra. At Parliament House we met guest of honour Paul Keating, and were recognised as a major player on the Australian export stage.

We didn't win the national finals in 1993, but the following year we won Northern Territory Agriculture Exporter of the Year and were overjoyed also to be named overall Exporter of the Year for the Northern Territory.

To achieve this within three years of starting our new business was something we had never dreamt of, and we were understandably filled with pride. We had made a success of ourselves and truly contributed to Australia with our new undertaking.

As a result of the business expanding at such a rate, my brother Shaan came to work with us in Darwin. He is a deep thinker, a straight shooter, polite, and methodical – and not a risk-taker like me. Shaan added his insights and business skills to ours, and his more independent perspective provided a different view on our activities. His contribution was one of a trusted outsider who could provide a perspective we valued greatly. After we moved to Díli, Shaan stayed on to run the Darwin office, but as the Díli business grew, there was less need for that Darwin office, so he accepted a position with the Northern Territory Police, where he stayed for almost eight years. He now lives in Perth and works for Border Force, working with refugees.

I am not sure that Shane Stone realises how influential he has been in my life. We could not have achieved our initial success without the support we received from the Northern Territory government export and business development initiatives.

At any time, there will be thousands of people, tens of thousands probably, trying to do business or people who have an idea they want to pursue, but only a handful of those will receive support. Those who are supported receive that support regardless of their colour, cast or creed. That, I think, in itself, is important to remember. For those who do not receive support, it is usually because the timing is wrong; the concept is not quite developed for market, or they haven't aligned their passion with their business ability.

I believe that I had a point of difference, and I was treated better than others because I had done my research. I knew my market. I knew my figures. And, importantly, I showed some oomph, some fire in my belly, a desire to succeed, to achieve and do more, so people got behind me. Without these people, I could not have achieved what I have with the business.

Shane treated me as an equal from day one, when he initially suggested I should look at moving into the TDZ. He takes great pleasure in helping people to develop personally, and in business, where he can. There is a common belief that those in politics or public service are often there to advance their own position and power. Then on the odd occasion you meet someone who is there to better their community, and Shane Stone falls into that category.

Shane has achieved so much in his life. He has been a government minister, chief minister of the Northern Territory, president of the federal Liberal Party, and served in many other offices. I know he feels that being Australian born meant that he had an easier starting point than others who came from outside.

'Look at you,' he has said to me. 'You have achieved so much with your business and life in this country, and you're from Pakistan. From the word go, as an outsider, you have additional hurdles to overcome, a new culture to embrace.'

It had been some years since I had last seen the Australian geologist Tim Hargreaves, so I tracked him down and invited him to visit us in Darwin. This was around 1994 when Pauline Hanson had begun spouting her vitriol against migrants. I was speaking at a conference in Darwin about my experience as a migrant, how I had been treated well and done well in Australia. After the event, Tim joined Neelo and me for a reception at Government House, where I introduced him to Shane Stone and others in my circle.

Despite our intermittent contact, Tim has always provided moral support since our arrival in Australia. Understanding the limit of my knowledge and experience has meant that I have always looked to those around me whom I trust for advice. Being in the natural resources world, his experience in business is different from mine, but he has always been there, behind the scenes, a clear and precise thinker, strategising with me whenever we meet up.

Those first few years were a whirlwind. People practically lined up to offer us money to expand. By 1997 we had borrowed $350,000. Business was good, very good. Our turnover was healthy. The margins were excellent. We had regular suppliers and buyers. All we needed to do was to hold on.

Leaving Sheraton meant that if I didn't work hard at staying in touch with the Darwin business and government community, I could easily have become isolated. With the export awards under our belt, and the business running smoothly and on track, it was time for an additional challenge. I had always looked at the role of an honorary consul general with some fascination. In Karachi, one of our neighbours was the honorary consul for Malaysia, and the pomp and ceremony associated with the role always impressed me.

The Northern Territory exported a substantial number of cattle to Mexico and, before I left Sheraton, the Mexican agriculture minister and Mexican ambassador to Australia had both stayed at the hotel. I looked after them both very well.

'If ever you need anything of Mexico, let me know,' the ambassador said when he left.

When I was in Canberra for the export awards, the ambassador attended the event, and later invited me to the embassy for a cup of tea. One thing led to another and I raised the question of honorary consuls. I had done the homework and knew there were various positions around Australia, but why not in the Northern Territory, I asked.

'Well, if the right person came along, we would consider it. There's no formal application for such a role, or a position description; you just have to have some rapport. If you're interested, send me a formal letter and I'll take it further.'

Over the years I had kept in regular contact with David Nicholson, Sheraton's part-time public relations consultant, so I called him on my return to Darwin.

'David, I want to become honorary consul of a country.'

He chuckled. 'And do you have a country in mind?'

'Mexico. I met with the ambassador in Canberra last week.'

'You? Honorary consul of *Mexico*?'

'Yeah. What's wrong with me? You have the words – can you help me formally present my credentials?'

He had successfully prepared submissions and helped Sheraton win several Northern Territory tourism awards. I briefed David and he set the process in motion. Three months later, the role was approved. I made a courtesy call to inform the chief minister at that time, Marshall Perron. There was something of a hold-up on the issue of my diplomatic car number plate, so I called the chief minister's secretary, Penny Lasette, to see if she could help. I knew Penny from my Sheraton days because, like all executive assistants and secretaries in Darwin, she was a member of the Sherry Club, which Sheraton regularly hosted.

'I've made the courtesy call and completed the required paperwork, but for some reason my diplomatic number plates are stuck in the system. Does it need approval from your office?'

'No. Give me a couple of minutes.'

I waited.

'Sakib, the chief of protocol is issuing a letter to you now.'

The letter arrived the very next day. I went to the registration office and was issued the plate 'C de C 8', which had been vacated by the then consul for Greece. I went on to hold the position of honorary consul for Mexico from 1993 to 2005.

David Nicholson became the voice and the pen for my ideas. When I wished to write letters, opinion pieces to newspapers, letters to ministers, or speeches as honorary consul or as chair of the Northern Territory International Business Council, I consulted him. He was knowledgeable about the operations of government and business and he knew how to push the right buttons with his carefully chosen words.

When he left Darwin to settle closer to medical care after having had a major heart attack, I gave him a fax machine as a farewell gift, which brought a smile to his face at this difficult time. He continued to help me with letters, speeches, and guidance on business and personal matters for several years, but tragically died young. He and his wife, Sue Schmolke, will always be remembered for the wonderful friendship we built over the years.

Juggling family and business

While Neelo was pregnant with Ismat, we went to Pakistan and then on a mini-pilgrimage to Umrah, in Saudi Arabia, where she picked up a severe cough. It was debilitating and, being pregnant as well, she needed a wheelchair at the airports. Her illness persisted after we returned home. As I had to head off to the Maldives, reluctantly, for business soon after, we found a volunteer from the Red Cross, Therese, to help around the house. As Neelo tells it:

It was the 25th of March, 1993. I was managing the office and had promised to take Zeenat and Saba for pizza that afternoon, but by the end of the day I had begun to feel uneasy. I called a friend who took me to Darwin Hospital and the gynaecologist immediately put me on a drip and said, 'The baby will be coming soon. You'll have to stay here.'

I panicked. Not only did I have to collect the kids from school but I was also responsible for a young Brazilian Rotary exchange student, Kika, who was staying with us. I called Therese, explained the situation, and asked her to collect Zeenat, Saba, and Kika from their schools and bring them to the hospital. The doctor saw me in my room at around 4pm and said that I seemed fine. He promised to return after his dinner.

Shortly after he left, the pains began. The nurses who were meant to be helping me had been called to an emergency elsewhere, so a midwife was sent. Ismat was born very soon after.

The girls sent a fax to Sakib to say that Ismat had arrived. It was a shock because it all happened so fast and he was not there. I remained in hospital for five days, partly because Ismat was a little jaundiced, but also because the hospital felt that it was too much for me to go home with a new baby when there were three other young children to look after.

The day after I was discharged, Sakib arrived home from the Maldives. To add to the chaos, that same day Sakib's whole cricket team turned up on our doorstep to say that he must come immediately and play an important match against an Indian team. Cricket! That day! Really! Men have a different view of pregnancy and birth. If men had babies, I think the world would end ... and we would have better ways for childbirth.

My mum, Nanoo, as we called her, had been there to help deliver Zeenat in Karachi, and then for Saba's birth in Islamabad, and we had planned for her to be in Darwin for Ismat's birth. We had lodged the papers in what we thought was good time, but days passed and her visa approval still hadn't arrived. I needed help around the house so we found an Aussie nanny who came each day from 8am until 5pm.

At first, I took Ismat to work and she would lie under my desk. But when she started to crawl, that was the end of that! The TDZ is a 20-minute drive from Darwin city, so approaching 5pm, I would hurry to end the day, because the nanny had to leave. Anyone who has had their own start-up business knows how difficult it is to stop what you are doing and walk out the door.

Finally, Mum's visa was approved. She arrived in May, and lived with us for the next 11 years, until 2004, when we moved to East Timor. She was a very strong lady, who always wanted people around her – the inverse of Sakib's mother. Mum was the front person to my quiet father and the more intimidating of the two.

When Ismat was very young, I would cook up huge, wonderfully aromatic pots of curry while holding her. I love cooking such dishes, but it can be difficult to do so on a daily basis, particularly when under the pressure of establishing a business. As the business grew, cooking became Mum's job. My father never liked the smell of garlic and onions on his wife, so her whole married life she had never cooked, and when they went to Saudi Arabia, they took their cook with them. Now that Mum was free to cook what she wished, she revelled in it.

Mum raised Ismat from a baby, and also cared for Zeenat and Saba while we worked. We were fortunate to be in Darwin over those years. It was a great place because the kids were always busy. It was safe, we had good friends, and we lived in a good neighbourhood. It had none of the pressures of Sydney with the traffic, the commuting, and the distances.

While Sakib was business minded early on, I had no experience with the ups and downs, the highs and lows of running a business, because my family had a secure monthly income from both my father and mother.

I would come home from my government job and work with Sakib on everything related to our accounts: the bank statements, daily transfers and deposits, and managing Sakib's salary. Sakib focused on bringing money in, because in a start-up, money is always going out. While Sakib was out marketing and selling, I saw to the bottom line, saying to suppliers, 'Sorry, we can't pay your bill today, but we'll pay next week.' It made me feel awful, but we got through it. After a few years, I left my government job to work in the business full time and eventually came to accept that, in business, you take each day as it comes.

That cricket match. Yes, I remember it well. I love my cricket, but looking back on the events of that day, it was an error of judgement that I still regret. Therese was helping out. Neelo was at home. If I were to relive this, I would do it differently.

We lost the match. I would do that differently too.

Nanoo's support was nothing less than heroic. Having her with us meant we could focus on the business 12 hours a day, six days a week. She cooked our meals and because she was such a worldly, intelligent, and wise woman, she supported us in dining table conversations about life and the business. Her contribution of personal support and wisdom to our family was immense, and without her, Neelo and I would not have achieved what we have.

Nanoo was a strong, independent lady. Well-travelled, well-read, and well-spoken, she harboured a love of daytime television shows such as *The Young and the Restless* and *Days of Our Lives*. She was a competitive player, whether it be draughts or cards, and had a wicked sense of humour that created a tight bond between us. Born in Goa, she remembered many Portuguese songs from her youth and could still speak basic Portuguese. During her final year or two in Díli, we had to call upon Australian military doctors on several occasions because of urgent, thankfully minor health problems. This made us aware that having medical support at hand was a priority and that Timor-Leste was not the place for her. At age 88, she went to London to live with her son and Neelo's brother, Javed and his wife, Maria.

Three years later, upon hearing she was gravely ill, we all flew to the UK and arrived within 24 hours of her passing. A wonderful, special funeral ceremony was held where my three daughters spoke and one of Nanoo's favourite poems was read. She was laid to rest in the beautiful Brompton Cemetery in London. Her memory now lives on in the school we built in Timor-Leste and named in her honour, under her maiden name: Avo Ana Irena Olimpia de Almeida. This Portuguese reference resonated with the Timorese community and commemorated Nanoo's heritage.

Nothing can stop us

In 1997, Asia was a financial powerhouse, and our sales in the region continued to grow. The so-called tiger economies of Thailand, Malaysia, Singapore, Indonesia, Hong Kong, Japan, and South Korea were growing, and Australia was in a prime position to ride this investment wave. Investors from around the world poured money into the region, including Australia. We were on the doorstep and supplied delicacies for high-end restaurants across Asia for those patrons funded by their ever-expanding wealth.

With business booming, we decided to find a house closer to the city and to the girls' school. As I headed out one evening for a diplomatic function, I passed a local agent taking down an open-for-inspection sign, stopped, and took a quick look through. It was a wonderful house, but we had no finance lined up and the auction was the next day. The agent gave me the number of a finance broker.

'Call him; he'll sort you out in no time. It shouldn't be a problem.'

I arranged to meet the broker the next morning before the auction and presented our financials. It was tight and there was no guarantee I would be approved that day, but we set the process in motion.

Later that day at the auction, the bidding was down to $1000 increments, back and forth between me and another party. I felt a tap on my shoulder. It was the broker.

'You know your finance isn't a done deal yet, Sakib.'

'Well, it's too late to tell me now. I'm all in.'

I signalled and raised the bid by $5000. My opponent shook his head. The house was ours.

The finance came through and we secured the house. However, we lived there only briefly because that same year we decided to design a new house for the block; one that would have a great high position on the road, looking out towards Cullen Bay. When the price of the rebuild came back, it was well beyond what was appropriate for the block. We knew that building it would mean we had overcapitalised, so we decided instead to rent it out. As it turned out, the new Northern Territory Police Commissioner became our tenant.

The Asian financial crisis

Then in July 1997, in quick succession, the tiger economies fell. In the short period after 2 July, when Thailand decided to float the baht, currencies and stock markets in the region crashed. Millions of people lost their life savings and their jobs, and were plunged into poverty. Trade all but stopped.

Qantas, in an effort to protect itself from the chaos, increased its freight prices from $1.50 to $4.70 a kilogram. They gave us one month's notice, and no one in the Darwin Qantas office would make themselves available to discuss it. We were a 100 per cent export company and relied heavily on air freight. We were completely at their mercy. The increase wiped out our profit margin in one fell swoop.

We sold the same mud crabs at two price levels: Hong Kong and Singapore received a low price, but the Japanese market demanded that the crabs be cleansed and purged of faeces in their digestive tract, a process that took several days. This meant we placed a hefty margin on crabs destined for Japan to cover the additional expense.

After cleansing, the crabs destined for Japan were placed into ice water to lower their body temperature and put them into hibernation before they were loaded onto the plane. This reduced the stress on the animal during the loading time but also during the necessary change of planes in Singapore. By the time they arrived in Japan, they were awake again, and fresh after their long flight. If only we could all travel like this!

Qantas knew quite a bit about the business because we had established a strong relationship with the key staff. They knew we sold the same crabs into two markets. What they didn't know about was the extra cost for handling and processing those crabs going to Japan. We explained the process, and begged for a break on the freight increase, but they just didn't understand – or perhaps they just didn't want to understand.

'If you charge so much extra for the Japan stock, you should be able to afford the new costs.'

James Strong, who was then chief executive and managing director of Qantas, was visiting Darwin to speak at the local International Business Council, of which I was then the chairman. I raised my problem with him.

'We run a business too, and these are tough times,' he said, shrugging.

He had clearly been briefed. He knew who I was, and that I had already raised my concerns with his local territory manager.

We had been on top of the world. Nothing seemed insurmountable. And then, in less than a month, the ground disappeared from underneath us. By August we had no business.

Just two years earlier, we had been Exporter of the Year. Now, the income that allowed us to live the life we had dreamt of when we arrived in Australia had abruptly vanished, leaving us with a debt I feared we could never repay. I had to do something.

We had few options. The best seemed to be to declare ourselves bankrupt.

Personal financial crisis

If I were to name one passion outside family and work, it would be my garden, my plants. Our house was surrounded by a lush garden, which was helped along by Darwin's tropical climate. It was the garden that attracted us to the house as soon as we saw it, particularly the two enormous trees that stood in the front garden, although it was desperately in need of attention.

I love that you can nurture a plant, watch it grow, and you are largely in control of the result. Our garden was my pride and joy. A garden in the tropics is particularly satisfying, because of the speed at which it grows. One never waits long for a result. Even though we now live in an apartment with no garden, I have orchids. I love the challenge of seeing how many blooms a year I can coax from one plant. Often, it is three.

A garden needs tending to remain tidy and presentable. While you might want to rest, a garden keeps moving forward, it keeps growing. To ensure it looks beautiful and remains in good order, you must give it careful attention. Devotion encourages growth.

When we entertained friends or professional contacts at home, we always made it a cultural experience. Our desire was to make friends and guests feel just as well-tended – appreciated and cared for. Formality is not customary in Australia, particularly in laid-back Darwin, but our dinners had a formal structure of courses, and the table would be laid with care.

When a guest walks into a hotel, they judge it first on the front-desk experience, followed by their initial impression when they enter their room. A perfectly made bed. Crisp new towels. An orderly family of tiny toiletry bottles resting beside the basin. To achieve satisfaction requires detailed, loving, careful attention. This was why I was hit so hard by Sheraton's action towards me in Darwin. I had given my time, passion, and dedication to that job. It was why the Qantas decision hit me so hard. In those first six years, we had given our all to establish our first business. We were in charge of the quality of service, of delivery, of relationships – who we dealt with and how we wanted to be seen. Qantas' actions were taken in response to the financial crisis we all faced and showed us that we were not actually in control. It had all been an illusion. Everybody was fighting for their own survival.

These were terrible days, without doubt the most difficult in my life. It was the first time my family, my children, saw me cry. The girls were too young to understand, but they knew something serious had happened.

Had I been wrong about ultimately being in charge of our own lives? A part of me knew I had to find a way to get back on my feet. If I didn't, the banks would foreclose on our substantial loans. There was no running away. I had done that once in my life when my father, in a fit of rage, demanded I leave home. Then, I had taken refuge at my friend Edgar Saxby's house; however, as an adult, there is no place of refuge. One has to face the consequences.

It's only natural that we have falls during our lives. When we are down, we have to find a way to get up. That's what I had learnt and always told my children. Now it was time to practise what I preached.

So many people had shown faith in me when we established ourselves in Darwin, and they continued to do so. To cave in to despair was not a route I could afford to take. I had responsibilities. I had a family. And I had supportive friends who had given me so much over the past years. These true friends stepped forward. Many of them were members of the Rotary Club. We found at every turn a Rotarian, concerned and willing to help, as we struggled to save the company.

Bankruptcy was one option. Another was social welfare. These were perfectly legitimate options in our situation, but I knew neither was for me. I had come to this country to build a life and to contribute. What would turning on that vision do to my self-confidence, my sense of worth? How would I live with that for the rest of my life? What impact would it have on the family and my children, and their children? Why would anyone trust us again if we walked away from our debts? These thoughts and many more twisted around in my mind.

I discussed our options with one of my fellow Rotarians and friend, Hugh Bradley.

'What would you do?' He was reluctant to impose his ideas on me, but because of my clouded head I was relying on friends such as him for guidance and advice.

'I would pay my debts,' he replied decisively.

I have always been someone who wants to act, to provide a solution to any situation. I will be the first to admit that it might not be the best solution, but it is better to make a decision and subsequently fix it than to procrastinate. I knew Hugh was right. So, that's what we did. We sold our beautiful home and everything of value, rented a house, and furnished it with what little we could afford to keep or what had no resale value.

I sat on the verandah of our house as the reality of our new, penniless life set in. Cries of hopeful wickets and laughter from the cricket pitch across the road would usually have given me great pleasure. Today this idyllic scene tormented me as my thoughts drifted to the many successful people I had met and I wondered what they might be doing now. I had always wanted financial independence. Now, where was I?

I closed my eyes. 'God, please let me die.' The lamps had burnt so low. If I died, Neelo would at least receive an insurance payout that was far greater than I could provide, so she could look after herself and the children better than I had done.

For the first time in my life, I faced the tangible consequences of failure: losing our house, losing our business, losing the good name that I had worked so hard to earn. I was now well known in Darwin. I could not hide. I had gone from being the talk of the town, with awards, articles in the newspaper, and people saying, 'Look what Sakib has achieved!' to abject failure. Those people who had placed their trust and faith in me to help establish the business would be disappointed. I didn't want my legacy for my children to be one of bankruptcy and failure.

Step-by-step

Neelo returned to a government job so we could put food on the table. Meanwhile, I continued to manage the business. We still had contracts, bills, and commitments that required attention. Step-by-step, I regrouped, pushing away the despair so I could focus. Selling our belongings and the house had covered the majority of our debts and, by being frugal, we were able to use Neelo's wage to offset our modest living expenses. Neelo's mother was still with us then, and she cooked and helped keep the house in order while Neelo and I focused on resurrecting our life, the first step of which came in the form of orange juice.

Early the following year, a trade show in Darwin presented us with an opportunity to pull ourselves out of our hole. One of the displays was for a family-run premium juice company in South Australia called Nippy's.

I discussed prospects for the Darwin market with its representative and he agreed to put in a good word for me at the head office. He requested that I back up our discussion with a distribution proposal, which I did. Soon afterwards, I was invited to visit the company in Berry, South Australia, to negotiate distribution rights for Darwin.

Little infrastructure was required. All we needed was a place to store the bottles of juice and a couple of chilled trucks from which we could deliver it in the Darwin heat. Yet, with no money, anything was a stretch for us.

Our friends Hugh Bradley AM and Sue Bradley AM came to our rescue. To know that people still maintain faith in you after a fall is a humbling experience. That gesture alone gave us the confidence to stand up and resurrect ourselves. We were determined not to squander the opportunity their kindness provided.

Each morning I filled the truck with boxes of Nippy's juice, drove the streets of Darwin, and visited the shops that had become my saviours. Every one of those shops, whether they bought six or 20 bottles, increased my confidence that life could return to normal, that we would recover and thrive and that I was again taking charge of my life.

In business, there will always be external influences that put at risk your very existence. To have friends who step forward and say, 'We still believe in you, we still have faith in your ability to run a business, and we want to help get you back on your feet', is something that leaves you forever humbled and determined to prove their faith is not misplaced.

Being so close to bankruptcy subsequently made us cautious of debt and borrowing money. While we had previously sought finance from banks, we now made sure it was within the bounds of measured and conservative accounts-receivable expectations. Taking finance from banks allows for faster growth, but we learnt that if we could consolidate what we had, invest slowly, and rely on organic growth, life was far less stressful.

As Nippy's is premium-priced, high-quality juice, we primarily distributed to smaller shops, rather than supermarket chains. Distribution grew, we learnt the processes and finances, and then tested the export market with a small sale to Brunei. However, the large amount of cheap juice coming in from other parts of Asia, plus the additional duties and taxes, meant there was only small demand for our product, so the export experiment proved to be short lived.

All was going well until heavyweights such as Daily Juice Co and Queensland United Foods, realising they had been missing out on this market, began to flex their muscles. Within a few months they had installed fridges across the city, from retail to takeaways, restaurants, cafes, and service stations. It is against the law to block other brands from your fridge, so they had to allow up to 30 per cent of space for other products. But of course, other products aren't given premium positioning.

Nonetheless, we had put our toe back in the water. We dominated Darwin for quite a few months, made some good money, and learnt about a new area of trade. This low-risk experience of retail distribution also gave us insight into a new business that we had not seen before. Our confidence was back, albeit this time laced with a new sense of caution and restraint. We had proved we could weather any storm and make a success of a new venture.

While I would not wish our experience on anyone, it was a valuable lesson. As a business owner, to find that you are close to losing everything, to understand how bad that feels, and to know how much you are willing to do to avoid it, changes everything, absolutely everything. Over this time, we learnt a lot about ourselves, about our tenacity, about our willingness to honour our commitments, and our determination not to relinquish control.

Despite our personal turmoil, I remained chair of the International Business Council, the international arm of the Northern Territory Chamber of Commerce, of which I was also vice president.

Chambers of Commerce are quite influential and central to the development of business connections, and are supported by state and territory governments. Darwin was, at that time, headed by chief minister Shane Stone, who had previously been minister for trade. Under his leadership, the Northern Territory government was building connections with the countries to the immediate north of Australia. The government was pushing particularly hard to create deeper business roots in BIMP-EAGA.

In 1997, I had visited the island of Timor with a delegation of Darwin businesses. We flew via Kupang, Indonesia, at the southern tip of the island of Timor. From there we took a flight to Díli where I signed a memorandum of understanding with KADIN, the local Chamber of Commerce, relating to future business collaborations.

As we travelled around the country, I saw opportunities everywhere. It was clear that East Timor would achieve independence from Indonesia sooner or later: walls were painted with 'Free Timor' and similar messages, and talk of independence was everywhere. Back home in Australia, too, there had been a great deal of media coverage about where East Timor was headed.

On that visit I met most of the people who are now the key decision-makers in government, and I came away with a good idea of who we should speak to, come independence.

The more I thought about the prospects for East Timor, the more opportunities I saw. There were echoes of the conversation I'd had with Neelo after hearing Sheraton Hotels' plans for Australia and the potential opportunities they would bring. So, the first thing I did on my return was sit down with her.

'Timor will win its independence soon. Nobody knows when, but everyone's talking about it. We should look at it, because a new country will start from nothing, which means that there would be opportunities right, left, and centre. The Indonesian distribution and agency agreements will no longer be valid. We could negotiate distribution rights there with a whole range of companies. They will need distribution services like ours.'

When Pakistan had been a relatively newly independent country, my father had seen an opportunity to buy real estate and to get in at the start. It was not just by being in the right place at the right time but about spotting opportunity when it knocked. I now see how my life reached a similar decision point.

Our introduction to East Timor

Díli is only a 65-minute flight north-west of Darwin. If you travel for the same time south within Australia, you will find yourself less than halfway to Alice Springs.

There is now enormous awareness and support for Timor-Leste from within certain communities in Australia: Rotary, church groups, schools, and local councils. Added to this is a network of friendship groups across the country designed to foster understanding and support for the Timorese people. These groups demonstrate enormous compassion for the Timorese and for what they have been subjected to in the past. Yet, as soon as you get to government level, the picture is very different. Powerful people, powerful countries, and powerful companies don't like it when smaller entities stand up to them and the Timorese people have a history of standing up – to Japan during World War II, to Indonesia, and later to Australia over the Greater Sunrise oil and gas fields.

Within the wider Australian population, there is a surprising lack of awareness and understanding of the suffering and violence that our close neighbour has endured since their world collapsed in 1975.

The Portuguese established a colonial presence on the northern half of the island of Timor in the 16th century, seeking to export the island's abundant sandalwood and coffee.

A relatively peaceful colonial life continued for centuries until World War II, when Australian troops were stationed there to defend the island from the Japanese. Their aim was to stop the Japanese reaching Australia, and the island of Timor was seen as a viable land barrier. The Australians would not have survived in the jungles were it not for the Timorese guides, and the Timorese would not have survived the Japanese invasion if not for the Australians who fought. This debt of honour, as it has become known, is a bond that still ties Australia and Timor-Leste today.

Fast forward to 1975. After nearly 500 years of Portuguese control, changes to Portuguese colonial policy in effect meant the colony of Timor was abandoned, left open and undefended. Political turmoil ensued as various groups formed to fill the governance void. The neighbouring nation of Indonesia felt that the eastern half of the island should naturally become Indonesian territory. However, this view was not shared by all, and on 28 November 1975, East Timor made its first attempt to declare itself an independent nation. While the Timorese people celebrated their first period of independence for centuries, across the border, the Indonesian government plotted to take possession of the Portuguese end of the island and bring it under Indonesian rule.

History now tells us that the day before the invasion, US president Gerald Ford and secretary of state Henry Kissinger met with Indonesian president Suharto. Documents from the US National Security Archive report that Ford's response to Suharto's disclosure of Indonesian plans for Timor was to say: 'It is important that whatever you do succeeds quickly'. While the Australian government initially chose to ignore the situation to the north, as the invasion drew closer, US pressure encouraged Australia to follow its lead. Only eight months previously, Saigon had fallen to communist forces, and the US feared that pro-communists in East Timor would take the opportunity to create another communist stronghold in the region. Another fear was that a left-leaning independent East Timor would become a member of the United Nations (UN) and vote against the

US on issues. It is now estimated that the US supplied 90 per cent of the weapons used by Indonesia in the invasion that followed.[4]

At 2am on 7 December, Indonesian troops launched a major assault on Díli. It began with a naval attack, followed by the arrival of troops and paratroops, 30 of whom landed in Díli Harbour and drowned due to the weight of their equipment. The attacks continued into the next year, and by April 1976 it is estimated there were around 35,000 Indonesian troops in East Timor.[5] The invasion also caused the deaths of 60,000–100,000 Timorese men, women and children.[6]

The Timorese called for international assistance, but no-one responded.

Throughout the second half of the 1970s, thousands more Timorese were killed as a result of the invasion. They were removed from their villages and placed in camps. Food supplies were destroyed. Then, in 1981, Indonesia launched further military action: *Operasi Keamanan*. Indonesian forces marched 50,000–80,000 Timorese men and boys through the mountains, using them as human shields against attacks by the Timorese independence group Fretilin.

In 1983, after a brief ceasefire, Indonesia again launched a series of attacks against the Timorese population: on one occasion, 200 Timorese were burnt alive in the village of Creras, with a further 500 in the surrounding region being killed.[7] Six hundred more Timorese simply 'disappeared' from Díli.[8]

---

4   Andrea Hopkins, 'Australia let Indonesia invade East Timor in 1975: Records show Canberra had 3 days warning but did nothing', *The Guardian*, 13 September 2000, https://www.theguardian.com/world/2000/sep/13/indonesia.easttimor. See also Wikipedia, 'Indonesian invasion of East Timor', https://en.wikipedia.org/wiki/Indonesian_invasion_of_East_Timor.

5   James Dunn, *East Timor, A Rough Passage to Independence*, Longueville Books, Sydney, 2003, pp 243–53.

6   George Washington University: National Security Archive, *East Timor Revisited*, https://nsarchive2.gwu.edu/NSAEBB/NSAEBB62/#17, accessed 4 February 2020.

7   Joseph Nevins, *A Not-So-Distant Horror: Mass Violence in East Timor*, Cornell University Press, Ithaca, 2005, p 30; Carmel Budiardjo and Liem Soei Liong, *The War against East Timor*, Zed Books Ltd, London, 1984, pp 127–28; James Dunn, *East Timor, A Rough Passage to Independence*, p. 292.

8   Amnesty International, *East Timor Violations of Human Rights: Extrajudicial Executions, "Disappearances", Torture and Political Imprisonment, 1975–1984*, Amnesty International Publications, London, 1985, p 23.

The Timorese must have felt their suffering would never end, but quietly, in the background, a resistance movement was building. Then, on 12 November 1991, Indonesian forces infamously opened fire on 2500 participants at a memorial Mass at Díli's Santa Cruz cemetery, being held for a pro-independence youth who had been shot by Indonesian troops. At least 250 people were killed. Present at this attack was Christopher Wenner, a British journalist and war correspondent who captured the scenes on camera. He buried the videos but later recovered them and transmitted the images around the world.[9] Such was Indonesia's fury that Wenner was compelled to change his name to Max Stahl when he returned to East Timor years later. This single act of bravery was a ground-breaking moment for the country and an event that made the world sit up and take notice.

Having the world's attention was one thing, the transition to peace and independence was another and it proved to be a painfully slow process. In 1999, the people of East Timor once again suffered from the kind of violence that had re-emerged at regular intervals in their recent history. In April, Indonesian troops left dozens dead in the city of Liquiça. This was followed by more towns and villages across the country being systemically razed by Indonesian troops. Some 200,000 people are thought to have been taken across the border into West Timor and held in camps.[10] On 30 August 1999, a referendum was held to decide whether East Timor would become independent. Indonesia was furious when 78.5 per cent of Timorese people voted for independence, seeing this as an act of betrayal.[11] Yet again, all hell broke loose. The Indonesian militia took to the streets, killing, burning, looting, and raping – again.

There were calls for urgent international intervention. On 20 September that year, a 4500-strong military force, the International Force for East Timor (INTERFET), led by Australia's Major-General Peter Cosgrove, arrived in Díli. By the end of October, the last of the Indonesian troops had retreated across the border into West Timor

---

9   A Schwarz, *A Nation in Waiting: Indonesia in the 1990s*, Westview Press, 1994, pp 212-13.
10 'Indonesia/East Timor: Forced Expulsions to West Timor and the Refugee Crisis', Human Rights Watch, December 1999, https://www.hrw.org/reports/1999/wtimor/.
11 Dunn, *East Timor, A Rough Passage to Independence*, p 351.

(Indonesia). During the peak of the conflict period, 11,000 troops from 22 countries were based in East Timor, helping to restore order and usher in independence.

For 24 years, from 1975 to 1999, the Timorese people suffered unimaginable brutality and violence. Determined, they continued their resistance with persistent guerilla actions against Indonesian forces launched from the jungles and hills. It was over these decades that the resilience of the people became clear, and people such as Ray Kala 'Xanana' Gusmão cemented his position as a leader of what would eventually become the new nation of Timor-Leste. Another founding father, Dr José Ramos-Horta, who had been in exile for 24 years, used his freedom to consistently plead for international assistance. Significantly, in 1996, Ramos-Horta was awarded the Nobel Peace Prize, jointly with Bishop Carlos Filipe Belo, for their efforts to secure peace for their country.

Gusmão and Ramos-Horta are extraordinary leaders who have since each held the positions of prime minister and president of the Democratic Republic of Timor-Leste.

Another founding father, who became the first prime minister following independence, is Mari Alkatiri. He served from May 2002 until his resignation on 26 June 2006, following civil unrest. His significant contribution and legacy were coloured by the events leading up to his resignation, although he has now been exonerated of any wrongdoing. At the time of writing, Alkatiri is still secretary-general of Fretilin, and holds a significant 30 per cent of the votes in a fragile, but ruling multi-party coalition, the Change for Progress Alliance.

José Maria Vasconcelos, also known by his *nom de guerre* Taur Matan Ruak, or TMR, has also served in both of his country's leading roles, being president from May 2012 to May 2017 and prime minister since June 2018. Before that, he was commander-in-chief of FALINTIL and, like Gusmão, is held in high regard as a leader of the resistance against Indonesia.

Various international organisations and scholars have estimated that the total number of deaths of Timorese men, women, and children at the hands of Indonesian forces lies somewhere between 102,000 and

180,000. We will never know for certain. What we do know is that the Indonesians persistently attempted to claim sovereignty over land they saw as rightfully theirs.

Finally, on 20 May 2002, the Constitution of the Democratic Republic of Timor-Leste came into force, and the nation was recognised as independent by the UN. On 27 September 2002, it was officially renamed the Democratic Republic of Timor-Leste. At the time of writing, the country is suffering some political growing pains, but it is fundamentally a stable and successful emerging nation that is slowly rebuilding itself.

Today, Timor-Leste on the whole has a very tranquil, laidback community, although there is evidence that the population has lived with trauma. On rare occasions, there are flashpoints. I believe that the Timorese people were deprived and persecuted for so many years that they are now determined not to risk their hard-won freedom. Virtually every household lost family members in the years before independence, and this can cause many people to have feelings of fear and anger.

Since independence, one of the strongest drivers of the country's success has been its refusal to seek retribution against Indonesia. One sign of the strong relationship between the two countries is the opening of a bridge in Díli, renamed in honour of Indonesia's president BJ Habibie, marking the 20th anniversary of Popular Consultation in 2019. This attitude has been upheld by astute and pragmatic leadership. Given that about 70 per cent of Timor-Leste's trade is with Indonesia, it would be a difficult relationship if the animosity were perpetuated. That is not to say that pressure was not placed on Timorese leaders to seek retribution against Indonesia for atrocities. However, to their credit, those in power have consistently refused to be drawn into taking such a stance.

The Commission for Reception, Truth and Reconciliation in East Timor, which was instituted not by the country's leaders but by the United Nations Transitional Administration in East Timor (UNTAET), has examined Indonesia's actions. The commission's brief was 'to inquire into human rights violations committed on all sides, between April 1974 and October 1999, and facilitate community reconciliation with justice for those who committed less serious offences'. 'Reception' addressed the repatriation of Timorese who had been displaced to the Indonesian half of the island. 'Truth' sought to identify human rights violations through more than 7500 personal interviews. And 'Reconciliation' was a community-based process designed to reintegrate those who had committed minor offences during the occupation years.¹²

It would be understandable for the Timorese people to be consumed by hatred. They are not. They generally say, 'That is our past; we now look forward', a liberating and brave stance and a lesson to other countries.

While I had been visiting the country and operating in the market since 2000, it was mid-2002 before we moved to Díli. We were acutely aware that we were entering what was then a fragile situation that would present many challenges and opportunities, but our overall attitude was one of confidence. We had seen how hard these people had fought for their independence.

My youth in Pakistan also gave me a useful perspective in terms of living in a developing country. To put Timor-Leste's achievements into some context, we can compare it to Pakistan, which achieved independence in 1947. Pakistan is still a political, social, economic, and environmental mess. Timor only achieved independence in 2002, only 18 years ago, and look at what it has achieved!

I often talk about how the Timorese people grew up with many mothers. They began with a Portuguese mother who said, 'We do things *this* way'. Then came an Indonesian mother who said, 'No, you must do as *I* say'. This was followed by hundreds of mothers in the form of the UN, with each member-nation providing advice. These mothers all had the best of intentions; however, they were all mothers who imposed their own views on the Timorese people. After decades, even centuries,

---

12   This Commission was more widely known by its Portuguese name and acronym CAVR, *Comissão de Acolhimento, Verdade e Reconciliação de Timor Leste* (archive sources: http://www.cavr-timorleste.org/en/ and https://en.wikipedia.org/wiki/Commission_for_Reception,_Truth_and_Reconciliation_in_East_Timor).

of confusion, frustration and shifting advice came independence, and the Timorese were able to consolidate what they had learnt. They were finally unencumbered and free to hear the voice of their own sacred mother, who originated from their ancient land.

Since 2002, they have lived independently, learning from their success and missteps. It is understandable that they may stumble along the way. Now, having held the reins of democracy for 18 years, they have established where they want to go. They have documented their trajectory in their Strategic Development Plan (2011–2030).

On the UN Human Development Index (HDI), which ranks 189 countries, Timor-Leste has already surpassed several larger, more established countries in the Association of South-East Asian Nations (ASEAN) and the region. The facing list provides some context.

In 2000, Timor-Leste's HDI value was 0.505 and since then it has generally trended upwards.[13]

When you look at these results in relation to older and more established nations, it is astonishing what Timor-Leste has achieved. After so much hard work, its people are now looking to fulfil the objectives of the Strategic Development Plan, using their knowledge and skills to consolidate all the good that has been done to date. They have a way to go, but they are certainly on a the right path.

---

13   Human Development Data 1980–2018, *Human Development Index.* http://hdr.undp.org/en/data.

UN Human Development Index

Country	Rank	Value	ASEAN, CPLP*
Indonesia	111	0.707	ASEAN
South Africa	113	0.705	
Vietnam	118	0.693	ASEAN
India	129	0.647	
Timor-Leste	131	0.626	CPLP
Bhutan	134	0.617	
Bangladesh	135	0.614	
Congo	138	0.459	
Lao	140	0.604	ASEAN
Myanmar	145	0.584	ASEAN
Cambodia	146	0.571	ASEAN
Nepal	147	0.579	
Pakistan	152	0.560	
Papua New Guinea	155	0.543	
Nigeria	158	0.534	
Mozambique	180	0.446	
South Sudan	186	0.413	

* Community of Portuguese Language Countries

Positioned in a densely populated part of the world, Timor-Leste sits amid several powerful nations who wish to align themselves with and support them on various levels, always bearing in mind the elements of national self-interest. The skill displayed by Timorese leaders in navigating these sensitive relationships and complexities is an exceptional display of diplomacy, a truly massive achievement. In terms of Australia alone, Timor-Leste's negotiation of the oil and gas agreement in the Timor Sea has been beautifully executed and transformative for its economy. Gusmão, as chief negotiator, and his team deserve to be extremely proud of their achievement.

Looking forward, the country clearly has great diplomatic and political skills and talents. The leaders now need to apply those skills to their internal political situation. They must fulfil the people's aspirations. They must utilise their resourcefulness and tenacity, characteristics that I have seen displayed throughout my time there, to capitalise on the positive economic and social potential they have created across so many sectors: oil and gas, education, tourism, and in the country's beauty, its agriculture, and its strategic location.

Successfully developing and managing these areas will secure national wealth, which in turn will ensure social stability and improved health and wellbeing for the people, now and into the future. Significantly, this has all been achieved despite ASEAN still not accepting Timor-Leste when many other nations ranked below it on the HDI are already members. While more than an HDI ranking is necessary to qualify for membership in ASEAN, I believe Timor-Leste must be given a chance. Its time has come and I would expect that after the COVID-19 pandemic has passed, it will soon take its rightful place as a member of this influential group. Timor-Leste comes from a small base, which makes transformation somewhat easier than if there were millions of people to raise up. It has an astounding position and record of success, and there is no apparent reason this trajectory should not continue.

It would be a tragedy if the internal political disunity, demonstrated in 2020, meant the country lost the economic strength and social stability it has achieved during its first years of independence. However, I continue to be optimistic because in my heart I feel that those in power will, in the end, act in the best interests of their people.

Ships to Timor

In Darwin, we successfully rebuilt ourselves over two years, and business was good again. By 1999, we had rented a larger family house with five bedrooms, a swimming pool, and a beautiful tropical garden on Darwin harbour. However, as we and our fellow residents in Darwin enjoyed comfortable lives, it is fair to say that few of us were aware of the brutality unfolding a short distance across the Timor Sea.

Only days after the East Timor independence referendum in August 1999, I awoke to a headline in the *Northern Territory News* announcing that a local company was to feed '4500 Diggers going to Timor'. Albatross Marine, which had won the contract to feed the troops, was right next door to us in the TDZ and so I went in that morning to congratulate Gavin, the owner. His company had partnered with Sealanes, another successful and quite substantial national business. I mentioned to Gavin that if he needed assistance with any aspect of the contract, we had the capacity, and would be happy to help out where we could. I had come to know him quite well. He shook my hand for longer than usual.

'Join with Albatross Sealanes,' he urged. 'We already have a small contract with the navy, and the new work will be an extension of that because they need supplies fast. They'll have to build a consortium to be able to deliver. If you can get prices on some of the items, you can be part of the arrangement. I'll need the prices by four o'clock today though. They're on a tight deadline.'

I was given a list of items required and went back to my office immediately to begin work. I called all around Australia to source bottled water, long-life milk, and a few other items, and arranged deals ready to proceed if we got the go-ahead. Whatever we had to do to get prices then and there, we did. We sent the prices to Albatross Marine by the deadline, and 30 minutes later I received a phone call.

'Sakib, thanks, mate. You're on for water and long-life milk.'

The shipping containers were 40 feet long. That's a lot of water and milk. But there wasn't just one container; the order we received was for 20 containers of water to be sent to Díli, two to three times per week, and 10 containers of long-life milk per week! On occasion, they would request other items, such as fresh cream or eggs. We didn't sleep for at least a week because of how much work there was to fill such an enormous order. It changed our life completely. It changed the way we did business completely. Here we were, steadily wholesaling one small box at a time to retailers in Darwin and, within days, we found ourselves preparing hundreds, sometimes thousands, of pallets at a time. With an eye towards the future, I started to fly in and out of Timor, looking for further opportunities.

Over the six-month contract, we sourced products from all around Australia, much of them from Melbourne. Everything was delivered to Darwin, where it was consolidated and repackaged and shipped to Díli. The repackaging was required because the original products were not delivered in the configuration required by the contractor for supply to Australian troops. When we received the stock, the containers had all been hand-stacked, hundreds of them. The contract required each layer of cartons on the pallet to be taped together and shrink-wrapped, before being palletised. All that shrink-wrapping had to be done by hand. It was an enormous task.

I employed a large number of casuals over this period. I even went to the Northern Territory government to explain that we urgently needed extra space. Fortunately, it had a larger factory in the TDZ sitting empty and, more or less on the spot, said we could use it. The government always accommodated our needs.

'Tell us what you want. We'll do it for you.'

As the situation in the country stabilised, the UN established UNTAET, which brought with it thousands of international police officers and civilian advisers. I now made regular trips to Díli to meet with various people in charge and said, 'We're here for you. What else do you want?'

People began asking if we could supply Coca-Cola, shaving cream, razor blades, toothpaste, snacks and chips, and so on. They wanted everything and anything you would find in a 7-Eleven. The orders didn't always specify a quantity, so rather than go to the suppliers, we went directly to the manufacturers of all fast-moving consumer goods wanted by the UN and non-government organisation (NGO) staff.

At the time, our sub-distributor in Timor was a local Timorese company. We knew that demand would only grow as more troops and NGOs arrived, generating even greater demand. We reasoned that if we signed distribution contracts with manufacturers now, we could enter this new country on the ground level. So, along with our orders, we presented a long-term proposition to the manufacturers: 'We want to be your distributor in East Timor. The country is about to gain its independence, but until then it's being managed by the UN. We already have a presence there, so we can distribute your products.'

We approached every major manufacturer and multinational we could think of, purely based on my gut instinct. It was the opportunity of a lifetime and we seized it.

Timor Sea commute

What on earth had I got us into?

For two years, Neelo and I slaved away to establish the distribution business in Díli. When I was at home, Saturdays were dedicated to a visit to Darwin's famous Parap Markets and Sunday afternoons were dedicated to cleaning the house, but one weekend morning was set aside as time for Ismat. One particular morning she suggested we go for a drive around the Cullen Bay area. Still dressed in pyjamas, we drove along Cullen Bay Crescent and saw a real estate agent setting up an 'open for inspection'.

We jumped out of the car, pyjamas and all, walked through, and decided it would make a wonderful family home for us. The agent must have wondered who he was dealing with. We put him in touch with our broker and, within 24 hours, what would become and remains our family home in Darwin was ours.

The house backed onto the Larrakeyah Barracks. It had no cable television connection and satellite dishes could not be placed on the roof because Cullen Bay management deemed such additions unattractive. The day we moved, someone suggested that Larrakeyah Barracks might have a cable TV connection, and perhaps a line could be run out to our house. In retrospect I'm not sure what we were thinking, but it seemed like a good idea at the time to just go to the barracks and ask. Note: this was not long after the terrorist attacks took place on 11 September in the US.

Shaan, my brother, was wearing traditional Pakistani garb, which probably didn't help. He and I pulled up at the gates of the barracks in my Land Cruiser and asked the guard if there was a cable TV connection. As soon as the words were out of my mouth, I saw the guard's reaction and realised how suspicious it must have looked.

'I can't discuss that. Please leave the premises now,' he ordered. As the only way to exit was to go through the barracks gate and then turn around, I motioned my intention to the guard. This only heightened his anxiety. Five minutes after we returned home, a team of Military Police (MPs) pulled up outside, with serious guns ready for action. Fortunately, one of them had a child in my daughter Ismat's class, and we were able to clarify the situation quickly. The MPs stood down. The crisis was averted.

I was also flying regularly during this period, and became resigned to the wary looks from other passengers and staff. It was a difficult time to be South Asian.

By late 2002 I began to divide my week: two to three days living in our new house in Cullen Bay, and the rest of the week living in half a shipping container in Díli. Although helped by her mother, Nanoo, it was tough on Neelo. She managed the business home base by herself, while I was on the front line in Timor.

In these early days in Díli, supplies were limited – as was my time – so Neelo and Nanoo would sit in the back garden at Cullen Bay preparing food to be frozen and sent to Díli. The scraps were fed to the goannas that gathered at their feet. Only in Darwin! Once a supply was prepared, Neelo would go to the airport and find someone travelling to Díli who would be kind enough to bring my food with them. Those were innocent, simpler times.

This arrangement was bearable in the short term, but in the long term the business needed a stable office space and I needed a base from which to live properly. I began looking around the city for a suitable rental. Foreigners are not permitted to own real estate in Timor-Leste, so a rental was my only option, which is still the case today. I found a terribly dilapidated house in the Díli suburb of Farol. For all its superficial problems and disrepair, it was a lovely old colonial building that I thought had potential to become a family home in the future.

It was owned by a Timorese-Australian man. I contacted him and explained our situation – that the UN was about to leave and that we needed an office and house. I mentioned that, as a landlord in Australia myself, I knew the importance of having a good tenant. He rented us the house on a long-term lease, and it has been our family home in Díli ever since. My daughter Zeenat and her husband, Sam, currently live there with their three children, Sofia, who was born in December 2012, Sakib (junior), born on my birthday in October 2015, and Isa, born in June 2018. With the arrival of each grandchild, I felt the same overwhelming emotion I experienced when my first grandchild, Zaydan, was born to my daughter Saba. The thought of my name living on in another generation, with Sakib junior, left me overcome with emotion when the idea was presented to me.

Farol is Portuguese for *lighthouse*, and the suburb is named after the Díli Harbor Lighthouse that sits on the harbour edge of the suburb. It was a neighbourhood of beautiful large houses but, as with much of the city, most had been partially destroyed. The only thing that saved this house was that it had been occupied by the head of the Indonesian naval contingent. As he was one of the last Indonesians to leave, there had been no chance to destroy the house. The Farol school is directly opposite, and many government ministers and ambassadors now have their residences here. Over the years we have undertaken various renovations to make it into a family home.

Originally, the garden contained five shipping containers that served as our warehouse. One of the first transformative changes for the business arose from a passing comment by one of four senior Pakistani bureaucrats who lived in the house before we took possession. Sher

Shah Khan had worked in customs with the Pakistan ministry of finance, but then found himself in Timor as UN secretary of trade. I can't imagine how he lived there during those years when everything around them was in such chaos. I struck up a conversation with him and he offered to assist if ever we needed help. His offer registered, but I had no idea at that stage what assistance he could offer. Then one day he commented on the amount of duty our agency products attracted.

'When you're trying to grow your business, and have to pay duties upfront on all the products you import, that's no good for your cashflow. You really must set up a bonded warehouse. Then you'll only pay duty on goods as you draw them from your bond.'

For example, if we had $500,000 worth of duty due on goods we imported, we were required to pay this upfront and hope that they would sell. It was risky, not to mention a cashflow nightmare. With a bonded warehouse we could import the goods, declare them inspected, maintain a record that noted what products we had brought in and their total value. We then needed to establish forecasts, for example, how much of each item we would sell each week, take that product volume from the bonded warehouse, and only pay the duty on the items as they were removed. As a result of his suggestion, we turned one of the containers in our garden into a bonded warehouse and transformed our cashflow overnight.

Sher Shah Khan is a very bright fellow with a master's degree from the London School of Economics. He now holds a senior position with the World Bank. We've become great friends. He is from the north of Pakistan, which I consider to be the most beautiful part of the country.

In 2005, we went on a family holiday with him and his family, driving from northern Pakistan up into the far western border with China. We drove a little Honda Civic along winding Himalayan roads, sometimes with a sheer drop of thousands of metres on one side of the road. We ate mangoes that we brought with us, which the kids cooled in the glacial river flow. Most people do not realise this, but that region of Pakistan resembles Switzerland: bright green pastures with steeply roofed little timber houses, rugged mountains, and blue-green glacial lakes.

Distribution business

The supply of goods to East Timor had previously been managed under Indonesian contracts. Following the acrimonious separation, the chances of Timor receiving goods from those contracts post-independence seemed bleak. Furthermore, post-independence, the contracts would no longer be considered legal documents. I knew we had an opening and a good story to tell. Independence was inevitable; we just had to sign contracts under this new country's name – whatever that was to be.

Our business model was based on the various Pacific Island neighbours of Australia – Fiji, Tonga, Papua New Guinea, and Nauru – whose agencies or distribution contracts have traditionally been managed from either Australian- or New Zealand-based head offices. We went to these offices and convinced them that it was in their interest to include the new East Timor nation under their regional management, so that they didn't lose their existing revenue or market share after independence.

Generally, we found that Australian companies were not focused on East Timor much at all because the margins were small, it was a small country, and they didn't think outside the box. To make it easier for them, we said, they could deal with us in Darwin and Díli. We just had to reassure them that once the country had found its feet, they could continue to sell those same products they currently sold under Indonesian contracts under new East Timor contracts. They were not without their concerns: *There might be thousands of UN forces there now, but what will happen once they leave? Who will buy our products then? It's a poor, developing nation.*

The population of Darwin was roughly 80,000 in 1999, while the population of East Timor was around one million. Five per cent of East Timor had disposable income, roughly the same as Australia. Because we sold to both the Timorese and to the expat community, this amounted to roughly 50,000 people, a sizeable population. As a result of these contracts our company is now one of the largest importers and distributors. In contrast, our percentage of the Darwin market was much smaller, with far fewer products, and yet our distribution business was viable. In addition, while the disposable income in East Timor might have been all but non-existent, there was a substantial UN and NGO market. Over time, this would shrink but, in the long term, East Timor would develop all the facets of any stable, growing society. And we wanted to be there when it happened.

Neelo and I worked day and night to build on the business foundations we had established, resulting in the operation growing faster and further than our skills and knowledge would serve. It was time to call in extra help. We needed our trusted Darwin-based consultant, Peter Anderson, to draw up another business plan. While we knew we had a good business, it was Peter who set us up with the right structure.

'This is a once in a lifetime, golden opportunity. If you do it right, you will do very well out of it.' Peter went on to describe the structure we needed, and how to refine our approach to the companies with which we sought distribution rights. After a two-month diagnostic analysis of the business and finances, he provided his recommendations. Our strategy would be to create our own intellectual property by developing a sales and marketing ecosystem around each product. Through this process, and after much research and many discussions, we became increasingly knowledgeable regarding the structures and strategies in dealing with distribution contracts from multinational corporations.

In these early days, our distribution covered only Díli, where shop owners opened their doors from 9am for morning trading, closed at midday, and reopened from 5–7pm for the evening trade. No one else delivered directly to shops, and the whole retail system was very laid-back and ad hoc. The companies with which we signed agreements, however, had rigid demands. This meant we had to work with the retailers to ensure the terms were strictly met, right down the line. Adhering to such requirements was a challenge, because it meant changing the whole culture of retailing in the city of Díli. We embarked on a series of discussions with retailers, where we explained that we could only supply them with stock if they followed specific rules. It was a struggle to re-educate them, but one which ultimately helped their bottom line.

In many respects East Timor was a Greenfields market when we began. The government was still in establishment mode and we were also learning, building our expertise and knowledge. In such situations, where manufacturers enter a new market, they need partners on the ground with local knowledge. Multinationals know that they cannot do everything themselves – set up warehouses, meet local regulations, hire staff, and the like. They also want to minimise risk. This is where local distributors like us come in.

We knew that distribution agreements were often used as short- to medium-term solutions for manufacturers to enable them to enter a new market with perceived potential. It is a common scenario in larger markets that the manufacturer then dispenses with the distributor after a number of years in order to move in directly itself.[14] This presented a risk. However, as this was a small market, and we were aware of the risk we were able to protect our investment. We built marketing knowledge, business systems and processes, market penetration, and market share, invested in merchandising, built strong relationships with suppliers and retailers, and invested in our people. All of this made us indispensable. We became leaders in every area of business. It was establishing these things in those early years that gave us our long-term strength.

As I have said, many of our early decisions were based on gut instinct, but we became increasingly strategic about which companies we approached to distribute. We looked at the market objectively in order to identify products with the best fit, those with a sustainable margin, and those which we felt we could develop over the long term.

In Australia, the Coca-Colas of the world have their own teams and so much power in the market that they wouldn't have even let us breathe. In Timor-Leste we did have a level of freedom, although Coca-Cola looked over our shoulder 100 per cent of the time. This was not in order to be supportive but rather to ensure we were doing the right thing by their standards. They were extremely protective of their brand. They knew the world's media was in force in East Timor, reporting on the troubles,

---

14 David Arnold, 'Seven Rules of International Distribution', *Harvard Business Review*, November–December 2000, https://hbr.org/2000/11/seven-rules-of-international-distribution.

and they couldn't afford to have any one of their distributors found doing something wrong. Any issue could potentially be reported in some foreign newspaper, such as an article published in Ireland, the US, or Australia, and that would impact the executive looking after that territory.

This level of control meant that some agreements, and not just Coca-Cola's, often ran to hundreds of pages, mostly covering what we couldn't do. We had to scale the business up enormously just to deliver what they demanded. I read every word of those agreements, so that I understood what was required of us, and consulted lawyers only when necessary.

One thing I learnt for sure during these early 'negotiations' was that flexibility didn't exist, that large and powerful companies do not like to change anything. Their attitude is: 'This is the contract. Take it or leave it.' And if you don't take it, someone else will. Most of the time, we simply accepted their terms. Back then, we didn't have the muscle we would later develop. Now that we are stable and respected, manufacturers approach *us*, which balances the power somewhat.

In these early days, there was one small hurdle to our grand plan: we had absolutely no idea how to actually manage the distribution we were signing up to deliver.

It was time to call my long-time friend and mentor, Mujahid Hamid, who was at this time chairman of Unilever China. Unilever is in the business of fast-moving consumer goods, distributing to every corner of the globe, so who better to seek confirmation from than Mujahid. We had reached a pivotal, life-changing point and so I presented him with Peter's recommendations.

Mujahid concurred with Peter on all counts, and he, too, was very clear about what we should do next.

'East Timor seems like a good opportunity, but you cannot do it from Darwin. You can't commute. You must move to Díli, establish your own infrastructure, and build your own team.'

One of the things Mujahid and I discussed was something he had learnt over his career. 'It is', he said, 'the issue of focus. The issue of "What is number one?" Choose the one thing that you want to do, and do it with focus and clarity.'

I took that advice very seriously.

'You will not be able to do East Timor if you do not move there,' he warned.

He was right. It was right from a business perspective, from a personal commitment perspective, and from a moral one. There are limitations to the fly-in, fly-out life, as can be seen in Australian mining towns. The workers do not have their heart and soul in the place in which they work. They are not committed to the local community. They simply turn up for the working week, then leave. On top of that, we needed to be on the ground to look after our processes, our contacts, and establish our own systems. Finally, besides being difficult for business, the commute didn't work for me, Neelo, or the children. We were meant to be together as a family. The advice to move to Díli was accepted unanimously.

I moved on 1 July 2002.

Our move to Díli

Díli, the largest city and the capital of Timor-Leste, is on the country's northern coast. It is on a beautiful, wide bay protected by Atauro Island to the north and overlooked by the famous Cristo Rei, a 27-metre-high statue of Jesus, to the east. The statue was a gift from Indonesia in 1996 and stands as a reminder that Timor was intended to be the 27th province of Indonesia. It was positioned to look towards the capital, Jakarta; however, it now diligently watches over the growing city of Díli, its protective arms outstretched, perhaps in mockery of Indonesia's original intention.

For the first-time visitor, it can be difficult to find their feet in Díli, primarily because it, too, is still finding its feet. Infrastructure is limited, and many buildings in the city centre look damaged and run-down, sit empty, or simply appear abandoned. Yet, every year the streetscape improves: holes in roads are filled, footpaths are smoothed and swept, traffic lights are added. On the same street you can see beautiful colonial buildings in the process of restoration and boarded-up shells from the decades of fighting alongside restaurants, shops, and NGO offices.

Adjacent to our Gloria Jean's at Colmera sits an imposing three-storey colonial building, virtually at the waterfront, but now sitting derelict. When the container terminal moves, as is the plan, it will occupy a prime position overlooking the bay. I can imagine that one day someone may resurrect it as a boutique hotel with a wonderful restaurant and bar, or perhaps a national art gallery and cultural centre. Now, however, it stands as a symbol of what Díli once was, and what it may become again when resources are available to rebuild such beautiful old residences.

Peter Anderson's primary recommendation was that we employ key staff, a sales manager being the first. Peter wrote up a job description and advertised for a sales manager to move with me to Díli and to begin work immediately upon arrival.

Several people applied, but Peter Berney was our preferred applicant. He didn't have formal business management training, but he was a natural salesman and he worked hard. He and I flew to Díli in advance of our first shipment to prepare the groundwork.

We arrived ready to start work. Our first visit on the way from the airport was to the office of a sub-distributor whose work we had already organised to take on. We had decided not to continue using them, and so we said to the staff, 'Anybody who wants to work with us, come now'.

Only one person took up the offer, the key staff member, Marcelino Sarmento, or Lino, as he's often called. He has remained with us ever since and is one of our senior and most trusted managers.

Next was a visit to the government trade office to collect the business registration papers for East Timor Trading, which I had lodged on my previous visit. We were about to become official. That meant I could open a bank account and begin trading. I went straight from there to the

ANZ bank to open our business account. That's where I met the general manager, Chris Durman.

'It's my last day today, so you're most welcome to come to my farewell party,' he said. 'It's at the Burnt House Restaurant.'

The Burnt House, as its name suggested, was just that: one of hundreds of buildings in the city left derelict by departing Indonesian forces. This one had been turned into a restaurant for the many expats in the city.

That night we attended his farewell. It was an enormous event with about 200 Australians, Europeans, and others. It seemed as if everyone's view was unanimous: 'You've missed the boat – the UN's leaving. There's no point starting a business here now.'

That was Peter Berney's first day, and now he was unsure about both his future and my judgement. Standing in that burnt-out shell, even I had to admit it didn't look good. There was so much negative sentiment and, given the number of UN staff departing, that view appeared to have some logic behind it.

'I'm not sure what's going on here, Sakib. You're saying it's all rosy, but all these guys have been here much longer than you, and they make it sound pretty grim,' he said.

Would a phoenix ever rise from the ashes of East Timor?

Here I was, a Pakistani via Australia, in a country where almost every building and piece of infrastructure had been razed by the Indonesians. And here was Peter, listening to all these Aussies saying the game was over. He was understandably dismayed.

'They have experience here, I know,' I argued, 'but we've done our research, and I disagree. Let's sit down and go over the business forecast and you can decide for yourself.'

We left the Burnt House and that night he and I sat down to discuss in detail my vision and the figures we'd set.

'I am completely confident that you will achieve at least half of these targets before your three years are up,' I said, 'and I'll be there to help you every inch of the way.' Peter ended up staying three and a half years, and did a wonderful job, achieving 70 per cent of the targets in our five-year plan.

With our core infrastructure in place, we hired a car, and within a few days had cleared our first shipment and moved all the stock to the containers in the garden at the Farol house. Peter began scouting the market to find out what was sold where, and at what price, and how many outlets there were around the city.

Each morning, Peter and Lino would fill the boot of the car and sell directly to the shops. We knew we had to be hands-on to understand each aspect of the business in detail before training the team behind the scenes. I cleared the shipments and detailed every step that each product took so we could set up the correct systems and workflow. Peter, two other staff members and I would unload one full container of goods by hand in just four hours. Anyone who has seen the amount of material a container holds knows that is fast work.

The processing of customs clearance and shipment documentation can be a stressful job. What's more, the logistical challenges of maintaining a steady supply chain while importing and distributing quantities of goods requires precise co-ordination and good teamwork.

In those early days, we had comparatively small quantities arriving on an ongoing basis, so while it was hard work, it was relatively straightforward. As we grew, we had to spend much more time on the logistics of getting containers out of the port. You can't rush the paperwork, and it requires patience not to get frustrated over delays. Over the years, as the number of containers we import has grown, we have developed good working relationships with customs officials and dock workers.

At the demand end, given the process and cost of importing products, selecting the items you wish to import requires a combination of market knowledge and research, gut instinct, and some hard-nosed calculations about margins. You want items that are in demand, easily transported, have longevity, and provide you with a sustainable margin. If you can establish all these elements, you have an ideal product.

When we began in 2002, we supplied only around 200 retailers in Díli. Now, our sales team serves about 2000, 70 per cent of whom are in Díli. Irrespective of the number of retailers we supply, these basic requirements of product line selection haven't changed.

Following the stroke of midnight on 19 May 2002, East Timor became independent. After four and a half centuries of external rule, the Democratic Republic of Timor-Leste was born. Xanana Gusmão became the country's first president. At an emotional ceremony in Díli, UN secretary-general Kofi Annan handed authority to Timor-Leste's new government. This ceremony took place in front of the people of Timor-Leste and visiting world leaders such as US president Bill Clinton, Indonesia's president Megawati Sukarnoputri, Australian prime minister John Howard, and Portugal's president, Jorge Sampaio.

President Gusmão's inauguration speech expressed the dichotomy this country would now face: celebration and ambition.

> *Today we rejoice as an independent nation governing our own destiny. Holding our own reins, we will improve our day-to-day living standards and we will build our nation.*

And a warning.

> *Our independence will have no value if all the people in East Timor continue to live in poverty and continue to suffer all kinds of difficulties.*

A helping hand

Behind our family business lies a great deal of considered thought and strategy that has developed and evolved over the years. While much of our success lies in long hours of pure hard work, it is interesting also to reflect on how much we owe to respected and accepted business thinking.

Michael Porter, renowned economist and founder of the Institute for Strategy and Competitiveness at Harvard Business School, has written much about competition, business strategy, and society. Among his institute's many areas of focus are the issues faced by companies in developing economies. Specifically, his institute has identified three stages of economic development. The first is competitive advantage based on labour and/or natural resources; the second is a company's primary competitive advantage, developing efficiencies in producing its products and services; and the third is changing focus to produce innovative products and services.[15]

I currently place us at stage two, but we have definitely begun to move into stage three in terms of service delivery, and our plans for the future identify new areas in which we will innovate.

The research indicates that lower labour costs in developing countries mean that companies operating there get by with a lower level of operational effectiveness. This is because investing in, for example, automated systems, has simply not been critical. Over time, as the economy grows, wages rise, the labour advantage decreases, and companies need to invest more in developing operations.

A common business experience in this environment is that companies start in an economy where it's OK to be opportunistic about business. Their products are often not distinctive, because in an undeveloped marketplace they simply don't need to be. They end up reacting to opportunities as they arise and they benefit from their first-strike position. We completely understood this from our personal experience.

However, for long-term survival, Porter notes that companies must ultimately change their approach to become more innovative and strategic – they must focus on identifying and building a unique position in their economy. 'This,' he says, 'means shifting from relying on a cost advantage to thinking in terms of value, ideally of creating unique value in the marketplace.'[16]

---

15 Michael Porter, 'Stages of Development', Institute for Strategy & Competitiveness, Competitiveness and Economic Development, Harvard Business School, https://www.isc.hbs.edu/competitiveness-economic-development/frameworks-and-key-concepts/Pages/shapes-of-development.aspx.

16 Michael Porter, 'Strategy in Emerging Economies', Institute for Strategy & Competitiveness, Strategy, Harvard Business School, https://www.isc.hbs.edu/strategy/related-topics/Pages/strategy-in-emerging-economies.aspx.

Why was this theory important to us? As a developing nation's economy grows and becomes more sophisticated, so, too, must the businesses operating there become more sophisticated. If we look at this in terms of the East Timor Trading Group, there was a distinct difference in wages between Australia and Timor-Leste. Coming with Australian dollars allowed us to enter this risky developing market at relatively low cost. The element of risk was compounded because we were not able to get insurance for the first eight years, as none was offered in Timor-Leste's unstable environment. However, we kept an eye on the long-term objectives, knowing that one day, amidst a more developed economy, we would have to develop our point of difference – to find our distinction.

We later determined our distinction would be in two areas. We would be a staff-centred business aiming to be the country's best and most desirable company at which to work, and we would follow Peter Anderson's suggestion that we create intellectual property by building our own distribution infrastructure.

What makes it all worthwhile is that, as a business that began in an extremely impoverished region which then became an independent country, we were not able or willing to ignore the plight of those around us. Poverty was everywhere. Rather than the traditional view that business and poverty alleviation are unrelated, research across a variety of developing economies has now revealed that the private sector plays a critical role in making growth more inclusive in developing nations. A strong and growing private sector fuels economic growth and thus helps lift people out of poverty by engaging members of the society as an integral part of the corporate value chain.[17] The logic is that as business in a poverty-stricken nation employs locals, they become part of the social chain as producers, distributors, retailers, and consumers, and the economy lifts to the benefit of all involved.

---

17 Mossavar-Rahmani Center for Business and Government, 'Business & International Development', Project Nurture: Partnering for Business Opportunity and Development Impact, Harvard Kennedy School, https://www.hks.harvard.edu/centers/mrcbg/programs/cri/programs/business-international-development.

Challenges in developing economies

Doing business in developing nations comes with risks and challenges. Some are common and recognised challenges that are familiar to us in Timor-Leste: under-developed countries lack the regulation for businesses to run effectively, there is limited physical infrastructure, and staff often lack the experience and skills to walk straight into roles.

There will always be unknowns, as we found out starkly in 2006 when civil strife erupted. But understanding these theories and knowing that others have gone before us, means we can develop our business strategy and trust the process. We can proceed with the confidence that, if we follow our plans, we give our business and our employees the best opportunity to thrive. Knowing that we are all part of the same chain enables us to see which links we need to strengthen. We are in control of the distribution link and have a plan for its development. We can improve the strength of the knowledge, skills, and education links through staff training. Plus, we regularly address our regulation/government links through strategic contacts and discussions with relevant parties.

Of course, some elements required for sustained economic growth and development, as identified in the UN University Policy Brief 'Achieving Development Success',[18] are outside our control as a business, for example:

- infrastructure networks such as roads, electricity, telephony, and potable (safe to drink) water
- diversification away from a focus on primary exports (currently oil and gas in Timor-Leste's case)
- development of strong government institutions
- human development, including education, health, and economic and political freedom
- social inclusion and progressive reforms for women
- a framework for political freedom.

---

18 Augustin Kwasi Fosu, 'Achieving Development Success: Strategies And Lessons From The Developing World', *UNU Policy Brief 2013/003*, UNU Press, Tokyo, 2013, https://www.wider.unu.edu/publication/achieving-development-success-0.

Timor-Leste has these elements and more at the core of its 2011–2030 Strategic Development Plan. Where possible, this plan allows us to align our business with wider national plans, such as ensuring that our staffing and board comprise a balanced gender mix.

It was not lost on us what a rare, arguably unique opportunity we had, to be able to create synergies between business and a new and developing government.

Legend-Nautilus

Leaving our lovely family home in Darwin for Timor-Leste was a huge adjustment, and at times I found myself wondering what I had got myself and my family into. I reminded myself daily that every business takes time to build, and we were doing so alongside the birth of a new country. The saying 'Rome was not built in a day' kept me on track. I just had to take little steps, every day, always forward, not backwards.

As victims of the Asian financial crisis, we had experience in weathering tough times, but the move to Timor-Leste was different. This was purely hard work. We were a family business and we aimed to build a business community, a family.

In many ways, the achievements of our first Timorese staff member, Lino Sarmento, mirror what we desired our business to represent for us and our staff. Lino worked hard and learnt much during the evolution of the East Timor Trading Group. When he started, we handled only a small number of container-loads of goods from the house in Farol, and he helped take orders by telephone. I was immediately impressed with Lino's work ethic, loyalty, and faith in my vision, and we frequently discussed our progress. With his finger on the pulse of the business around him, he was an ally to whom I could turn when I needed guidance from a local perspective.

He and his sectional sales and marketing team have been instrumental in extending the company's wholesale distribution network nationwide, encouraging small businesses, shops, and guest houses in various districts to stock a wider range of products. He has convinced them it's time for them to grow, so as to cater for the needs of the tourists who are starting to visit. It's a new market. It's going slowly, but now's the time to think of the future, the next generation.

During our first 12 months of living in Díli, we continued to develop the companies from which we had acquired distribution rights, and we pitched ideas to those that we still hoped to acquire. Our approach was: 'Take the management of East Timor under your control and we will be your distributor in Díli.'

It wasn't long before foreign companies noticed that we had tapped into a whole new market – a whole new country to potentially add to their budgets – and began contacting us. None of the companies we initially approached had considered this, as they knew nothing about East Timor. We steadily built up our contracts and at one time had distribution agreements with around 30 companies. Some were valuable immediately, but others, such as Apple, were way before their time. It was not yet the time for luxury goods in East Timor.

In these early days of transition, the UN was still on the ground in large numbers, essentially running the country. Following independence on 20 May 2002, the UN remained as a guiding hand behind the scenes in key areas such as the justice department, the police department, and the military. The expat community that surrounded the UN was our primary market, as the Timorese struggled to afford even the most basic supplies.

Now that the country has developed so much and business is growing, there are some agreements that I regret we let go because the time wasn't right, or because we weren't doing as much as we could have to market them. One of the larger ones was Nestlé, another was Proctor & Gamble, which bought Gillette, one of our biggest-selling products at the time.

Another major transformation for the business came in 2003 when Legend-Nautilus Australia, an Australian Stock Exchange-listed company that operated throughout Australia, Singapore, New Zealand, and East Timor, went belly up. It had maintained the biggest warehouse in Díli to wholesale fast-moving groceries, stocking 300–500 items at the time. One paragraph in its 2002 annual report reflected the very concerns that Peter Berney and I had heard from those at the Burnt House event:

> *East Timor saw a decline in business in the second half of the year. This is a result predominantly of general market conditions ... and an exodus of expat personnel with the handing over of government to the local people. As a result of what the Directors see as a permanent change in the landscape of the local economy, provision has been made against the carrying value of the assets and a consultant has been appointed to seek expressions of interest for the sale of the Díli operations.*

It appears the company had committed to certain investments based on its longer-term experience in the East Timor market. In contrast, we were new and had based our expectations on our own fresh and independent assessment. This was another golden opportunity for us, so we purchased their operations, leased their facilities at Rua S. José, Delta 1, Comoro, in Díli, and away we went.

While we retained some of the Legend-Nautilus stocks, we pared them down, because we didn't intend to continue the range of products it had imported. Our model was different. What we predominantly wanted was the facility, which was large enough for our office and for container-based accommodation for up to five people.

I moved into the premises and let my house in Farol to CNN Timor correspondent Carolyn Robinson with the agreement that in a couple of years, when my family arrived, we would take possession again. Whenever we met, Carolyn and I would discuss the country and I would express my views about the future.

'You must meet José Ramos-Horta,' she would say, 'because everything you say about the country matches what he says; that is, with the tiniest little problem, everyone beats the drums of fear, and turns it into chaos, mayhem, and fighting again.' It was true. If a purse were snatched, or there was an act of civil disobedience, it would be whipped up by the media into a major event.

Carolyn arranged an introduction, and I organised a lunch at a Japanese restaurant in Díli to meet Ramos-Horta. We got on very well and, after that, often ran into each other at various business events around the city. He has given us valuable support over the years, and speaks highly of our business. I think he realised early we were in the country for the long haul, because of our significant personal and financial commitments.

Neelo and Ismat to Díli

Living and working across two countries, I was keen to have a stable Australian base for my family. I wanted us to own a family home again, as we had done before. As described above, in 2000 I found the ideal house in Cullen Bay Crescent.

Cullen Bay is a beautiful man-made marina development less than two kilometres north-west of the Darwin CBD. It's a little like a waterfront international hotel: clean, new, and luxurious. The development contained some of Darwin's finest restaurants and bars and homes. My dream a few years earlier had been to live in an international hotel in Nusa Dua, and this was as close to that as I could find in Darwin. Neelo loved the lifestyle. Ismat loved life by the beach, she could walk to school and her friends were close by. My elder daughters, Zeenat and Saba, left for university in Sydney and Canberra respectively, in 2002 and 2003. With this house we finally achieved the lifestyle I had hoped for when we first moved to Australia.

Eventually, we decided it was a suitable time to relocate the family home from Darwin to Díli, although we were determined to keep the Darwin home. The family business would at last have its family around it.

When Neelo told people in Darwin we were going to Díli, seeing the colour of our skin, they assumed she meant Delhi, in India. Nobody knew where Díli was. They knew about Timor, but not its capital. We heard a similar story when the US president Bill Clinton and other dignitaries from around the world attended the official Timor-Leste Independence Ceremony on 20 May 2002. One of the visiting foreign ministers had asked his secretary to book his travel for the event, and she mistakenly booked him to go to Delhi. In the nick of time he found out and corrected the error.

I had been slowly renovating the Farol house. There were still containers in the garden and the bathroom was absolutely terrible, so a few weeks before Neelo, Nanoo, and Ismat arrived, I had the whole house painted and the bathroom updated.

Neelo had never been to Díli, so she moved there sight unseen. However, I was not too concerned about the move for her. We had moved countries together before, and she had always taken it in her stride. Her parents, the experienced expats that they were, had always taught her that you need to be flexible in life. If you have a bed, you sleep on a bed; if there is no bed, you sleep on a mattress on the floor; if there is no mattress, you sleep on the floor. We both had that flexibility. We needed to be together as a family – it was as simple as that.

Neelo turned up with all our belongings. We had tried to sell some of our household items, but nothing sold. This turned out to be a blessing. Virtually all the contents of our home in Darwin went to Díli and we rented out the house in Darwin. We even shipped my car.

We were understandably worried about how Ismat would settle. Cultural shock was inevitable for a child of 11 who had lived her whole life in Australia. To move from Darwin to a country where you can't drink water from the tap, your electricity supply comes from generators, making it unreliable, and you can't walk down the road to the shops to meet your friends, was going to be difficult. It wasn't new to us, but it was to her. (Every time Ismat and Neelo returned to Darwin, the first thing they would do was visit the supermarket to look at the fruit and veggie section, because there was limited variety in Díli and most of our vegetables and meat came from Darwin in a general chiller container.)

We were also quite concerned about Ismat's studies. However, our family friend and teacher to my elder daughters, Norma Grant, said that we should not be worried.

'What she will learn from books is nothing compared to what she will learn from life in Díli.'

Nevertheless, it did worry us. She did not enjoy school, because the educational offering in Díli was not good. She went to high school for a period, then we tried an American correspondence course, which turned out to be extremely outdated. After that, we employed a home-school teacher from Sri Lanka for her year 10 equivalent studies. We turned one of the offices at the business headquarters into a classroom. Together, she and Neelo would head off each morning to the East Timor Trading Group's facility.

While Ismat's education was solved with this patchwork approach, fixing her social life was more challenging. It was difficult for her to meet and make friends because the children she met of her own age had grown up in radically different environments – the Timorese had lived with an undercurrent of trauma that affected every person in every family. Common ground was difficult to find. As a result, Ismat did not experience what most would see as normal teenage years. That is, until she went to study in Australia. To make matters worse, she resembled an Indian actress who played a character in a movie that was quite popular in Timor-Leste: *Kuch Kuch Hota Hai*. Everywhere she went, people called her by the character's name, which she hated. As a foreigner, it is difficult to hide. Everybody knew who we were. In Darwin, Ismat could go to the shops or for a bike ride and be free from attention. While we never felt there was a safety issue in Díli, the constant attention worried us.

As far as personal security went, Neelo was initially worried because people told her not to wear jewellery or carry a large handbag in case of theft. She took the recommended precautions, but it soon became clear that no threat existed. In contrast, she had her handbag stolen from under a restaurant table in Sydney.

Norma Grant was eventually proved right. Ismat has turned out to be an extremely capable all-rounder, culturally sensitive to everybody's needs, and she mingles comfortably with people of all ages. These qualities and abilities do not come from books. She has chosen hotel management and food as a career, and has excelled. So, while her education might not have been as conventional as it would have been had we remained in Darwin, it has provided her with a world view that she would otherwise not have. In a hospitality career, that is a distinct advantage.

During these early days in Díli, we held an intimate dinner party one evening. It was the first time José Ramos-Horta came to our home. We also invited the Australian and Malaysian ambassadors. Neelo's mother, Nanoo, was introduced to our guests. As a military wife she was used to mixing with people from various levels of society and was known for always plainly speaking her mind. On this occasion she looked directly at José Ramos-Horta and said: 'Foreign minister, I hear there is corruption in your government.'

I was mortified.

'Where do you hear such things?' I said, trying to lighten the tone.

'I have my sources,' she replied, and continued to press him.

Neelo managed to defuse the situation, and we later explained to Nanoo that this was not something she should have said to a guest.

José was gracious, as always. However, I became concerned when several weeks passed and I had received no response to my apologetic messages. We eventually ran into each other at an event in Díli, whereupon Neelo and I took the opportunity to apologise again, saying that we feared the comments had perhaps damaged our still young relationship. He assured us that, no, this was not the case.

'You haven't met *my* mother,' he joked.

Neelo, an extremely practical, organised person with an innate sense of how things should be done continued her deep involvement in the business. Her corporate experience was invaluable to our growth and on top of that, her business administration diploma provided her with a detailed understanding of how business works. Handling decisions effectively together gave each of us confidence that what we were doing was correct.

We balance each other. I have always had a more anxious personality. Neelo's attitude is that if one door closes, another 10 will open – whereas I worry about finding even one door to open with success!

To manage my anxiety, I have developed my own *Awan Stress Scale*. I try to identify the worst possible result of a situation and grade it from one (minor/simple) to 10 (major/worst). With anything near 10, I sit down and think about how to reduce it down to one or two. I do this by looking at things objectively, identifying solutions, and reminding myself, 'This problem doesn't end here. It's OK. We will pull through.' It can sometimes take a few hours, even overnight. During those times when I'm 7+ on the scale, it can be really unpleasant – I don't want to be there. However, the process works well for me, and utilises elements of sales negotiation training strategies: to be objective, look at the wider picture, and identify the situation's strengths and weaknesses in order to make the best and most informed decision. My anxiety does not come out of fear of the result per se, but because I want to make the optimal decision for us as a family, for the business, and for our staff. So many people's lives depend on my decisions – not only my direct employees but their extended families too.

Human resources management is time consuming and each business has its own unique issues to deal with. In addition, when your business is based in another country, you can also have a cultural layer to place on top of that. We have found that, as a rule, open discussion sorts out most situations.

Lucio, the third Timorese I hired, and who is still with us, sought me out one day.

'Boss, I have to tell you something, but I don't know how, because it involves a lot of people.'

'Tell me, Lucio. Whatever it is, I'm sure we can deal with it together.'

'They're stealing from the till, Boss. They've offered some to me, and I said, "No, I don't want to take the money", but the girls outside take $10, $15, sometimes $20 each, and don't punch in the coffees and teas they sell. They say, "Shut up and keep it. Don't talk about it".'

It turned out that a large number of staff was involved in taking cash generated by coffee and tea sales – items where it is difficult to estimate exactly what's been sold, versus products that can easily be inventoried, such as cans of drink. I called in those involved, one at a time.

'Tell me the truth about what's going on. I already know what it is, but if you tell me the truth, I won't report it to the police. Although I can't guarantee your job.'

One by one, they all admitted to having stolen money. In that one day, I replaced the entire service staff, except Lucio. It was an unpleasant experience and, thankfully, my only major experience like this.

When we began employing Timorese staff, the types of jobs we offered had never existed before so it was a completely alien environment for them. We had to train people on the job and quickly, which was stressful both for us and for them. Part of that included developing a process/procedural call sheet that staff could regularly refer to until they learnt our systems. In Australia, when you employ people in the hospitality industry, all of them have experience, if not in employment then at least as a customer. They eat in restaurants. They often stay in hotels. In Timor-Leste, that wasn't the case. On top of that, the trauma of the Indonesian occupation years is something Australian employees have never experienced. We found an enormous amount of personal support and hand-holding was initially required, but overall, our low staff turnover reflects that we handled this well.

It is also rare in Timor-Leste for women to be in charge, so anticipating this when Neelo was still in Darwin, I organised forklift driving lessons for her. On her first day, without anyone else's knowledge, I organised the warehouse staff roster to ensure the forklift operator was out on a delivery when a truck was scheduled to arrive, full of palettes that needed to be unloaded without delay. I went into the office and innocently asked for our usual operator.

'He's gone on a delivery. The truck will have to wait,' I was informed.

'No, we can't wait that long,' I insisted. There were worried looks all round. 'Call Madam,' I instructed, which was what all the staff call Neelo.

She came down and I explained the situation. Without hesitation, and to everyone's astonishment, she stepped into the forklift and smoothly transferred the palettes from the truck to the warehouse. Mission accomplished! The staff's confidence in her rose stratospherically. Today, just over half our workforce are women and attitudes have changed.

The Timorese are incredibly tenacious, resourceful, and quick to understand what is required of them. My team effortlessly employs lateral thinking to solve any obstacle they may face. One day, for example, I wanted a cabinet maker to build a walk-in wardrobe in a spare storeroom, something that would cost several hundred dollars. One of my team members, Salvadore, stepped in and built me something for $20, and it is still there today. Such tenacity and resourcefulness is undoubtedly a result of the horrendous obstacles they faced for decades. Most of us have never faced anything like what they had to endure, and God willing, they will never face a similar situation again.

The United Nations

In 2004 the opportunity arose for us to take on the Post Exchange (PX) operation near Maliana, 140 kilometres south-west of Díli, and only four kilometres from the Indonesian border. PX is an American term for a duty-free supermarket from which soldiers and personnel, posted on a mission, buy their essential consumer goods.

PX Maliana had been operated by Eurest, called Compass Group in Australia, a multibillion-dollar company that operates on large-scale corporate and government catering and food service contracts around the world. It operates various international PX facilities, including in Díli, but was no longer interested in Maliana and the 600 or so troops stationed there. It was simply too small. Eurest submitted a tender, no doubt with pricing that indicated it had little interest in winning the contract. The solders at Maliana were not happy. If the PX closed, they would have to make a trip of nearly three hours to Díli for basic supplies.

I suggested we run the PX, pointing out that because we already stocked the needed items, we could be operational in 24 hours. Senior staff approached the force commander at Maliana to say a company was in a position to make a swift and smooth transition, although we were not an approved UN supplier. The commander, primarily focused on the welfare of his soldiers, argued our case and we were soon approved to apply for the tender.

There was, however, no profit in the arrangement for us. Six hundred is a small market and food rations and other essentials were already being supplied, so all they needed from us were consumer goods. Moreover, the UN was extremely hard-nosed, and had a well-deserved reputation for pushing margins ever lower with its suppliers. My friend Tim Hargreaves and I discussed how to deal with the situation. As an isolated town, Maliana was also difficult to supervise with just an experienced part-time manager, and too small an operation to which to commit a full-time manager.

That year I had met with Tim when I visited Islamabad on business. He took me to a UN function where I spoke to one of the managers about the UN operations, particularly in East Timor. We had a foot in the door, but I thought there might be more we could do with them. I saw that the Maliana contract, while challenging, could be a loss leader. Indeed, the contract for the UN Commissary in Díli was due to expire within 12 months so here was an opportunity to deepen our involvement.

In 2005, the tender documents for the Díli Commissary were released. It turned out to be a particularly complicated document that I suspect might have been so designed to keep us out. As well as the usual financial and commercial strategies, it included a safety plan, a hygiene plan, an employee benefits plan ... The list went on.

We brought Peter Anderson on board to prepare this mammoth submission, which cost us a small fortune in consulting fees. At almost 10 centimetres thick, with around 800 pictures, it stood in stark contrast to Eurest's 30-page submission. Perhaps it assumed its contract would be renewed without question.

We also received the tender documents quite late, and so the window in which to reply was tight. We worked long hours to get it done and completed it at the 11th hour. To be sure it would arrive safely, we produced two complete sets of documents, one of which I would deliver by car and the other which was to be delivered by my finance controller by motorbike. We agreed the first of us to arrive at the office would submit the tender. It was a dramatic rush through the rough and broken streets of Díli, but we made it.

I soon received pushback on our prices because the UN believed we had made mistakes. How could gin be USD7 a bottle? Our prices were so low! We explained that our figures were, in fact, correct. The difference between Eurest and us was that for most items, we were the local distributors, and so we paid distributor prices. Eurest, in contrast, had to pay wholesale, which was substantially more. As with the Maliana PX, we said we could have our service up and running in 24 hours.

Our hard work and the foresight that helped us obtain distribution rights across a range of essential items had paid off. We won the tender against Eurest, one of the world's largest suppliers of its type, and what a sweet victory it was. Eurest was furious. Its apathy and sense of entitlement had backfired. We had the operation up and running in only 12 hours.

In the end, it turned out that we had to buy all of Eurest's onsite equipment, even items for which we had no use. That was disappointing, but not enough of a distraction to take away the satisfaction of the win.

While we were grappling with the stress of UN contracts, the year closed with an altogether different stress: the horrendous Boxing Day tsunami of 2004, that killed around a quarter of a million people across 14 countries in the region.

Timor-Leste was spared from the main tsunami, but the community – in fact, the whole region – remained on edge. Would there be another? Was Timor safe? The tsunami had been triggered by a 9.1-magnitude earthquake off the north-western end of Sumatra. While this was some distance away, the world shrinks in our perceptions under such circumstances. After all, Indonesia is our neighbour.

The lack of information and communication from and about the region, coupled with relentless media coverage showing the devastating death and destruction, were a major source of fear. A couple of days after the large tsunami, we were at the beach all day, with no phone connections. We returned home to find Díli residents fleeing en masse to the high ground of the mountains, just behind the capital. Not being able to get any details because the cellular network was blocked, we jumped in the car and sought to navigate the chaotic roads out of the city. It turned out to be a false alarm; someone had seen waves crashing onto the road and started the panic, which was then advanced by others. When so many people fled, there followed a great deal of looting of houses.

Growing pains

In early 2006, the UN began downsizing. In two years it would pull out altogether. We had trained 35 or 40 people to work in the Commissary near the corner of Rua D. Fernando and Rua Caicoli. The last thing we wanted to do was to let trained staff go without jobs to go to.

The Commissary was labour heavy, because it comprised a pizzeria, bar, coffee shop, and duty-free supermarket, for which we imported about 200 products. At the withdrawal of the UN, the staff on the distribution side could go to the East Timor Trading Group, but that still left the service-trained staff without employment – good people whom we were reluctant to lose.

I said to Neelo, 'Let's do something that we're trained for, something I'm trained for.'

We began to search for a building in which we could create a hotel. After a career in the industry, this would be a dream come true. Long hours were spent building our new expanded business.

Then, on 24 April 2006, all hell broke loose. The military opened fire on the police in the streets. The police retaliated.

This time it was internal, there was no Indonesia in sight. This unrest was merely the growing pains of democracy. Many people died, and street violence turned into full-scale civil unrest. Overnight, the city virtually shut down. People stayed home. The port closed. Banks closed. Díli airport was under UN military control.

Xanana Gusmão was president, with Mari Alkatiri his prime minister. Regardless of Gusmão's calls for unity, the violence would not abate. In May, international assistance was requested by foreign minister Ramos-Horta.

The result was Operation Astute, an Australian-led international military response of around 1800 troops. It was coordinated by the Australian Defence Force, headed by Brigadier Bill Sowry and included troops from Australia, Malaysia, New Zealand, and Portugal.

The troops arrived on 25 May 2006. Throughout that month, the violence continued. Troops were flown from Darwin to Díli, with the returning planes evacuating civilians to Australia, creating an air bridge between the two countries. Ismat went to stay with her sisters in Australia. The lack of internet and telephone communication out of Díli meant that our children were unable to find out what was happening, including where we were from one hour to the next.

As fighting raged across the city, Neelo and I, along with the management team, were moved to the UN compound for safety. We remained there for 10 days, sleeping on the floor with several hundred families of other UN staff. What meagre supplies we had were shared among those trapped inside. One of our staff was so terrified for his life that he hid in the freezer room. Like all Timorese, he had experienced this before. The prospect of continuing violence was simply too much for him. All we could do was to provide the UN personnel, our staff, and several hundred others with basic survival rations. Thousands of slices of bread, butter, and jam were made available every day.

We shifted some of our most valuable items into the UN compound, and increased security at the East Timor Trading Group compound from two guards to eight. They were as scared as anyone else, and to provide solidarity, I went there to supply them with two meals each day, regardless of the situation. A gang approached our office compound on one occasion. I had a brief chat with an Australian commander at the PX in the early hours of the morning and he assured me they would do what they could to protect our staff and the facility.

The next morning I awoke, assuming the worst, that our business had been torched. Instead, my security guards called to say that whatever I'd done had worked. A couple of army vehicles had turned up and scared away the gangs.

By 16 June, rebel Timorese soldiers had begun handing their weapons over to the Australian troops. Then on 22 June 2006, Alkatiri stepped down. Ramos-Horta assumed the role of prime minister on 8 July. Calm returned to the streets, and 10 days later the violence had all but subsided. Alkatiri was ultimately exonerated of any wrongdoing in the events. It had been, no doubt, a terrible time for a man who previously had contributed so much to his country.

The long-term result of all of this was that a Memorandum of Understanding was signed by the East Timorese government, Australia, and the UN, under which Operation Astute was to continue. It was decided that the United Nations Integrated Mission in East Timor (UNMET) would remain to help develop East Timor's police force.

The continuation of the UNMET mission meant a huge expansion of personnel, up to around 2500. This was another turning point for us, with our newly won UN contract. The numbers instantly jumped from 250 to 2500 customers. We were no longer concerned about finding new jobs for our staff, who had been destined to be retrenched.

To describe those months as frightening would be an understatement. Following the country's independence, everyone foresaw peace, stability, and prosperity for the Timorese people as they settled into their new lives. Experiencing such events welded us to the country. No one could have been unmoved by the subsequent desire for reconciliation or failed to admire the fortitude of the Timorese people. Violence, however, continued sporadically throughout 2006 and into 2007. Gangs of youths threw rocks at passing vehicles, and occasional gunshots echoed around the city. When the port reopened, our supply of products resumed, which led to the hiring of Reinato de Araujo and Angelito da Costa who would become key staff members.

Neelo conducted the interviews for new staff. Reinato admitted later this was a challenge for him as it was not customary in Timor-Leste to be interviewed by a woman. Still, he, like the remainder of our staff, soon realised that Neelo and I worked together as one, doing whatever needed to be done, whenever it was needed. Although we remained outsiders in the eyes of the Timorese, seeing Neelo and me working so closely together gave our staff great confidence that we were 100 per cent committed to both the business and their country.

Reinato and Angelito unloaded our containers at the port, reloaded the goods by hand onto trucks, and navigated the still-dangerous streets of Díli with their valuable cargoes. Quite often, it was not a simple trip, as Reinato later recounted to me. 'I had to focus on the job,' he said. 'I had been part of the Resistance in Indonesian times and so I knew how to avoid trouble spots, but I found myself afraid sometimes, making those trips. People threw stones and fired guns, but we went straight to our destination, loaded up, came back and, fortunately, nothing happened to us.'

As stability improved, the volume of imported goods steadily grew, as did the workload for Reinato, Angelito, and others. Everyone was stretched to their limits as growth continued. Reinato and Angelito did a wonderful job and, as we expanded and took on more employees, they were both promoted to senior positions in logistics, and sales and marketing. Our days were consumed by the single most important thing: to keep products moving from the port to the retailers and, ultimately, on to the customers.

I stopped going to the office regularly, as I found that I could do by phone or email in two minutes what would have taken me much longer in the office because I would stop and speak to so many people. I loved doing that, admittedly, but there was so much to fit into my day that I needed to prioritise my time, so I worked from home as much as possible.

Discovery Inn

Díli is a small city and it didn't take long to find a suitable building for our new hotel, 84 Rua 30 de Agosto Aldeia Grilos, the former Galaxy Hotel. The building was vacant and because the contract had been breached early, litigation was under way between the building owner and the hotel operator to agree upon early exit settlement terms. In what was excellent timing for us, the owner had just won the case, so we approached him.

'We'll sign a lease if you can provide written confirmation that the court case is over and that the building may be released to us.'

It was an almost ideal building for our new hotel. The essential services of plumbing and electricity were in place, but nothing else. It was not much more than a shell.

As soon as we received written confirmation, we signed a long lease and began work. Minor external work was required, and internally it needed a complete refit. The plan was to open for business in the first half of 2007. There was a great deal to do, but I believed it was manageable if I was hands-on from day one with everything from refitting, to employing and training staff, and serving customers once we opened.

While the building is old, and we were not able to make structural changes, we did what we could. The core of the hotel would be our people. They would go through a thorough training program in service, personal grooming (how to look smart, clean, hair combed, a clean, crisp black uniform), and how to talk to guests. For example, how do you speak to a guest personally if they are seated in a group? You do it discreetly, in a voice not much louder than a whisper.

It was a priority for us to find a builder, fast. A Chinese contractor named Ben Chang was recommended to me. All reports indicated he was a reliable and conscientious worker. He proved to be excellent. However, he spoke no English and little Indonesian. We began work via a translator, but I soon found that the translations failed to convey my requests accurately, so we settled on sign language. With hand signals I would describe what I wanted, and where it would be placed, and he would go off and do the work. To explain where the basin would go in a room, I would stand in front of the desired position and pretend to turn a tap on and wash my hands. To show where the toilet should go (with much amusement to all concerned), I would squat where it was to be placed. Very few drawings were used during the whole renovation.

Hotels have been a core passion throughout my career. I love the experience of staying in hotels around the world, seeing how they operate, testing the room's acoustics, checking whether the layout works well and, while my family laugh at me, measuring the room size with steps.

Due to the lack of resources in Díli at the time, we sourced most of the fittings in Indonesia, which meant dozens of trips were required. There are many changes I would still like to make to the hotel structure, but as we only rent, there are limits to the work we can undertake. I started with a very small budget and things continued to evolve as we moved through the construction to create the style and quality of hotel we wanted.

It took time to settle on a name. Whatever it was to be, I wanted it to be known as an inn, not a hotel. Eventually we decided upon 'Crocodile Inn'. I was not completely content with this name, but time was of the essence, and I was eager to make a choice. I turned up to register the name 'Crocodile Inn' at the government office.

'You can't use this name. The crocodile is our sacred animal.' To upset the gods and alienate the locals would not be a good start. I turned to Neelo.

'Let's make it Croc Inn,' I suggested, knowing I was moving further away from the style of name I had hoped for my first hotel. It sounded so downmarket, so kitsch. No, it would not work. I returned to the hotel and called a brainstorming session.

'How about Discovery?' Neelo suggested.

The Discovery Inn. That was it.

One of our favourite features of the original building upon taking possession had been a large dead tree trunk in the centre of what would become Diya Restaurant. We planned around it for some time, and seriously considered leaving it there as a feature. It would have been spectacular, but would have caused too many potential problems long term, not to mention being full of termites, so we reluctantly removed it.

Our hotel is somewhat of a landmark building on Rua 30 de Agosto because of its height and salmon-coloured paint. The building's design enabled us to create a quiet haven in the city. Upon entering, it imbues a sense of peace. An entrance hall extends along the left side of the building, taking you through reception to a leafy private courtyard, from which you enter Diya Restaurant and the upstairs Deck Bar. The rooms are very comfortable and offer all one expects of three- to four-star hotels.

Our staff members are trained to speak to guests as I was trained to do, in a soft voice conveying a feeling of tranquillity. We have 23 staff, and most have been trained across a wide variety of roles, so they can step up and fill positions if another member is away, sick, or looking after family.

Diya is recognised as one of the best restaurants, if not the best restaurant, in Díli. We combine the best of Timor produce and cuisine with the best of our own South Asian cuisine, along with more traditional Mediterranean dishes. We seek to cater for the variety of guests who visit. It has built a reputation as a lovely restaurant, where you will often run into government ministers, ambassadors, international celebrities, heads of state, royalty from various countries, or even the president having dinner.

The Diya menu, while comparable to those of quality restaurants you'll find anywhere in the world, manages to be distinctive, with its hint of Timorese and international flavours. When my family ate at the restaurant, we would usually ask the chef to create an off-menu meal of six small dishes with roti or naan bread, rice, and condiments. Some guests saw us eating this and asked if they, too, could have it. So, we now offer the Family Style South Asian Banquet, which is popular with groups.

My number one at the hotel is Ryan Saputra, our innkeeper. I met Ryan, Indonesian by birth, on a trip to Bali and was so impressed with him that on the spot I offered him a position at the Discovery Inn. He accepted, moved to Díli, and began as duty manager in our first year, 2006. Ryan is an extremely capable and enthusiastic innkeeper, who now has responsibility across the whole of the hotel.

Marcea Exposto also started in our first year, and she and Ryan helped to set up the hotel from scratch. They have seen it transform from what was a shell to what it is today. They are part of my Discovery Inn family. Some of our staff there, such as Marcea and Ally Alianca, had their first training in any kind of hospitality at the PX Obrigado, where they worked serving customers in the café, the supermarket, and as cashiers, which meant they had some experience in customer service.

When Marcea was at PX Obrigado, I offered her the role of manager of Diya Restaurant, but she was convinced she could not do it. I knew she could, however, and looking back now, I am happy to have been proved right – she has excelled. The greatest learning curve for most of our staff has been their lack of English. They had to learn on the job and now have wonderful, marketable language skills that will serve them well into the future.

2007 elections

One day in early 2007, shortly before we opened, I walked into the hotel as three official-looking Europeans were walking out.

'May I help you?' I asked.

'You are the owner?'

'Yes.'

'We're from the European Commission. We're looking to rent a property for six months to house staff overseeing the elections. We need everything onsite – office facilities, accommodation, function spaces, briefing rooms, and a restaurant.'

'We can provide all of those facilities for you here. At the right price, it's yours.'

Following Alkatiri's resignation in June 2006, Ramos-Horta had been appointed acting prime minister until a successor could be named. In 2007, two major rounds of elections were to be held. The first was

March–April to appoint a president, followed by a full parliamentary election in July. Ramos-Horta announced that he would run for president in this election, which he won decisively.

The European Commission delegation was in Díli to forestall any outbreaks of violence that might occur during or following the elections, and their arrival could not have been more impeccably timed for our hotel. Within days we had signed a six-month agreement to rent them whatever space or number of rooms they needed for a flat-rate monthly payment. The Discovery Inn became the headquarters of the Embassy of the European Commission mission and a UN flag now waved above the front door.

It was a dream deal for us in those early days, not only because we had guaranteed guests but the delegation hosted hundreds of people for briefings, meetings, lunches, and dinners, all of whom got to see and experience our new hotel.

We opened the restaurant daily from midday, except when it was booked for briefings. All of Timor-Leste learnt that the Discovery Inn was where the European Commission was based, and that we had a beautiful restaurant in the back as well as an upper deck with a bar. From day one, there was no competition. We offered all the little touches that I was used to providing in a major international hotel, and which were all but unheard of in Díli at the time. As one General who came to stay commented, 'When I was in Timor, I was picked up at the airport by an extremely courteous driver who presented me with a local newspaper, a cold white towel to refresh me, and a bottle of iced water.'

I have always taken note of services offered by any of the hotels or restaurants around the world that we visit, with an eye to adopting the same exceptional services at the Discovery Inn. The smallest detail can make a huge difference to someone's experience. For example, when we were on holiday in New York City, I thought it would be wonderful for Ismat, who was developing her future career in hospitality, to experience what was then the world's number two restaurant, Daniel. Saba was reading the menu to me because I had left my glasses at the hotel, when the waiter came over.

'Sir, you don't have your glasses with you? Let me see what I can do.'

He swiftly returned with a set of +1.00, +2.00, and +3.00 spectacles. In that instant, my esteem for what was already an amazing dining experience rose higher. Immediately after dinner I called Ryan at the Discovery Inn and asked him to go and buy a similar set of glasses, and introduce this service at our hotel. Such a simple gesture costs very little, but it will be remembered by guests for years to come. That Manhattan restaurant's service is now immortalised in Díli.

Díli was still very rough and war torn, however, word got around and people said to us, 'When we walk into this place, it doesn't feel like we're in Timor-Leste. It feels as if we're somewhere else. The service we get, the quality of the rooms – it's a wonderful hotel!'

I believe it is our attention to detail that has contributed to the Discovery Inn's number one rating on Tripadvisor in Díli for more than six years, and why it received the Tripadvisor Excellence Award in each of those years. It is also why prominent people such as José Ramos-Horta is our greatest ambassador. He has said that the food we serve and the service we provide make it one of his favourite places to visit.

Solidarność

I was honorary consul for Mexico in Darwin from 1993 until 2006. When we moved to Timor, I became interested in another honorary post because such a position would provide an additional level of contact with the diplomatic corps and the opportunity to meet international guests that I might otherwise never encounter.

In 2009, I mentioned my interest to the foreign minister. Not long after, a Timorese gentleman and I were recommended to the Polish ambassador for the role of honorary consul general for Poland. While my competitor was a high-profile and successful businessman, he had no experience in such a role and did not speak English, which was a priority, as the working language in the Polish embassy was English, not Tetum or Portuguese. Accordingly, the Polish ambassador to Indonesia, Tomasz Lukaszuk, invited me to Jakarta, nominated me for the position and it was approved. Diplomatic approval was also required from the

Timor-Leste government. Ramos-Horta, then president, approved it and I received the appointment.

The role meant I would represent Poland and, in commercial negotiations, would look after the interests of Polish companies that wished to do business in Timor-Leste. There were also official and ceremonial functions and a certain amount of travel. On one occasion I accompanied Timor-Leste's chief of army on a visit to Poland. I paid for such trips myself, but I was included in all official delegation appointments.

Shortly before my induction, I received a communication from Tomasz Lukaszuk informing me that president Lech Walesa would visit the region, and that he was keen to include Díli on his tour. He would take this opportunity to inaugurate me in the role, he said. What an honour! I immediately called the foreign minister, who organised and hosted a special function in the Ministry of Foreign Affairs, and we invited every ambassador in Timor-Leste. Lech Walesa was a big name at the time, and I remember the Brazilian ambassador saying to me, 'I have to pinch myself! Am I really in Timor-Leste in the company of José Ramos-Horta *and* Lech Walesa?'

Everyone attending met regularly with Nobel Laureate Ramos-Horta, but having Lech Walesa, who had been awarded the Nobel Peace Prize in 1983 for his campaign to free Poland from the tyranny of the Iron Curtain, would be a major event in any country. Walesa spoke for a few minutes through an interpreter and proved to be an unexpectedly humorous orator.

The connection between Poland and Timor-Leste was partly due to the two Nobel laureates. However, there was a greater bond that reflected Walesa's 1980 Solidarność campaign and aspects of Timor-Leste's own Solidarity movement for independence and freedom from tyranny under Indonesian rule. This is something that was further cemented by Pope John Paul II's visit in 1989, because he was of Polish origin. He is now memorialised with a statue in Díli.

Ramos-Horta invited Walesa to stay at his home, but Walesa, concerned about the heat and possible lack of air conditioning, said he would prefer to stay in a hotel. He stayed at Hotel Timor, but we hosted a dinner at the Discovery Inn with the two Nobel laureates, several ambassadors, and foreign minister Zacarias Albano da Costa and his wife, Milena, now Timor-Leste's ambassador to the UN.

José Ramos-Horta kindly offered to take Lech Walesa to the airport the next day and they agreed that he would be collected at precisely 12.30pm from his hotel. The driver arrived, as scheduled, in a bulletproof car, but there was no sign yet of Ramos-Horta. At exactly 12.30, Walesa went and sat in the car.

'Where is he going?' I asked the ambassador. 'José is not here yet.'

'He's a man of his own mind. Half past 12 was the agreed time.'

'Can you do something?' I asked.

'I think it would be preferable if you invite him back inside.'

I tapped on the car window and explained that the president had been held up and should be here soon.

'This is the second time your president is late,' he observed. 'I will not be late for my own funeral.'

'Let's not be so morbid, Mr President,' I suggested.

I invited him back inside. Within five or 10 minutes, José arrived and the four of us proceeded to the airport.

After my retirement, the current Polish ambassador suggested that my daughter Zeenat assume the position of honorary consul general and Ramos-Horta concurred. Having assisted in the role since 2016, her position was finally approved in August 2020. It was an honour to have served Poland in this distinguished position for eight and a half years, and it makes me extremely proud that visitors to Timor-Leste from Poland will now be capably looked after by Zeenat.

In May 2021, I received unexpected news from the President of Poland, Andrzej Duda, that I am to be awarded the Gold Cross, Medal of Merit in recognition my services to the state as Honorary Consul General. This is a great honour and as I reflect upon those years, it makes me proud that I was able to help Poland establish a presence in Timor-Leste.

Photographs | 1

△ My parents: Nabi Dad Khan Awan (*Abba Jee*, Dad) and Ismat Jehan Awan (*Ammie*, Mum).
▽ Neelo & I at our wedding, 1983.

△ Me in Montréal, 1978.
▷ A red 1976 Honda CD-175, just like the one that transformed my life (facing).

△ **Karachi in the 1970s: Another world**
Luxury Beach Hotel (centre), The Metropole Hotel (above).

Two of Pakistan's most recognisable landmarks:
△ Faisal Mosque in Islamabad (Photo: REUTERS/Mian Kursheed)
▽ Mohd. Ali Jinnah's Mausoleum in Karachi (Photo: Haroon)

▷ Facing: The glorious north of Pakistan, unknown to most of the world. Filled with spectacular mountains, lakes (Centre photo: Waqas Afzal) and glacial rivers, including K2, the world's second highest peak at 8611m, compared to Everest's 8849m.

This page:
△ Intercontinental Karachi, now the Pearl Continental Hotel, where I did my training in 1975 (top).
△ Taj Mahal, Karachi, now Regent Plaza, where I had my first international hotel job in 1981.

Facing:
▷ Sharjah Continental Hotel, UAE, now Radisson Blu (top).
▷ Holiday Inn Islamabad, now Marriott Hotel Islamabad (centre).
▷ Sheraton Hotel Karachi, now the Mövenpick Karachi (right).

△ Greeting Prime Minister Bob Hawke at the Sheraton Hotel, Darwin, 1989.
▽ Neelo and I with Prime Minister Paul Keating, as winners of the Northern Territory Export Award, at the 1993 Australian Export Awards.

Photographs | 9

△ Darwin (L-R): Me with Pakistan President H.E. Farook Leghari, and Northern Territory Cheif Minister Shane Stone.
▽ Meeting Prime Minister John Howard, late 1990s.

△ Meeting United Nations Secretary General, Kofi Annan.
▽ Neelo and I with Nobel Laureates, President of Timor-Leste José Ramos-Horta and President of Poland, Lech Wałęsa, at my inauguation as Hon. Consul General for Poland, Díli, 2009.

△ Honorary Consuls for Mexico from around the world meeting in Mexico City with the Mexican President, in the mid-1990s.
▽ Saba, Prime Minister Xanana Gusmão, me, and Zeenat.

△ With Timor-Leste Foreign Minister Zacarias Albano da Costa and Prime Minister Kevin Rudd, 2011.
▽ Neelo and I meeting the Australian Governor General, Dame Quentin Bryce, in Díli.

△ Receiving the Order of Timor-Leste from the President of Timor-Leste, José Ramos-Horta, May 2012.
▽ Neelo and I at the Order of Timor-Leste investiture ceremony, May 2012.

△ Our warehouse in Darwin's Trade Development Zone, with the Sealanes office visible behind.
▽ A view over Díli Harbour, Timor-Leste.

△▽ Discovery Inn, Díli, and a Díli sunset.

△ Our original Burger King restaurant and Gloria Jean's Coffees, Timor Plaza.
▽ Gloria Jean's Coffees, Colmera, Díli (L). Our Burger King, Operator of the Year Award and export awards from Darwin, Northern Territory.

△ Gloria Jean's, Colmera, Díli: Domingos Da Silva and Justina Magno.
▽ A page from our 2014 Burger King Timor-Leste calendar.

△ Our Early members of the East Timor Trading Team in Díli.
▽ Some of our ETT staff. Front: Norlyn Ngo, Eligio Perreira, Celina Soares. Back: Elvis Pereira, Pedro Gomez, Lucio Sarmento.

△ The East Timor Trading Group Headquarters, Comoro, with some of our delivery fleet.

△ East Timor Trading Group Family, Christmas 2018.
▽ East Timor Trading Group sales training, Bali, 2019.

△ CEO of East Timor Trading, Sam Aluwihare.
▽ The Late Renato, one of our early employees, who was Regional Sales Manager when he tragically died on **23 June 2021.**

East Timor Trading Group's future plans
▽ Our next step in hospitality: The Discovery Hotel, Díli.

▽ An architect's drawing of our new warehouse and office facility in Comoro.

△ The family together.
▽ Enjoying my semi-retirement in 2019.

Part 2

Business

His Excellency Xanana Gusmão

To be a successful and prosperous country we need to build a robust and sustainable private sector that creates jobs, supports economic growth, and provides opportunities for our people.

East Timor Trading Group plays an important part in our economy as a leader in hospitality and retail. We need more businesses like Sakib Awan's so that we can reach our economic potential. And so that we can provide hope and opportunity, grow our economy, and build our nation.

Sakib has built a business that has provided jobs and training to many Timorese, and supported the growth of supplier networks throughout the country, from the coffee areas of Ermera to the hospitality sector in Díli. This has contributed significantly to our economic growth.

Sakib is one of the most successful businessmen in Timor-Leste. It is his strong belief and commitment to Timor-Leste, his focus on growth, and his patience, that have allowed him to succeed. Sakib is not here to make quick money – he is dedicated to building a sustainable business. He has a strong but sensible risk appetite, and he knows that hard work and dedication over a number of years are required to build a lasting business.

Government can only build our nation in partnership with the private sector. It is only together that we can establish a strong economic foundation for our country. Two of our greatest nation-building challenges are to develop our human resources – the skills and experience of our people – and to create jobs. Sakib is doing both.

As one of our largest private-sector employers, and one that places importance on building and enhancing the professional development and skills of his staff, Sakib is making a substantial contribution to our nation-building endeavour. However, even taking into account this contribution, it is my view that the greatest impact Sakib and his company, East Timor Trading Group, are making on Timor-Leste is inspiring investor confidence and showing what can be done in our country with hard work, dedication, and vision.

Timor-Leste

> *The Timorese spirit of community is similar to that in Pakistan; I think that's why I have found working here fulfilling. We are on the same page with our community spirit and social expectations.*
>
> – **Neelo**

One unique challenge of doing business in a country managed by the UN is the disparity created by the exorbitant wages the UN pays its staff and the salaries of local staff. This creates a false economy within the country that generates unrealistic income expectations among non-UN staff. The word gets out quickly that if you get a job with the UN, you'll be paid handsomely, with little or no pressure to work hard. While we've had wonderful experiences with NGOs, the UN culture is quite different. East Timor is classed as a hardship posting for UN staff, and still holds the second-highest hardship rating, which translates to even higher wages, something we simply cannot afford to match.

The wage hierarchy starts with the UN at the top, embassies below that, moving on down to the private sector. The East Timor Trading Group set its wages between those of the embassies and the UN. In addition, we provide an array of other benefits to our staff, including good-quality meals during their shifts. Initially, in the early 2000s, fresh food was hard to come by, so such meals were prized.

Thankfully, the business and employment landscape has now slowly readjusted to more normal levels, based on the local economy since the UN left. However, Timor-Leste, like every country, still has its share of challenges; unlike most countries, it's only early days and it's learning to walk.

The standard of living in Díli has improved, but there is still a long way to go. If you walk through the back streets from Timor Plaza to the parliament building, only a block or two back from the esplanade there are some terrible housing situations, many of them makeshift, where people moved in after the buildings were abandoned. Yet, new housing is being developed as earning opportunities increase. As more people move into the country it should continue to improve.

Most of my employees have their own houses now, the result of stable employment and the loans that we provide. It's still not easy for some people to make ends meet, especially when everything is so expensive. Still, there are signs of improvement. One of our staff, for example, redeveloped a block of land and is building a new house on it, a project that employs local people and builds capacity in the city.

It has been a process of evolution, but it is working. Gaunt and malnourished, the staff I hired in 2002 showed many signs of a poor diet. Now, they are healthy and happy, with full faces and bright eyes. As a result of their new, more prosperous lives, many of them have become respected elders in their communities.

Community in Timor comprises one's immediate family, extended family, those who live nearby, those one works with, and those who attend the same church. If you are a wage earner, it is considered a family responsibility that you provide for your parents, siblings, and the siblings' children, whether through buying food, giving them housing options, or paying for their education.

The Timorese community is quite different from those of many Western countries, although in many ways the thinking and social challenges are similar to those in Pakistan. Both cultures value their elders and the close family unit, and they share the challenges of the developing world. I believe it would have been less of an adjustment for us if we had come to Timor-Leste directly from Pakistan. After living in Australia, where there's a system for everything, where you pick up a phone and things get done, life in Timor was a challenge. We knew that being in a new country would require patience and represent a learning curve. All the laws, the systems, training of the people, the bureaucracy, the political system – everything had to be built from scratch.

There are also cultural sensitivities and a social hierarchy in the Timorese community that one does not face in more developed countries such as Australia. If I employ someone from a lower position in the hierarchy to supervise someone societally senior, it can place them in a challenging position. Yet, times are changing. I have noticed that the sense of hierarchy is somewhat less inherent in the younger generation, as the country becomes more of a meritocracy, at least in Díli.

As businesses grow, change is required, and it is human nature to greet change with a level of resistance. In Timor-Leste, it is no different. One of the greatest human resource challenges has been to help our staff understand why we make certain changes and decisions, why we move staff around, or why we sometimes employ people from outside, rather than simply force change upon them.

We have almost 300 staff, including around 250 Timorese and 45 from Indonesia, Malaysia, Sri Lanka, Pakistan, the Philippines, Singapore, India, Australia, and Bangladesh. We count our security guards, whom we have hired from outside contractors over the past 15 years, as part of our family, which means they are provided with meals during their shifts, just like our regular employees, and they also receive employee and Christmas bonuses based on length of service.

One of them retired recently, after having a stroke. I was out of the country at the time, but when I returned, he was given a retirement bonus equal to his annual salary as a gesture of our gratitude for his years of service. We now employ his son who, of necessity, has become the financial anchor for the family. It is gestures like these that I wish to continue so that we remain true to the genuinely human organisation we created. I know this is not everyone's attitude to running a business, but we see our business as integral to our family. In Timor-Leste, the young people are ambitious and eager to work hard and learn, and we wish to celebrate that attitude.

Good jobs are hard to come by, and you must be smart to stand up and get a job so as to advance your prospects. There is pressure on us to employ locals, which is not just understandable but also laudable. However, most of our executive committee members have MBAs or CPA certifications, or a graduate degree in accounting or marketing. While these jobs were open to all, few people in Díli possessed the necessary education and skill sets to fill them. Accordingly, we had to look farther afield to qualified foreigners who were willing to move to Timor-Leste. However, unlike the UAE or some Gulf countries, it's not easy to find people willing to relocate to Timor, or to obtain work visas for them.

Despite the skills gap at our senior level, many of our staff have progressed despite little formal education, because they are naturally street smart and deal well with people. We try to give them opportunities to move up and we see that they are promoted on merit. For example, Lino Sarmento, who was originally hired to be my driver, is now the sales and marketing manager, while Martin Fernandes, who initially replaced him, is now the shift manager in Burger King. Marcea Exposto, initially a waitress, is now duty manager at Discovery Inn, and Eligio Pereira, who was once a cashier at PX Obrigado, is now our head auditor.

We are by no means the only employer in Díli, but we have strived to be the most supportive, and to provide the greatest opportunities to build experience and education. Notably, we believe and promote gender equality. As Melinda Gates says, 'If you want to lift up a family, a community, a society, you employ women'. Neelo and I are a team, and our belief that our staff are all equally important and our desire to be inclusive led to our decision to maintain a relatively equal ratio of male and female employees. Our management committee and board are also gender balanced, something not many boards in Australia can say. It makes good business sense. Satisfied employees translate to a lower staff turnover rate and lead to significant long-term loyalty, a great asset to any enduring and sustainable corporation.

At board level, there is a reasonable amount of microeconomic evidence to show that gender parity improves the financial performance of a business. It has now been shown that men and women bring quite different attitudes to risk, and also to collaboration, in a workplace. What this might mean for the macroeconomic growth of a developing nation has only recently been examined.

In 2018, the International Monetary Fund (IMF) found that having more women within a labour force brings greater macroeconomic gains to the economy than adding the same number of male workers, and that upskilling and educating women while lowering the gender inequality gap can increase a developing nation's GDP by up to 35 per cent.[19] Eighty per cent of these gains come simply from new workers entering the labour force; the rest stems from the results of diversity in productivity. Upskilling and educating women on par with men is just one piece of the puzzle for employers, and we are pleased to see that Timor-Leste has reinforced this by including gender equality in its 2011–2030 Strategic Development Plan.

We see it as important to give our staff a quality of life in Timor as well as opportunities to broaden their horizons, which they might otherwise never have had. As a result we rarely say no to getting behind a cause that will clearly benefit a specific sector of a community, be they large projects such as a school, or small, family-level projects.

Another primary focus is health. We provide healthcare for staff and their immediate family. Access to healthcare in Timor-Leste is still difficult and so providing these benefits means our staff live better lives, which is good for their jobs and families, and of course also for the security of the business over the long term.

When we moved to Díli, only extremely limited resources were available to the populace, and so we started contributing additional forms of support to our staff. For example, we pay all of their medical bills. For extraordinary causes, such as an illness that can't be treated in Timor-Leste, we even send staff overseas for treatment. When we do this, they usually need to be accompanied by somebody who knows their way around Singapore, for example, to assist them. So, another senior staff member usually goes with them as a carer.

We have also organised and provided catering for the weddings of several staff members. We have helped many staff with financial issues too, at first with interest-free loans and now with a rate far lower than banks offer. However, these loans are subject to certain rules: 1) if someone has taken a loan in the preceding five years, they can't take any further loan; and 2) every person making use of a loan needs to have two staff members as guarantors, and while the guarantee is in place, those guarantors themselves are not able to apply for or have a loan.

---

19   Emma Newburger, 'Employing more women could boost economies by 35 percent, says IMF chief Christine Lagarde', *CNBC Make It*, 5 March 2019, https://www.cnbc.com/2019/03/05/imf-chief-employing-more-women-could-boost-economies-by-35-percent.html.

More than 50 or 60 staff typically have loans at any one time. More importantly, we train staff about how to save money and be self-reliant so they can pay off their loans.

To attract international staff to more senior positions, we offer additional benefits; for example, accommodation, a laundry service, utilities, housekeeping, even a car, depending on the position. Except for breakfast, all meals are provided. These individuals work hard, and they have left their home countries to come and work for us, so they deserve this added level of comfort.

Many years ago, my mother heard about some of our activities in Timor-Leste and she said, 'Why don't you come and provide some of your assistance and further your charity work in Pakistan, instead of Timor?'

'I earn my income here,' I explained, 'so it should be spent here. We provide money to improve education in Timor, which is very close to your heart, to father's heart, and to my heart. So, that's what we're doing.'

She replied with an old Pakistani expression: *'Jangal mei more nacha kis ney dekha?'* Literally, 'Who sees a peacock dancing in the jungle?' She meant that while I was dancing in Timor, nobody in my homeland could see what I was doing.

In later years, we undertook charity work in Pakistan; for example, we drill boreholes in the more remote areas of the Sindh Province, so people can access clean water. Sindh has one of the largest irrigation networks in the world, comprising 14 canals and more than 40,000 channels that direct water to fields for crops. This water distribution system extends across almost the entire province, except for the Thar desert and the Kacho area. This equates to uneven, unequal distribution of water overall and therefore a great number of people do not have food and clean water. Our boreholes help provide some of these areas with access to clean water.

The importance of education is one of my core beliefs. In conjunction with my brother's foundation in Pakistan, we have provided housing and funded children's education in Karachi. In Timor, we provide courses and training for staff, whether it's general education about hygiene or more specific training relating to IT skills and languages. We built a preschool in Timor-Leste in association with Kirsty Gusmão's office (UN goodwill ambassador for education in Timor-Leste), and the ministry of education. We also provided funding for education and housing in and around Díli. We are now establishing another preschool. It is our earnest desire to have a preschool in every district in the country.

Our aim is to continue to initiate and establish various financially sustainable projects in Timor-Leste and Pakistan. Neelo and I both believe that there is no point taking your money to your grave.

An eye towards the future

Many years ago, when I was driving home, I turned into our street and was astonished to see the streetlights illuminated. I was jubilant and rushed inside.

'Neelo, we have streetlights! The streetlights are on! They're working!'

The small, simple things that are taken for granted in developed countries represent great leaps in Timor-Leste that bolster our faith that the country is moving ahead. Success in infrastructure means that the wheels are turning, that all the government planning and spending has paid off, resulting in tangible improvements. Whether it is business registration, customs reform, taxation, education, health, or infrastructure, Timor still has a long way to go, but for a nation that has been independent only for a few short years, it has already come far.

The confidence I have in Timor-Leste is reflected in our plans for the business. If we didn't have faith in the country's ability to grow at a sustainable rate, we wouldn't continue investing. Our head office at Rua San José Delta 1, Comoro, is only 100 metres from Timor Plaza. It has served us well since 2003. At around 4000 square metres, it has been expanded in various directions over the years to accommodate our growth. It remains efficient for now, but as we continue to invest in the country, we will no doubt need more space.

I see this growth occurring in two main areas: tourism and domestic consumption.

Tourism

Like many Timorese who work in hospitality and come face-to-face with visitors, our Discovery Inn staff see so much more that could be done to show the world the beautiful places there are in this country – we simply need more tourists to experience our hospitality. My son-in-law, Sam, is vice-chairman of the board of the newly formed Hotel Owners of Timor-Leste (HOTL) association, whose role is to encourage the private sector to support the government in its tourism ambitions.

I do not believe that luxury tourism will take off here in the foreseeable future. Instead, adventure holidays and eco-tourism are where I see the growth potential. However, much work needs to be done before more tourists will come. Airport arrivals must be streamlined to reduce queues. Repairs are needed on pavements and roads around Dili.

The main beach needs to be kept clean. Only five minutes east of the city, towards Cristo Rei, there are beautiful clean white beaches speckled with tables and chairs from which you can sit and watch the sunrise and sunset across the bay's crystal-clear waters.

The Dili CBD waterfront needs to be similarly cleaned up, so that visitors can gaze over the bay without containers, drain outlets, and rubbish spoiling the view.

Roads to the districts are improving all the time, for example, one can now drive to Baucau in less than an hour and a half – a trip that took many hours only a few years ago. Challenges remain, but with each passing year the infrastructure improves.

None of these things present insurmountable problems. We need only to make manageable changes to increase the country's appeal. There are a couple of specific actions I believe the government could take. First, it should spend money on a world-class advertising campaign to attract international conferences. Secondly, the cost of getting to Dili by air must be reduced. Until this is done, I can't see that any tourism will grow significantly.

If just one per cent of the approximately 35 million tourists who visit Indonesia and Singapore annually could be given a three-night add-on stay in Dili, the number of international tourists coming into the country would require eight to 10 new three-, four-, or five-star hotels to accommodate them. The same could be said of tourists from Australia. These are tiny percentages, but they represent an enormous potential boost to the economy. Currently, most visitors to Timor-Leste are professionals who come for business purposes. Only one per cent are tourists, so there is huge room for improvement in this sector.

Domestic consumption

I believe growth in domestic consumption will be fed through foreign investment and increased government expenditure. As a result, we are focusing on developing commercial and residential real estate and expanding our hospitality offerings. Given that the stability and longevity of multinational distribution agreements are largely outside our control, this diversification is also a risk management strategy to ensure we remain profitable over the long term by creating a broad business base. This also suits the lifecycle of the local economy, which is now relatively stable and becoming more sophisticated. We will move with it to develop our business with innovative products and services, so that we can capitalise on growth in domestic consumption as it occurs.

These plans are based on expanding our existing strengths, so that they reflect the fundamental concept of our business as one of organic growth. With these developments in place, our aim is to take the company from current staffing levels of almost 300 to at least 700–800 people in the next 10 years.

However, despite all my confidence, I am always on the lookout for risk. I see now that our greatest existential risk is also our greatest potential, if handled appropriately. With Timor having been around for essentially 20 years now, there's a whole new generation who are very close to graduating with new skills, qualifications, and experience who will be able to move directly into junior management positions in both government and business. This is a very different and much more positive situation than the one we faced 10 or 15 years ago, but it does mean we face pressure to review our human resources policies. As this new Timorese talent comes through, we will naturally want to employ them, yet we do not want to lose the faith of, or be seen to abandon, existing employees who have worked extremely hard for many years and have their heart set on achieving promotions to more senior positions. We know this balance must be handled sensitively for the benefit of all parties concerned.

Because the East Timor Trading Group works at a grassroots level providing fast-moving consumer goods, we experience economic and social change early. We are heavily reliant on domestic consumption, and the majority of that comes through government spending. If that doesn't happen, we notice very quickly that all is not as it should be.

The patronage of supermarkets provides a good indicator of the local growth, wealth, and stability of the population in Díli, and it has changed dramatically: in early 2000, 90 per cent of people who patronised Western supermarkets were foreigners – UN and NGO staff, and so on. Only 10 per cent of customers were Timorese. Now the situation has more than reversed and around 95 per cent of customers are Timorese people who have achieved a level of prosperity in their lives, with secure employment and homes. The same cannot be said for the whole population yet, of course, but change begins in the larger cities. In time, such change will filter through to smaller districts and cities across the country.

Such heavy reliance on government spending can, however, be a curse. In a democracy, sometimes politics gets in the way of these wider goals, and it becomes a little harder for simple things to be achieved. As I write this in 2020, there is a political standoff in which the budget has not been approved. It has gone back and forth for months, the result being that there was only essential government spending from July 2018 through 2019 and into 2020. The World Bank's *Timor-Leste Economic Report* in April 2020 showed that government expenditure had plummeted due to the standoff.[20] The result has been that the economy has all but stopped. Every businessperson we have spoken to has said the same thing.

Back in October 2018, even after that budget had been approved, there were glitches, and payments were further delayed. A further

---

20 The World Bank, *March 2018 Timor-Leste Economic Report: Lower Public Spending Leads to Slower Growth*, 20 March 2018, https://www.worldbank.org/en/country/timor-leste/publication/april-2020-timor-leste-economic-report-a-nation-under-pressure.

complication is that if allocated money isn't spent within the financial year, it is returned to the Treasury. As a result, the money didn't really start flowing through the economy until early 2019. The World Bank's Economic Report from April 2019 showed some improvement,[21] however, it was mid-year before we began to see the economy stabilising. That makes for a very short business year.

From July 2017 to June 2018, dozens of well-known businesses in Timor closed or reported financial troubles. In addition, as a result of the extremely young population (the median age is only 19 years whereas Australia's median age is 39), there is a great number of people moving from school into the workforce. What jobs will they go to when there are fewer businesses to employ them?

From our planning perspective it is also extremely difficult. If we order stock to fulfil expected demand based on our experience and then find there is less demand due to lack of spending, we end up with inventory sitting in our warehouse that we have to pay for. This is potentially a huge strain on our cashflow. This instability related to doing business in Timor-Leste is one of our major risks. Many businesses close because they fail to manage such issues.

Going solar

With an eye towards the future, the East Timor Trading Group was one of the first private companies in Timor-Leste to go solar. My son-in-law, Sam, became CEO in 2017. One day, as he was looking at the sun beating down on our warehouse roofs in Comoro, it hit him that it would be the perfect place to install solar panels.

The Comoro facility is particularly expensive to run, with around 100 pallets of power-hungry cold storage in 13 reefer containers fed by diesel and gas sources. Now, solar cells power 100 per cent of the lights, offices, and warehouse air conditioners. This investment will pay

---

21 The World Bank, *April 2019 Timor-Leste Economic Report: Moving Beyond Uncertainty*, 22 May 2019, https://www.worldbank.org/en/country/timor-leste/publication/april-2019-timor-leste-economic-report-moving-beyond-uncertainty.

for itself within two years and marks our first step towards becoming 100 per cent renewable. We haven't yet invested in an on-site battery, but that will come once we have the next stage of our warehousing expansion plans finalised.

One exciting part of the project involved sourcing a team of young Timorese technicians who were trained at the CNEFP Vocational Centre in Tibar. Once they had familiarised themselves with the models we had chosen, they installed the panels, cabling, and all the other electrical work. That part of the project was completed within 12 months. They did a great job, and we have now engaged them on a monthly service and maintenance contract. They, too, have become an integral part of our team. These young graduates have been able to develop their skills and experience in the renewable energy sector, so they can provide this service to others wishing to follow our lead and install solar. There's been a definite flow-on effect, because we receive emails and calls from other businesses asking how they can do what we've done.

We were particularly keen to undertake solar because, as well as making financial and environmental sense, it also aligns with the UN's Sustainable Development Goals and the sustainability goals in Timor-Leste's 2011–2030 Strategic Development Plan. What's more, the energy cost savings will enable us to reinvest in expanding the business and creating more jobs.

Despite the recent turbulence, the economic climate in Timor is very good. Before 2017, economic growth was positive and business was flourishing. There was a steady stream of investors, and the country was perceived as an increasingly safe place in which to do business. That view is not lost; the clouds will part in good time and the economy will return to growth.

A post-conflict country poses every kind of challenge imaginable, but I believe the greater the challenge, the greater the opportunities. Risk and reward go hand in hand. For me, being raised in Pakistan to the age of 20 and living in a megacity like Karachi (20-plus million people), Díli was manageable. However, for those people coming from developed Western countries, who haven't experienced sustained power outages, water shortages, and unsafe tap water, living and doing business in

Timor-Leste is unquestionably testing. Nonetheless, I firmly believe that over the next 10 to 15 years, Timor-Leste has the potential to become a prosperous nation.

Managing franchises

Managing a range of agencies and franchises across diverse sectors presents an array of difficulties, both logistical and financial. Franchises, in particular, are a major logistical exercise, because products are sourced globally to supply outlets worldwide. For example, Burger King supplies its franchises around the world with beef from Australia, chicken from Malaysia, chips from America, and sauces and buns from India and Singapore, respectively. This makes for a complicated supply chain and ordering strategy to ensure everything arrives together and is used within the use-by dates, thereby ensuring minimal waste. To manage this, we established a distribution centre specifically for this franchise, a major commitment for so few outlets.

The company's rapid expansion, following the acquisition of the widely recognised Burger King and Gloria Jean's franchises, meant the East Timor Trading Group gained a high profile in Timor-Leste. From a procurement perspective, we wanted to achieve a critical mass to achieve economies of scale for our orders. However, forecasting in a small, developing city such as Díli, which is also a new territory for such enterprises, proved difficult. Initially, we were quite bullish.

To supply our four outlets, we deal in enormous quantities: a container-load of chips; a container of burger patties; a container of burger buns. Other burger shop businesses allow a 12-month period in which to store and use beef patties, but Burger King restricts this to a four-month window in which you have to use the meat. Although it's safe for another eight months, the quality reduces after four so the taste is different. Coupled with delays at the supply-chain end, where clearance from the Díli port may take one week or longer (if we are lucky), we can lose the opportunity to sell supplies we have paid for. That really makes these kinds of franchises expensive to run. Accordingly, we continually look for better ways to operate.

Yet, there's always that unpredictable component of the time spent at the port that makes it very difficult to plan and budget. The first year we were caught out on our planning and lost $50,000 worth of various perishable items. We learnt the hard way that when you add shipping time to items with only a three-month shelf life, the actual selling period becomes very brief. We made that mistake only once. Now that we have established and streamlined our logistics, it is rare that we experience this problem with foods. However, we do try to share as much as possible with staff and their families leading up to the expiry dates so that not too much food is wasted.

All these aspects of the business involved steep learning curves. As our experience grew, we became increasingly careful about the agencies we took on, and began to focus on products with longer use-by dates. I can understand the need for use-by dates on some products, but so many of them are perfectly usable beyond these dates; for example, shampoos and soaps come with a *best before* date, which is crazy. They're not harmful after that date, but we have to throw them away. We soon decided to rationalise our products and focus on those with longer shelf lives.

Now that we have several long-term contracts and a good record with many of our suppliers, our relationships have become more about trust, the amount of market penetration achieved, and a good rapport with someone senior in the company. I now find that we can begin to propose minor changes to a contract – these might be *minor* changes, but at least it's something.

At one annual regional conference for one of our franchises, I took the opportunity to speak to some regional managers.

'Establishing the business has been difficult,' I pointed out, 'but we are focused on making this work over the long term. However, if I had made the same investment elsewhere, I would have been far in front of where I am with your product.' I then requested certain changes and said that if they weren't made, I would walk away. I knew our numbers and possible competitors who could come in, and I really had nothing to lose. 'I just need a clear answer that you will allow me to do what I propose.'

To their credit, they respected my position and agreed. In this case it was a win–win. One of several changes we wanted was to reduce the floor space of the operation. The agreement specified a minimum size, but given our rent and the size of the customer base, it wasn't viable and we wanted to reduce by one third.

This was a great lesson for me and showed me that even in a David and Goliath situation, everything is negotiable, given the right argument. Know your position, and make realistic requests.

Challenges ahead

The government carefully continues to establish laws that will be good for the country over the long term. I understand the need to proceed cautiously and thoughtfully. Due diligence takes time, and when you start from nothing, it is an enormous task. A great deal of thought has been put into regulations to encourage and allow local and foreign companies to do business smoothly and in a balanced fashion. By balanced, I mean not opening the floodgates to foreign investors when there are so many Timorese who would like to start businesses themselves.

The government is, however, streamlining the process of establishment of businesses for foreign companies. The government agency, TradeInvest, provides advisers and anyone wishing to establish a business with a portal for information and documents. It's a great initiative, although we often find that government staff haven't kept up with processes and changes in the law. Progress is delayed when staff of a government office either apply the wrong law or are not sure which aspect of a particular law to apply to a given situation. We then have to send lawyers in to discuss and interpret, which is an expensive and time-consuming process. If new companies arrive in the country and find starting up too onerous, they are likely to walk away. I have met many people who come from Australia who say, 'But at home I can register my business, open a bank account, and have an operation started within a day!' Timor-Leste law, on the other hand, is based on the Portuguese system, which can be quite bureaucratic. It's not like New Zealand, Singapore, Australia, or some of the Nordic countries, which hold the top positions in the world for ease of doing business.

Being able to turn paperwork around fast can be critical when, for example, we unexpectedly find we don't have a valid clearance certificate to have a shipment of consumable goods released from customs. On one such occasion we had stock sitting on the wharf for four weeks awaiting clearance as its use-by date drew inexorably closer. This meant our sales window shrank, all over a minor piece of red tape – a process that we usually undertook weekly on other shipments without any problems. Eventually, things get sorted out, but until they do, the current system inhibits greater foreign investment.

For example, the country still lacks a legal basis to determine land ownership. This is a legacy from two periods of the country's history. Under Portuguese colonial rule, few land titles were issued. Then came Indonesian occupation, where forced displacement meant that thousands of people were removed from their traditional lands. In addition to this, in yet a third layer of complexity, the Timorese people's understanding of 'ownership' of land is quite different from that of commercially based Western cultures. Villagers perceive that they 'own' the land on which they live as a community, but there is no actual title. Ownership by title is very much a Western construct. The result is that because ownership cannot be shown by a land title, banks do not easily offer mortgages. Until the land law is clarified so that banks can give loans with confidence of title, it will remain very difficult for local and foreign real estate investment to become established. At present, only citizens can buy land, not foreigners, and this further restricts investment. Ultimately this will need to change, both for the financial security of the citizens as well as foreign investors.

The flow-on effect of such a change within the economy will be huge. I believe that once this is sorted out, we will see liquidity in the market and the economy will really start to move. Hopefully, once land law reform and the streamlining of business establishment are effected, banks will view Timor-Leste as a safer place in which to lend money. At present, interest rates are far too high for most businesses (sometimes up to 15 per cent), and this does nothing to encourage investment. These rates are not held artificially high by government; it is purely a commercial decision by the banks. Before COVID-19, the Australian bank rate was one per cent, and for business it was four per cent. In the European Union, it was below two per cent, and in the US, below four per cent. This has now changed. Central banks around the world have lowered their rates close to zero to try to halt businesses failing en masse as a result of the pandemic.

Timor-Leste offers a frustrating circle of problems. It is risky to invest in the economy because of the lack of liquidity in the market and because the economy is so beholden to government spending. The banks have no security against which to lend money, which means their interest rates are high to cover their risks. Many of my staff aspire to be their own bosses one day. They have the drive, the ideas, and the passion. All they lack is money. Yet, even if their family occupies land, they have no security to offer the banks; and if they did receive a loan, who wants to pay 15 per cent interest or more? This makes for a stifling scenario for start-ups with no initial cashflow. I believe, once this circle of insecurity is resolved, we will see many more Timorese people establish themselves as entrepreneurs.

One huge win for Timor-Leste, under its chief negotiator, Xanana Gusmão, was the signing of the Maritime Boundary Treaty with Australia in March 2018. This was followed in April 2019 by Timor Gap, Timor-Leste's national oil company, purchasing a majority share of the Woodside-operated Greater Sunrise oil and gas field from Shell and ConocoPhillips. Greater Sunrise is now a joint venture between Woodside (34.4%), Osaka Gas (10%), and Timor Gap (56.6%).

This resolution should remove the county's biggest obstacle to growth, and provide Timor-Leste with financial security for decades. The country has acquired an asset from which everybody wants a piece. It could bring in another partner – the Brazilians, Chinese, or

Malaysians – or develop the asset themselves, list it, and then sell its share of the equity. Financially, it would be better for Timor-Leste to liquidate when the resources are already pumping, because the country would then receive top dollar compared to what it gets now. That income could then be used for other national priorities listed in the Strategic Development Plan.

However, at the start of 2020, it faced a perfect storm of new challenges in this sector. Fossil fuels are generally dropping in price as renewables become cheaper and more cost-effective to produce when compared with the cost of extracting oil and gas.

ConocoPhillips moved out of northern Australia and the Timor Sea, and a stalemate ensued about where the raw materials would be sent for processing. Joint venture partner Woodside wanted the gas brought to an existing LNG plant in Darwin, a relatively cheap solution. That plant has now been sold to Santos, so it is unclear if that is still an option. Timor-Leste wants to build a processing plant on the southern shore of the island, but has yet to secure finance for such a large project. As an active investor, China is an obvious source of funding, although this presents a strategic dilemma for Australia about whether it should act on the opportunity to help Timor-Leste develop such a plant. During the World War II, Australia's deep ties to Timor-Leste were forged, and I believe we should now consider our moral obligations to help a neighbour in need.

Also in March 2020, the Saudi–Russia oil discussions collapsed as the economic disaster and global inactivity brought on by COVID-19 took hold. This caused the price of oil to fall to an unprecedented negative US$37 a barrel on the futures market – meaning that you had to pay people to take oil off your hands. This will be short term, but for now, demand for oil has dried up.

Timor-Leste still has options for its oil reserves, but given the current state of the economy, it will take time for those to be negotiated and any successes realised.

Despite all of the challenges Timor-Leste has faced, and still faces, there is no violence in the streets. There is no martial law. The Timorese people have basically achieved their goal of establishing a peaceful country. They have been competently led by leaders with a deep desire, first and foremost, to do better.

In our hearts we all want peace, prosperity, a stable life, stable income, employment, education, and health providers – all of the things we take for granted in developed countries such as Australia. The Timorese people worked hard for independence. They faced challenges. They worked through them. They fought. And then, when the country won independence, they looked to the future and forgave. To view the future through a lens of forgiveness is arguably their greatest attribute. Now the country is theirs and they are shouldering the responsibility to rebuild so that those still without jobs and housing can live better lives. If the leaders do not succeed with this, the fight has been for nothing. They have no choice but to succeed.

As I move towards retirement, I'd like to think I, too, am leaving a legacy for the country. At present, it is unclear who will be the new Gusmão, Alkatiri, Taur Matan Ruak, or Ramos-Horta. It is my fervent hope that as a younger generation of political leaders emerges, there are people among them with a vision to shape the country for the benefit of all, just as there were during the early years.

Entrepreneurship

In business I have always found it an advantage to be an outsider. Not only do you bring knowledge of at least one other country, if not several, but you also do not view things with the accepting eye of a local. Instead, you bring a fresh and unbounded perspective that I believe lends itself well to entrepreneurship.

When I started the East Timor Trading Group, I brought with me the experience of four countries – Pakistan, the UAE, Canada, and Australia – as well as a life of extensive travel. I immediately spotted opportunities. Living in Australia again now, I see opportunities both here and in

Timor-Leste. It's the same when I visit Pakistan. Opportunities abound there too, although because I have been out of that country for more than 40 years, I am not eligible to work within their system and I have no desire to do so.

Opportunities are everywhere and it becomes easier to start a business when you have experience under your belt. When people ask me about a start-up, I usually say, 'Well, you could make it work, but financially speaking, it is a hell of a ride. You need to be prepared for that.' One day you could be up on top of Mount Everest; the next day you could be at the base. One thing is for sure: what you put in is what you get out. If you're smart enough and do it right, and you have some luck on your side, you can earn a year's salary in a month. However, it is more usual to take 20 years on average to reach a point of stability and growth, under normal conditions.

If you can develop an extraordinary business, and you have extraordinary opportunities, as I've had in Timor-Leste with major international contracts, that is different. Ours was a once-in-a-lifetime opportunity and most people do not experience that. I often see that when people start a business, they begin with grand expectations that within a year they'll be working just a couple of days a week while the money rolls in. For most people, that is simply not the case. If you enter with that expectation, you should expect to be disappointed.

Experience teaches you a lot: which button to press when, where to go knocking, and discovering where the niches are. When you're young and energetic, your heart often bursts with ideas, but it should be your mind that processes them and decides on their viability. Your heart might well say, 'I want to own a chain of hotels,' but your mind should ask, 'OK, how should I go about achieving that?'

The failure of a business often means that the business owner will face very hard times, possibly bankruptcy. Losing something in life teaches you how to survive. In this case survival is, of course, having to watch every cent and not going over and above what you can afford. It is very easy in the early days not to think things through and not to focus on every cost saving. Poor financial planning decisions are what force most businesses to close.

When I reflect on our disastrous 1997 when we lost virtually everything, it gives me a renewed sense of perspective and priorities. I don't believe we had the wrong priorities in our life before this experience, but I do think the fall made us more aware of the life we led. It made us more grateful for what we had in our lives – and I don't mean material possessions. Twenty-plus years later, Neelo and I are still mindful of the consequences that can follow poor planning, or negative external forces. We are far more mindful of our actions and what we need to do in terms of planning for tough times to protect our business, ourselves and, of course, our employees and their families. We now understand the process of planning to survive tough economic times.

Unions

With business comes unions. Timor-Leste is no different. Unions are important in that their purpose is to advocate for the worker who might otherwise be exploited. For the most part we work well with the various unions with whom we interact. However, not all of them are easy to deal with, particularly if they stir up trouble simply to garner attention. Even the government finds such union administrators challenging at times. One must simply deal with them calmly, conceding to some demands, but not to others.

We had particular concerns about one such union. It wanted us to pay it the value of the benefits we provide to our employees so that it could disburse them, instead of our doing so directly. Concerned that our employees might not receive their due, we refused. This has created tension.

However, even our employees were unhappy with this union's representatives. Recently, one of our female employees, who is the secretary-general of this union, had an altercation with another female member of staff. While on duty and in front of customers, she slapped and pulled the hair of the other employee. The woman who was slapped resigned within 24 hours. The union official all but took over our Timor Plaza outlet, closing the doors, and declaring that nobody was allowed to leave. We decided there would be no appeasement policy and that she was to be removed from our staff. Of course, that upset the union, and it made personal threats against my son-in-law, Sam. We took this threat seriously because the union office sits opposite Sam and Zeenat's home. We immediately boosted security at their house. In terms of the employment issue, we stood our ground and finally managed to terminate her services by outlining the legal processes available. Everything had to be done by the book.

Facing multinational corporations

Multinational corporations drive hard bargains and, as a result, we sometimes decide to withdraw from contracts that no longer provide a suitable return on investment. Over the years, we have learnt how to deal with them, and this often requires us to be forthright. As recently as 2018 we gave up one agency, and the whole experience was an interesting study in the power and processes of big business.

It had built a bottling plant in Díli, based on sales forecasts that didn't add up to us. We believed that only around 30 per cent of the quantity it claimed was coming into Timor-Leste was actually arriving, and the rest must have been ending up elsewhere. Yet, the company seemed uninterested in hearing about this from us.

When it sought approval to establish the plant, it promised the government it would employ so many thousands of people. Based on our sales figures, we believed its plans were not financially viable. It's possible that the company used a formula that included not only its direct employees but also staff in the entire supply chain right through to retail – thereby portraying the aggregate as all its staff. In essence the company must have said: 'If we consolidate under one roof, we will need [this number] of employees ... *Won't that be great for the Timorese economy!*' On the strength of those figures it received government approval to build the plant, along with huge tax and financial concessions. However, because the factory was built based on inflated figures, it is lucky nowadays to operate two or three days a month. Perhaps that's karma.

At their 2018 conference, I ended up in conversation with our regional manager's boss. He asked me how things were going.

'Well, if you want to hear me out, I'm happy to talk, but it's not good news,' I said.

We talked for a while, but I soon realised nothing would change, so I sought out my regional manager.

'I'm walking away. I wanted to tell you face-to-face. All of your bosses are here, so if any of them wish to discuss this, they are more than welcome, but I can't see a resolution.'

And that was that. I don't think the company believed we would really drop it, but we were serious about cutting our losses and dropping unprofitable deals. We had sufficient, more viable business in other brands. Years before, we had signed an agreement to be the same company's official distributor for Timor-Leste. However, the terms were tough, and it was cheaper for shops to buy from unlicensed distributors in the market. This is called a parallel trade, and while it's not illegal, it is unethical.

Parallel imports do make for a very competitive market. Although we have exclusive contracts in place, many people import those same products on a parallel basis and undercut us. Managing this risk to our business requires constant vigilance. We have several direct competitors and countless parallel importers, so we are not alone in facing this pressure. They are able to undercut us because we bear the complete responsibility for – and cost of – inventory, distribution, marketing, and more.

Then there is the black market trade across a variety of consumer products. I accept that this will always exist. It is a small element that compromises your bottom line and, ultimately, should be the focus of greater attention as the economy grows. For now, the government has many higher priorities. I have confidence that when the time comes, it will tackle such issues.

Mentoring

One of the critical aspects of running a business is understanding your knowledge and skill limitations. You must be able to clearly identify where you need assistance and seek the services of professionals in those areas. It is tempting to hold your cards close to your chest when developing ideas, but it's also important to remember that a strong team of knowledgeable, skilled people is essential to your success. It is a valuable lesson for anyone in business to know when to ask for advice and when to listen.

Mujahid Hamid is one of the people in my life about whom it is difficult to quantify exactly how influential he has been and the depth of gratitude I owe to him. Although he is highly experienced in international business, there was something in addition that endeared him to me from when we first met. As a mentor, Mujahid felt like a wise elder brother, and I had great respect for his views on life.

Mujahid's core belief is that your primary objective in life must be to understand yourself, and that perspective struck a chord with me. If you find what motivates you and what desires drive you, you will experience organic growth, both personally and in your business life.

In early 2017, we were negotiating new distribution licences and tenders with some of our major clients. Sam had just taken over as CEO. My health was not good. We needed additional strategic assistance. It was time to call on Mujahid.

As a mentor, Mujahid is a confidant. He gives you the opportunity to brainstorm and raise issues, and he helps give clarity to your thoughts. He is very strategic and applies best international practice to ensure that you harness the potential within the organisation and its people. These days, Mujahid knows more about my business affairs than I do. He and Sam have weekly Skype meetings and he asks Sam probing questions to guide him in considering options, finding answers, and drawing his own conclusions about appropriate actions. A true mentor, he helps Sam discover and understand who he is.

Mujahid proposed that we establish a formal board, with me as chair, Sam as CEO, and Neelo, Zeenat, and himself as board members. Before our inaugural board meeting in Bali, Mujahid and I met in Sydney for a week to discuss plans. The week after the meeting, Mujahid flew to Timor-Leste to see the operations for himself.

'My goal is to see yours as the best-run company in Timor-Leste,' he told me.

Thanks to Mujahid we now operate like a small multinational company and we are on track to achieve this goal.

Mujahid on mentoring

When I go into a business, I usually know in advance 90 per cent of what I'll find. I'll be categorical about that. The remaining 10 per cent contains some good and bad surprises, and that mix depends upon the lifecycle stage of the business and the temperaments of those involved. This is why it is vital to understand the people before you consider what direction to take.

In my experience, small organisations and sole proprietorships have a certain way of being run, much of which is based on the instinct to stay alive. The owner says, 'OK, I've done this step. Now let me do the next step.' It's day-to-day, one foot in front of the other, solving one crisis after another.

When I come into a business, I look first at the small crises and say, 'These will not kill us, but let's solve them in the context of the company as a whole, and its direction'. Managing organisational change is one of the first things we work on.

The manager often asks me what I think they should be doing in a given situation, and I reply with, 'Well, first, tell me what *you* think'. That gives them time to consider their question and their possible responses in more detail. My role is not to tell a person how to run their business. It's about being a mirror and a guide. Ultimately, I am there to talk, ask questions, and make it a pleasurable experience – I'm not there to wield a stick. Everyone wants to enjoy life. If someone is not enjoying running their business, they should be doing something else.

Most small companies have no planning process and no goals outlined, so the first thing we do is create an annual plan. This is a serious and critical document that outlines everything for the business. Most businesses tend to underestimate the importance of this plan and the amount of work required to write it. A large amount of leadership is required from the manager to motivate the people around them who are, perhaps, not used to this kind of thinking.

A new plan must be created annually: 'What are we going to do this year? What are we going to achieve?' It should be made into a booklet that is given to each member of the management committee, and they need to sign off on it. It's not something to look at every day, but once a month we need to refresh ourselves about what we were supposed to be doing in a given year. Are we on track? If not, how do we get on track? Often, I find people have a great idea, and then, three months later, they've completely forgotten what it was, because they never took the time to write it down.

The plan is used to remind members of the management committee what is to be done that year. It also means that even if the CEO is not there every day, the business will run on track, because it has a documented direction.

Just as the plan means the business can run efficiently without the CEO, it is also important to have a process and agenda for board meetings, so if the chair is not available for some reason, the meeting can still be held to ensure processes are followed and reviews completed.

What we are really trying to do with these systems is to take ourselves outside the organisation and towards the point where, regardless of what happens, the plans we put into place will be achieved and board meetings will continue. The system will run on its own and the targets will be achieved. That has to be the goal. Why? Because then the CEO can be otherwise engaged!

The company becomes a series of layers: board, management committee, and CEO. Get the right people, and the right structure, and the company begins to turn on its own. This is where it moves from being a pure business into becoming a philosophical process. This is where it's not just about running a business, it's about how much you can contribute to your business, to your personal goals, and to the broader environmental goals that you wish to achieve.

It is also important to accept that people won't necessarily stay with your business for the rest of their lives. Some people move on, and you should be proud that they are now contributing to another company and therefore to the country in a different way.

Finally, the ultimate goal of the CEO of a well-run company – as a matter of priority – is to identify their successor. Any good CEO must have a succession plan. This plan will depend upon how well the CEO has employed and developed good people within the company, or identified an outsider.

Sam says he found the process very smooth at East Timor Trading Group. What he describes as smooth is actually a measure of how well he grasped all these new concepts. He'd never run a business before, but has been very accepting and trusting of the process. Conversely, he could have been a different sort of a guy, somebody who would feel threatened. Then things would have been much more difficult.

> The mentee must be willing to open up and learn, and to trust the process. Mentoring is not about judging how you work. 'What type of person is Sam?' was topmost on my mind at our first meeting. It's very easy for somebody trying to run a business to feel threatened when an outsider comes in. Mentoring is about building trust from the word go.

Mujahid and I continue to talk but he is very good at saying to me, 'Take a breath, step back, enjoy your retirement'.

One of his key mentoring messages is: *If you don't enjoy your business or career, don't do it. We all want to have fun. Business is fun. Profits are fun. Respect is fun. Enjoy yourself today because there is no tomorrow.*

These days, living in Australia, I am positioning myself to mentor young, aspiring businesspeople. One such opportunity arose recently, not long after I'd had a heart attack when Neelo and I were flying from Díli to Sydney. We had a stopover in Darwin and there was our old friend, Shane Stone, standing in the airline lounge.

'I've never had the opportunity to thank you enough in my life,' I said. 'Life is short; I've just had a heart attack. I want you to know that I can never thank you enough for the role you played in our success. I'm not sure you know how much we hold you in our hearts.'

He replied: 'Well, now, then maybe it's time to do some wider good. Let's talk about philanthropy. I'd like you to come to the Duke of Edinburgh Awards luncheon.' With that, he set the wheels in motion for Neelo and me to become Duke of Edinburgh Award ambassadors.

The ambassadors program is an Australian addition to the awards and was launched in 2009 at a ceremony in Sydney by Professor Marie Bashir AD CVO, when she was governor of New South Wales. It was attended by HRH Prince Edward, Earl of Wessex KG GCVO. It seeks the support of passionate people in the community who can use their skills and positions to help promote the value, relevance, and importance of such an achievement for young Australians.

It was a simple decision. We became ambassadors in 2018 and were recognised for our contribution at a formal dinner at Buckingham

Palace, where we met Prince Edward. Our involvement in the Duke of Edinburgh award program is an ongoing commitment to mentor youth in Australia, and we look forward to being involved over the coming years.

Part 3

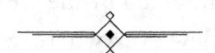

Home

Polar year: 2012

There are years in one's life when the best of times is coupled with the worst of times. My polar year was 2012.

While Neelo and I were establishing the Discovery Inn in 2007, our eldest daughter Zeenat was getting to know a young man, Sam Aluwihare, back in Sydney. In January 2012, Neelo and I were proud to host Zeenat and Sam's wedding, *Nikah*, in Sydney.

It was held at The Station function centre and the Waterfront Park, at Pyrmont, with around 80 guests, followed a week later by a reception at the Sergeants Mess in Mosman. Pyrmont's streets can be wind tunnels, and when poor Zeenat left our apartment to walk down the hill to the *Nikah* ceremony, she was buffeted by the wind roaring down the street. Her carefully tended hair flew everywhere. She was nearly in tears, but we made it and were able to hold a lovely ceremony for close family at the water's edge.

It's wonderful to see your daughters marry men whom you love and respect; men you know will look after them devotedly throughout their married life. As the father-in-law of two such men, I feel blessed.

The second celebration that year was in Timor-Leste. On 20 May, the country celebrated the 10th anniversary of its independence. As Xanana Gusmão said in a speech in Sydney that year that the people of Timor-Leste had 'established a free and democratic state, with the rule of law and a safe and secure society'. To reinforce this, the country experienced four years of unprecedented economic growth, and was listed in *The Economist* magazine's top 10 fastest-growing economies, with a growth rate of more than 8.5 per cent.[22] I was honoured to be awarded an Order of Timor-Leste by then president Ramos-Horta for ongoing commitment to and services in Timor-Leste in this momentous anniversary year.

On 31 October, the resident six-year International Stabilisation Force, comprising hundreds of Australian and New Zealand soldiers, came to an end. This was followed, in December, by the withdrawal

---

22 'Top Growers', *The Economist*, 18 November 2013, https://www.economist.com/news/2013/11/18/top-growers.

of UNPOL, the UN Police, which had been an integral part of the UN peacekeeping mission.

During our years in Timor-Leste, we had witnessed so much social, political, and economic change. When we arrived in 2002, Timor-Leste was a country very much in survival mode. Now, in 2012, it had taken its place on the world stage.

Because the banks publish their annual reports in the newspaper, I know that in the 2011–2012 financial year, our company paid more aggregate withholding, excise, sales, salary, company, and import taxes to Timor-Leste than all of the banks put together. We were a stable and established business, and excluding the oil and gas sector, we were one of the top 10 taxpayers in the country. All in all, it had been a good year.

On 21 August 2012, I had just returned to Sydney from a client conference in Bangkok. Neelo, Ismat, and I were on our way home from dinner, enjoying a gelato as we walked. I began to feel unwell – unwell enough to throw the gelato away – quite unlike me. By the time we arrived home, I felt terrible. Neelo and Ismat were so worried that they called an ambulance, which arrived in no time.

Neelo didn't know Royal Prince Alfred Hospital, or how to get there, so the ambulance staff, who were incredibly kind, said, 'We'll take him downstairs, assess, and stabilise him. You collect your car and follow us.'

I was having a heart attack.

Early the next morning, after monitoring me through the night, I underwent a cardiac procedure to install two stents. Other surgical options were rejected, because the build-up in the left artery presented too high a risk. It was decided that maximum medication levels would have to suffice to keep any troubles at bay. Two days later I was discharged; in and out fast. The Australian health system has some amazing technology and truly dedicated and talented staff.

My doctor's advice, and Neelo's instructions, were clear and succinct: I was to pull back from day-to-day involvement in the business, otherwise I would be taken from it, and my family.

Until this point, succession had not even been a footnote in my business plan. My heart had been on a roller-coaster ride and I was not ready to think about this. I was not ready to retire. Any business you build from nothing comes with huge, often unrelenting stress. We put everything on the line, every day of the week. On top of that, in a developing environment such as Timor-Leste, our world was neither stable nor predictable, raising the stress levels immeasurably higher. It was clear my heart had dealt with this for many years, but now had come a time when it had had enough.

The problem is that running a business of our size needs someone with experience, skills, and know-how to keep it on track. I had talented staff on their way up, but they were not ready, not right then. However, with my heart the way it was, I needed an option *now*.

As if on cue, in June 2013, Zeenat, Sam and their five-month-old daughter, Sofia, came to visit us in Díli. Smart, polite, and a great communicator, Sam has the ability to remain calm and collected, but he also has a passion and a fire in his belly. He studied software engineering at the University of New South Wales and had begun an MBA while working as an innovation manager at the Commonwealth Bank. After seven years in that role, he expressed dissatisfaction with the job. He and Zeenat told us that they would like to work for the East Timor Trading Group, if any positions were available.

If they wanted to work for us, I told them, they had to apply like everyone else. We were no longer a small family business – we were now a medium-sized company that had corporate and staffing commitments that required specific expertise. After some discussion, they returned to Sydney with the idea of beginning a new life in Díli.

In July that year, with the help of Judith Fergin, the US ambassador in Timor-Leste, I secured the contract to open Díli's first international-brand fast-food restaurant, a Burger King. The initial conversation took place at the Fourth of July celebration, which we co-sponsored. I spoke with her about how we might secure such a restaurant. Then I held conversations from August to October with Burger King about starting the build. The agreement stipulated that the franchise would be open by 31 December 2013. I knew I would need a manager and, given the discussion we had just had with Zeenat and Sam, it was clear that Sam was a candidate.

In September, I flew to Miami for the Burger King convention where I met Jack Cowin, the franchisee of the Hungry Jack's chain in Australia. It is called Hungry Jack's there because when Cowin went to register the name 'Burger King', it was already registered by a small takeaway shop in Adelaide. Jack is a Canadian but has lived in Australia for decades.

'As you know, I'm here as the franchisee for Timor-Leste, and we open our first store in December. I'd like my manager to be trained by one of your regional managers, someone who has set up several outlets from scratch,' I said, and Jack kindly agreed.

I told my son-in-law of the plan and offered him the position of manager. If he were interested, he would undertake 10 weeks' training in Sydney before he and the family moved to Díli and he assumed the role. In their minds, the decision to move had already been made, so Sam leapt at the opportunity. He resigned from the bank, dropped his MBA, and in a matter of weeks began training at the Hungry Jack's outlet in George Street Sydney. His friends wondered what had got into him: why had he left his banking job to flip Whoppers?

The Sydney manager controlled several restaurants in the area, so Sam was exposed to all of the roles across a variety of outlets, from mopping the floor and making the burgers to manning the drive-through. He was fully trained on the ground, and 10 weeks later was accredited to run a Burger King restaurant. He impressed his Sydney trainers greatly and they even offered him a regional manager's role controlling several restaurants. That didn't surprise me at all.

Sam, Zeenat, and Sophia arrived in Díli during the first week of December 2013 and, on 9 December, Sam officially became manager of the Timor Plaza Burger King restaurant. Zeenat would be a director of the company, but for the time being would focus on family life. She needed to be aware of what was going on in order to step into a role in the company when the children were older.

If I knew then what I know now about setting up a Burger King, I would not have agreed to this tight deadline. One does not simply purchase equipment from any supplier for a franchise like this. Each item is manufactured to specific standards and all materials are supplied under existing contracts from all over the world. We had to liaise with more than a dozen suppliers to build the restaurant. On top of that, having items shipped to Timor-Leste was no simple task, particularly in the lead-up to Christmas.

As well as the construction challenges, we also had to establish the ongoing supply of all the food ingredients from buns, burger patties, chicken, to cooking oil and condiments, right down to pepper and salt, all of which came from various approved suppliers around the world. The biggest issue of all was to predict the quantities required in a new market, where there had never been an international fast-food outlet before. We had some research from Australia, Indonesia, Malaysia, and Singapore at hand, but most of our purchasing decisions were based on gut instinct – to what degree would people support a new restaurant like this? As always, I would rather have more supplies than to run short, so we ordered based on a best case scenario. My team's optimism on this occasion went too far and we were caught with $50,000 worth of overstock that we were forced to dispose of as the items reached their use-by dates.

I had arranged with the president of Burger King Asia Pacific that he would attend the launch, and he agreed to drop other engagements to fly in for the event. He suspended family holidays in Spain to fulfil this commitment. What he witnessed was an event with around 300 people attending and a huge success all round. We had delivered on our promise and the founding team is to be commended for its herculean efforts. The restaurant has been enormously successful and won the Burger King Asia-Pacific Operator of the Year award in 2015.

I thought Sam had done an admirable job and was ready for a promotion. I appointed him chief operating officer of the East Timor Trading Group. While the role is operational in focus, it also includes marketing, human resources, supply chain, and finance. Human resources presented the steepest learning curve, and it took him about two years to understand the dynamic of the business and get to know every member of the staff. On top of that, the move from a highly systematised Sydney banking environment with established IT to what was virtually a blank slate opened up his world view.

By 2015, Zeenat and Sam had settled into their new lives and had their second child, Sakib junior, followed in mid-2018 by their second son, Isa.

Paris

While Sam had been training at Burger King in Sydney in September 2013, not far across the city our youngest daughter, Ismat, was completing her eight-month internship at what was then Australia's number one restaurant, Rockpool. She had also applied for entry to the Grand Diplôme at Le Cordon Bleu Paris, a comprehensive course on cuisine and pastry, with internships in top establishments. As her time at Rockpool came to an end, she received confirmation of acceptance.

Although we had only recently acquired and furnished our new apartment in Sydney when Ismat received the news, we decided this was too big an opportunity to miss. Neelo and I had always wanted to live in Paris, so it was a simple decision. Now was the time.

It's fair to say that I've been a person of excess all my life – I'm always all in. If you ask the girls and Neelo, they will say that I have always been active: playing cricket, travelling, volunteering in the community, and super engaged in business. I always loved spoiling the kids on my return from travels with the latest music or clothing, and I derive enormous pleasure from hosting people. My attitude has manifested itself in the freedom that my daughters have had to be anything they wished to be, not necessarily a doctor or lawyer, as most Pakistani fathers would have strongly suggested, but to do whatever they were passionate about.

Travelling gives me great pleasure. Part of the pleasure is that I love the opportunity to meet and speak with new people. Hence my career in hotels. I also get great pleasure from the surprise of catching people off-guard and addressing them by name, when they assume I don't know who they are. My aim is to leave each person I meet feeling better than when I walked up to them. This sometimes leaves my children reeling with embarrassment.

Although my business travel schedule was hectic, my workload, together with other self-imposed activities and a practice of never taking weekends, meant family holidays were a rare luxury. In the early days, we went on a holiday to Pakistan to visit family every couple of years, and this continued until our daughters were about 14 or 15.

The opportunity to spend an extended time in Paris was therefore not something that could be passed up. Timor-Leste was stressful and not good for my heart, so even my cardiologist should have been overjoyed to hear the news.

We moved to Paris in February 2014. For the next year I travelled between France and Timor-Leste, spending two weeks in Paris, followed by two in Díli – arguably not the most relaxing of schedules.

We had a brief stay in one apartment while we waited for our apartment in the 16th arrondissement to be available. This is my favourite area of the city. We were located at 10 Boulevard Émile-Augier opposite the Italian embassy. It is a beautiful residential area near La Muette Metro station and full of wonderful apartment buildings from the late 1800s, as well as fashionable boutiques and cafes. As a tourist living in Paris for a year, there is no more wonderful area in which to settle. The apartment was ideal and provided space for the whole family.

Our time in the city reinforced my view that I would live permanently in Paris in a heartbeat. A key Parisian pleasure, of course, is the enormous number of wonderful restaurants. We dined at local restaurants, at traditional bistros, and spent hours walking the streets, taking in the scenery.

What is uniquely imposing about the streets of Paris is the uniformity of the architecture. We have Baron Haussmann and his extravagant vision for grand boulevards, parks, and public facilities across the city to thank for this. Haussmann was employed by Napoleon to redesign great tracts of old Paris. Over nearly 20 years, the city was transformed from a mediaeval city of lanes and ancient housing into a modern city on a grand scale. Parks were a major new feature and, as a tree lover, one of my great pleasures is walking in those immaculately laid-out city parks with their beautiful trees, all inspired by London's Hyde Park.

That Paris contains more than 100 kilometres of canals, I think, must be one of the lesser-known facts about this city. They were originally built to deliver Parisians their fresh water but are now used purely for leisure activities. We travelled along the nearly five-kilometre-long Canal Saint-Martin, which runs through parts of central Paris, making it the longest underground river in the city. Its banks are lined with cafés and restaurants. However, the most amazing elements are the system of nine extraordinary locks and the two-kilometre-long tunnel that, in my recommendation, make it an essential journey for anyone visiting Paris. The locks create rushes of water that allow barges to move through the canal under many bridges. The Panama Canal offers a similar concept on a grander scale.

Neelo's only frustration during our time in Paris was not knowing the language. I was a little familiar with French, because I had learnt some in Montréal all those years ago. Even though I found I could understand much of what was being said, I had difficulty finding the words to reply. Luckily, Saba, Rayeed and their son, Zaydan, took five months off to come and stay with us. Saba speaks French, so when we did need help, she was there for us.

While we enjoyed our family time, the trip was about Ismat's education. It was her turn now and being in Paris was a bonus for the rest of the family. She spent her days studying at Le Cordon Bleu on Quai André Citroën, just across the Seine from our apartment. She also secured a three-month internship with Pierre Hermé, a world-renowned pastry chef who has several patisseries scattered throughout the city. This was a major achievement and a wonderful experience for Ismat. In 2016, Hermé was voted by the *World's 50 Best Restaurants* as the world's best pastry chef. Based on her training in Paris, Ismat has now created a beautiful, rich, chocolate fondant dessert for Diya Restaurant at the Discovery Inn, demonstrating how yet another aspect of the wider world can be experienced in Díli.

Paris turns my mind to one of our dear friends, Norma Grant. I have mentioned several people who have had a resounding and long influence on my business life, but Norma was always there for us as a family. She was the preschool teacher for our daughters Zeenat and Saba, and we invited her to come and stay with us in Paris after her husband unexpectedly passed away.

Through her teaching, Norma has been a role model for many young people across Australia's Northern Territory. Many of her students consider her a second mother, our children included. I think she is best summed up by Zeenat:

> *When I think of growing up in Darwin in the 1980s and 1990s, there were a few families that were quintessential Territorians and part of the fabric of the Territory. The Grants were one of those families. Mrs Grant has a gentle, quiet strength about her, a way of making people, especially the children in her charge, feel completely at ease, loved, and valued in her presence. The lifelong effects of having a teacher as wonderful as her inspired me to be that person for other children, so I, too, became a teacher.*

I am pleased to say that Norma, for her lifetime of dedicated community work, was awarded a well-deserved Order of Australia (OAM) in the Queen's Birthday Honours, June 2021.

While Ismat studied, I was still running the East Timor Trading Group, and although Burger King was settling into its first year under Sam's capable guidance, there was still much to do. It turned out that commuting between Paris and Díli is far more stressful than commuting between Darwin and Díli. It is essentially two days of travel each way, with gruelling flights of 14 hours, usually to Singapore, then on to Timor. This began to take a further toll on my heart.

I had arranged in advance that if I needed a specialist in Paris, I would be looked after by Dr François Tarragano, the cardiovascular diseases specialist at the American Hospital, not far from our apartment. We had been strategic in our selection of where to live. I told him about my ongoing discomfort and he called me in for an angiogram.

The verdict among the team of French specialists was the same as those professionals in Sydney: my condition was too risky to treat with anything more than medication. However, after much discussion and the signing of a waiver, the decision was made to add two more stents *and* for me to manage my stress levels better.

I am, today, nowhere near as aggressive in my ambition as I used to be, even a decade ago. When you've achieved something in your life, building it brick by brick, it's very difficult to visualise losing all of that – and your livelihood. You can become very protective and conservative in your decision making.

I asked my brother to invest in the company so we could pool our resources. This was at my 50th birthday, when he was 58 years old. I thought we would go much further that way.

'No, it's not for me,' he said. 'If I can spend what I have now on charitable purposes, I'll be the happiest man alive. I don't want any stress. I want to deliver a better life to other people now.' I look back now and realise how wise he was.

It took two key things to inspire my change in perspective. One was my health. Having two heart attacks and four stents necessarily changes your life. I enjoy good food and I like to travel. No one, including me, likes stress. Second, and more importantly, I don't want to lose what I've built, because that would impact the lives of many hundreds of people.

In 2014, the business was at a stage where it had become important to consolidate and protect what we had achieved, and not let everybody down.

Hotel management, Lausanne

Around mid-2014, Ismat received the news that she was to be interviewed for a place at l'École Hôtelière de Lausanne (EHL), one of the top hotel management schools in the world. We were abuzz with excitement. With a new business suit and a bright scarf to set it off, she was ready to catch the train to her interview in Lausanne. After several long, anxious weeks, we received the news that she had been awarded a place. She would start in February 2015.

We concluded our year in Paris and then moved to Lausanne for nearly two and a half years. We found a beautiful apartment only a 15-minute drive from Ismat's college, which meant that Neelo could drop her off each day. Our apartment had a view across Lake Geneva to Évian-les-Bains, a brief 30-minute ferry trip to the far shore and source of the famous Évian water. The lake, rimmed by the Alps, offers truly gorgeous scenery. In contrast to Sydney Harbour, which is always busy, Lake Geneva is tranquil, and it is rare to see much activity unless it is a sunny day when people come out for a swim or to sail.

I could only have dreamt of attending EHL as a student and I wouldn't have been admitted, because I didn't have the grades.

Ismat's course was a bachelor of science in international hospitality management. Her internships and training at Le Cordon Bleu, Rockpool in Sydney, and Pierre Hermé in Paris, meant she received several credits, reducing the course from four years to three. At her graduation ceremony, Ismat and her dear friend, Lauren Loh, were selected to speak on behalf of their cohort of graduates. It was a great honour and a testament to her hard work and natural people skills. She has worked extremely hard and done well over the years. For better or for worse, it seems she has inherited her parents' tenacity.

Saba, our translator, Rayeed, and Zaydan, had returned to Canberra, and so we had certain language frustrations living in Switzerland. However, we were lucky enough to have a wonderful group of neighbours to help us.

The building in which we lived had six apartments, and offered an intriguing variety of neighbours who could provide enough stories for me to write another book. In one apartment lived a New Zealander who spoke to us only in French. Perhaps he was making a point, or didn't want to speak to other antipodeans, who knows? Then there was Nagwa and Omar, a Swiss-Egyptian couple and their two kids who now live in Dubai, whom we have since visited. During one of my heart scares, they came in the ambulance with me to the hospital to help communicate in French with the staff, while Neelo followed in the car. There were also two slightly older couples, both in their 70s. The French couple, Gilbert and Danni, moved between various houses around the world depending on the time of the year and became our friends and translators for anything important. He was the retired head of an international pharmaceutical company. The other couple included the Swiss-German inventor of Nespresso pods, Frank, and his wife, Daniella.

We experienced a wonderful sense of community with these other couples, which made our time in Lausanne so enjoyable. Nothing was too much trouble. While I was travelling frequently I had a great sense of security knowing that Neelo and Ismat would be looked after, should they need anything at all, from a cup of sugar to a lift to the airport. It was quite unlike our experience of Paris. Regardless of the language barrier, we had long dinners together, laughing and talking using body language or translation apps. These three families were our rock.

It was also interesting to see the difference in cultures and civic pride between France and Switzerland. Switzerland displays a great deal of trust and pride in itself as a country. We didn't see the same in Paris, although admittedly that is a much larger city. In Paris, we found that only the main tourist-area metro stations were stylish and clean. As soon as you strayed beyond these areas, the stations were old and in need of upgrading. We felt there were two cities: one for the tourists to say, 'Oh, it's so beautiful!' and one for the locals.

While we were in Switzerland, we travelled around the country to small villages such as Interlaken, where, when you get up in the morning, you can find yourself in the clouds. On one side street we saw a shopfront with honey and other homemade foods for sale. A sign next to a box said, 'Please leave your money here'. There was no shopkeeper in sight. We saw the same in front of a house selling eggs and cheese. Each item was priced – you simply picked what you wanted, and left the money. It's a wonderful feeling to find yourself in a country that exhibits so much trust in its citizens.

We travelled around this perfectly formed little country on its immaculate trains, and used it as a base from which to explore countries a little further east: Austria, the Czech Republic, and Poland. While I would live in Paris again tomorrow, given its romance and cuisine, I still feel a particular affinity with Switzerland. In the 18th century, Switzerland was a key destination for European travellers coming to take the waters and purify their lungs with the crystal-clear alpine air. The country became the hospitality centre of the world, so it seems natural that my heart would feel at home there.

As countless people have done for generations, Switzerland became a place of health consolidation for us. My heart required it. Both Neelo and I focused on walks, exercise, and making the most of our time in the mountains. We explored as much as we could of Switzerland's classic towns and famous mountains and resorts, but my particular favourite was Bürgenstock Resort, perched high on the southern side of Lake Lucerne. It is an incredible old building, now modernised, that appears to be stuck to the side of the mountain, and is accessed from the lake by a funicular railway. Its height affords a dramatic view across the lake to Lucerne.

I continued to travel between Díli and Lausanne and, given my frequent travels, it was inevitable that I would encounter the odd recognisable or famous person. On one of these trips I looked up to find an extremely glamorous woman seating herself next to me. It was Sophia Loren. We chatted politely for a few minutes, and always one to tease, I mentioned to her that as a nervous flyer, I usually held my wife's hand for take-off and landings, suggesting that she could perhaps take Neelo's place this time. We exchanged pleasantries and she smiled politely, each settling into our seats.

Crunch time

Our two-and-a-half-year stay in Europe drew to a close in mid-2017, and instead of returning to Timor-Leste, we decided to move back to Sydney. I needed to be close to a hospital. I have severe sleep apnoea, anxiety, thalassaemia minor, and even after these wonderful relaxing years, I remain a heart patient. To be close to an emergency department of a major hospital was critical.

My first heart attack had been in 2012 and every time I went to Timor, I would see things that were wrong, and my anxiety would soar sky-high again.

'You want to live?' my doctor asked. 'Reduce this stress or you will have another heart attack.'

It was time.

My stepping down had now been planned for some years. I did not just disappear overnight. I kept preparing the staff and informing them of my thoughts: I'm going at 50, at 55 ... When I found myself over 55 and still not retired, I felt I just couldn't handle the stress any more. I had navigated the business to this level and now it was time for the young ones to drive. I had Sam in place. He possessed the experience and skills, and I was confident he would fulfil my vision and expand on it.

Retirement & restructure

Officially, I retired in December 2016, at 60 years of age. For my 60th birthday, Neelo and my three wonderful daughters compiled a memory album – people from throughout my life sent letters and provided comments and photos. It was a heartfelt compendium that allowed me to reflect on the important people in my life. This was particularly poignant, given it had been such a momentous year for me professionally.

Sixty was a doubly significant turning point, and a challenging marker. I told Sam that if he achieved all his 2017 goals and key performance indicators by the close of the year, I would promote him to chief executive officer. This move would allow me to step down from my day-to-day management and operational responsibilities and become chair of the new board.

As I expected, Sam achieved his goals admirably and we embarked on a strategic three-stage process to ensure that all aspects of the role would be covered and dealt with sufficiently:

1. The official 12-month handover, beginning in December 2016, with him shadowing me to learn.
2. My old mentor, Mujahid Hamid, becoming Sam's performance coach to provide him with guidance and strategy.
3. Sam assuming the role of chief executive officer in January 2018.

The one-year handover ended up taking almost three years. It was a complex process for several reasons. Perhaps the most important is that the business has been my baby from day one. I started from zero and built it into what it has become. I know every nook of the business and I value the relationships I have with my neighbours, government ministers and bureaucrats, my driver, and my employees. To relinquish that, to hand that over, was difficult. This is by no means a reflection on Sam, or my confidence in him. I simply felt that Sam and Zeenat did not have the same impact as I did when dealing with situations. They didn't have 17 years of knowledge of Timor, or nearly 30 years of business experience as I did. However, with their youth, energy, and commitment came new perspectives and vigour, as they successfully made the business their own.

In the end I realised that I had to accept that I would never be 100 per cent satisfied with anyone taking over. They would never be me. However, I now know that Sam and Zeenat have a willingness to learn, a respect for their role, a vision, and respect for the staff. They also have the strength and confidence to weather the perhaps unpalatable fact that I will always be looking over their shoulders – both a blessing and a curse. I have never been someone to sit and be hands-off.

Sam's natural talent and vision make him a good leader to take the company forward. I'm confident he can multiply the turnover five-fold over the next 10 years, as long as we diversify and capitalise on opportunities as they arise. However, to set the East Timor Trading Group on the right path for future growth, and for me to step out, would require a major reworking of the business structure. Rather than remaining a set of isolated business units, we determined we would create two operational arms, sales and distribution, and hospitality and retail, each with its own general manager. We then identified the support functions required to allow the growth of the operational arms: HR and corporate affairs, finance and IT, and supply chain. This would all be overseen by a new management committee, where each member was accountable and responsible for the growth and direction of their profit and loss and, in turn, for the company as a whole.

Sam's focus since he took over as CEO has primarily been on people and management systems, of which a major part is working together as a team. Under this structure, the management committee discusses every issue that arises and decides as a team, aware of the implications to their relevant department. Sometimes this slows down the process but, overall, it has improved our decision making enormously.

The coronavirus

Over the years Neelo and I have faced many challenges, but our life together has been enriched by each obstacle that we faced. We, and all our staff worked hard, and overall, our businesses have grown each year. Then came the budgetary stalemate that began in 2017, which caused us to reduce our income expectations significantly. Now, as I write this in 2020, the world faces the COVID-19 pandemic, which has required us to reassess again.

In February 2020, Neelo and I travelled to Pakistan to be with my family. It was to be a 10-day trip dominated by family reunions and birthday celebrations. However, a few days after we arrived, I was admitted to intensive care because of heart issues, and I remained there for three days. This was only a short-term solution because the attention my heart required was better performed back home. In Sydney I have access to my regular cardiologist, the aftercare I need, my medical insurance and, of course, the support of my immediate family. We decided to fly home as soon as I was judged stable enough to do so. We were also aware that we had only a few weeks to have my heart attended to by my usual doctors, as we were booked to go on a cruise on 28 February.

However, in mid-January, the world began to wake up to the existence of a SARS-type infection originating in Wuhan, China. Although it started relatively slowly, cases soon appeared around the world, and the first case outside China had appeared in Thailand.[23] International teams were investigating the outbreak, but views on its severity were not consistent.

In the meantime, after several inspections, my cardiologist decided against installing another stent. My heart had stabilised, and she agreed that the prospect of enjoying several weeks on a cruise, away from undue stress, would do me good. We would float around the South Pacific, safely away from this new virus.

As our departure day approached, the reports coming from China about the spread of the virus increased. I did some extensive research to confirm that the tiny islands we were due to visit had no reported cases. They were isolated and it appeared unlikely that they would suffer from this new threat. We talked about whether we should go or not. No refund or change of date was allowed, so we would have to wear any loss. We had to decide.

If it were like SARS, we reasoned, it would not be too bad, and of course we would take precautions. Our ship, the *Norwegian Jewel*, had been in the Pacific Ocean for a month, and in New Zealand for the preceding 12 days before we were to board, and appeared to be a clean virus-free environment. So, we settled into our suite and sailed out of Sydney Harbour on what was a beautiful sunny afternoon.

---

23 World Health Organization, 'Archived WHO Timeline – COVID-19', https://www.who.int/news-room/detail/27-04-2020-who-timeline—covid-19

Two days after we left Sydney, the emergency committee of the World Health Organization (WHO) reported that the new virus constituted a 'public health emergency of international concern'. Three days later, the WHO released preparedness plans for developing and weaker nations about how to deal with the virus. It appeared to be spreading fast. We know now it was faster than most people expected, and faster than the public was told. COVID-19 hit a largely unprepared world. In response, country by country, international borders started closing. The world was shutting down. Then, on 11 March, the WHO declared COVID-19 a pandemic. By mid-March virtually all international travel had ceased. Soon after, towns and cities around the world began locking down their citizens. All but essential services were shut down and an eerie silence descended on our cities.

Stories of cruise ships being turned away from ports around the world increased. Our captain desperately tried to find a port that would allow us to dock and disembark, so we could fly home. We made countless reservations for flights home via the limited shipboard wi-fi service, during which time we crossed the International Dateline four times, approaching no fewer than seven ports. We were met with protesting locals at some of these ports, shouting at us to go away. No one wanted us. No port would let us off. We were prisoners on the *Norwegian Jewel*.

While sailing around the Pacific, I was in communication with Sam in Díli. Tourism and hospitality were the first businesses to close, as countries declared increasingly stringent national lockdowns, first borders, then internally. Bars, restaurants, and shops were closed. I found myself having to make major decisions that affected hundreds of people's lives from a ship in the middle of the ocean, as our business disappeared virtually overnight.

We closed the Discovery Inn. We shut the Gloria Jean's cafés, Burger King restaurants, and other retail outlets. We temporarily laid off 200 employees, and arranged to supply food to them. We didn't close the business, but nearly all staff were sent on annual leave until we learnt more about how things would play out.

On the family front, Zeenat and the children flew from Díli to Darwin while Sam remained to manage the dramatic transition. Saba, Rayeed, and Zaydan, in Canberra, along with Ismat, in Sydney, flew to Darwin for us to be together as a family.

Meanwhile, Neelo and I were still sailing around the Pacific, our ship desperately seeking a port. On 15 March, we were scheduled to arrive at Lautoka, Fiji, at 5pm the next day. We were informed of the quarantine procedures by Fijian officials and booked a Qantas flight from there to Sydney for 17 March. But by the evening of the 15th, the promise of Fiji was off, our entry refused. Around the world, things were very tense.

That night, there was a great deal of anger and anxiety on board and, to calm the situation, the company announced it would fully refund all 2000 guests' fares. Our stress-free trip was looking increasingly like the plot of a disaster movie.

The next announcement was that we would head to Hawaii. Why, we wondered, as it was a five- or six-day sail away.

It turns out that the US First Lady, Melania Trump, is the godmother of the *Norwegian Jewel*, and strings had been pulled. We just needed to refuel to ensure we had enough fuel to last the distance. American Samoa came to our rescue, allowing us to purchase enough fuel to sail to Hawaii.

Media outlets around the world were, by now, covering our ship's story. According to *The Guardian*: 'As countries scramble to close their borders in response to the global COVID-19 pandemic, thousands of passengers are stranded on the high seas while their vessels seek a port at which to dock.'[24] By this time, we had been refused entry to Fiji, New Zealand, Bora Bora, Papeete, Tahiti, and Australia, when there was talk for a while of us sailing back to Brisbane. (I found myself wondering whether this was a divine intervention for the rest of the world to experience what the Kashmiri people had lived with since August 2019, when India moved to rein in some of Kashmir's autonomy. We had lost control of our destiny.)

---

24 Ben Doherty and Dom Phillips, 'Coronavirus: cruise passengers stranded as countries turn them away', *The Guardian*, 17 March 2020, https://www.theguardian.com/world/2020/mar/16/cruise-ships-scramble-to-find-safe-harbour-amid-covid-19-crisis-as-countries-turn-them-away

By 20 March, we had booked and been forced to cancel five flights and all the accompanying hotel reservations. I had even undertaken several ABC interviews discussing our predicament, and pleading with the Australian government to step in and help us to get home.

On 21 March, two days out of Honolulu, we ran into a heavy storm. The ship rocked all night, and our chances of disembarking in Hawaii became grim. Miami, we were told, was now on the cards, yet another 10 days away. Our ship was possibly now the most talked-about ship on the seas, with coverage by the *Sydney Morning Herald*, CNN, *The Guardian*, and the ABC, to name a few. Information was patchy, but as the night drew on, Honolulu remained a plan, and on 23 March we arrived and tied up at the docks, waiting to hear how we would return to Sydney. Everything looked good, until we heard our flight was cancelled. And then another one was cancelled. So much for reducing my stress level. This was not what we signed up for!

We waited overnight to find out whether a new flight would be approved. Everyone on board was calling their embassies and relevant government offices, seeking passage back home. We did the same, helped by our daughters, contacting the Department of Foreign Affairs and Trade (DFAT) and other relevant offices.

Charter flights were arranged by NCL, owner of the *Norwegian Jewel*, to a number of countries. For the 278 Australians on board, the Australian government arranged a Qantas charter. We disembarked and then sat in a bus for three hours on the tarmac at Honolulu airport, waiting anxiously for approval to fly to Sydney. Finally, the news came that we could leave.

There was just one problem. Australia had quarantined all arrivals from cruises. Information was sketchy, but it appeared we would now face 14 days of mandatory quarantine – detention – in a city hotel. Ours was to be a room in the Swissôtel, Sydney. A chartered coach collected us at the side exit of Sydney airport and took us directly to our hotel, although we were given little information about how this was to work. The hotel had, in effect, become a quarantine station, run and patrolled by Border Force and the NSW Police. Hotel staff were not privy to details and there were guards on every floor. We found it difficult to find anyone with any knowledge or authority that we could speak to about what to expect. All we knew was that there would be no housekeeping service and that food would be left outside our door three times a day. We were told little about protocols, but it appeared we would be arrested if we left our room. Meanwhile, all our family was now in Darwin, in isolation and under lockdown, going out only to buy essentials.

As state borders closed, one after the other, the next question was whether we would be allowed to fly to Darwin after our quarantine. If we did get to fly, would we face another hotel quarantine for 14 days when we got there? We also heard that the Northern Territory government had decided those in quarantine would have to bear the cost themselves.

Many calls later and after much negotiation, we were finally permitted to self-isolate in our house at Cullen Bay, based on excessive hardship and health grounds. We would be together as a family, with three generations in one house. Neelo and I have weathered much, both together and apart, during our lives. Now, together with our family, we weathered this quarantine period, hoping, like millions of other households across the globe, that this pandemic would be over reasonably soon, with as few deaths as possible and that the freedom, the normality, we take for granted would soon return.

Trying to keep the infection rate down is a global priority because in severe cases of COVID-19, patients require a ventilator and most hospitals have few of these machines. During March, as cases in cities around the world grew so fast that there were not enough ventilators for everyone who needed them, thousands of people died.

The terms 'lockdown', 'social distancing', and 'flattening the curve' became mantras as the fear of contagion from crowd transmission hit home. We were required to remain at home, or be no closer than 1.5 metres from another person, to discourage the spread of the virus. We were also encouraged to wear masks when out in public. Shops that remained open had crosses marked on their floors with tape identifying where one should stand to avoid close contact with others. By mid-April, it was estimated that one-third of the world's population was in lockdown at home, only venturing out for groceries and other essentials.

The other side of this pandemic was the resulting chaos that hit every major economy.

Supply chains were disrupted, manufacturing all but halted, and international trade collapsed. On a more local level, non-essential shops, cinemas, restaurants, and cafés were closed, sports matches ceased, schools were shut and students home-schooled. None of this was the result of individual choice; instead, it all happened by government decree, something most developed countries have not experienced since World War II. By the second half of April, it was estimated that half a billion people would be plunged into poverty due to the economic impact of the virus. As I write, the economic consequences of the shutdown and forced isolation have been devastating to the global economy, and we are not over it yet.

Like countless other cities around the world, Díli is essentially closed. At the East Timor Trading Group, we have retained a skeleton crew to keep the essential business services operating. The Discovery Inn is still shut, but we have recently reopened six retail outlets as things begin to stabilise a little. Sadly, we have had to lay off 200 of our wonderful and dedicated staff, but when we begin to emerge from the crisis, we are aiming for a staged reinstatement of employees. The timing of this is as yet unknown.

What we do know from experience is that downturns are not permanent; we have seen them before. It will pick up, and we'll see spending again. We have learnt in the past that one must ride these waves in business, adjust expenses accordingly, and aim for the smallest possible impact on staff. Having an ear to the ground to identify potential risks to the business, downturns in the economy, or anything else that might put business stability at risk is vital. This strategy of caution is a direct application of the lessons Neelo and I learnt in 1997, when we narrowly avoided bankruptcy due to the Qantas freight price increases and the Asian financial crisis.

Overall, we run an extremely lean and streamlined operation. The government slowdown from the budget stalemate in 2017 allowed us to embark on a period of consolidation. However, the global downturn from COVID-19 is on entirely another level. In a dramatic and humbling fashion, it is a stark reminder that we are part of a wider web of life that we cannot control. COVID-19 will no doubt alter the business landscape forever, although the world will return to some form of normality eventually. Right now, we watch and wait, with trepidation for those most at risk in our community.

In March and April 2020, the early days of the pandemic, Italy, Spain, France, the UK, and the US suffered terribly, and we looked on with horror.

As I write this in early 2021, we still do not know how, when, or even if things will return to pre-COVID-19 days. We now have vaccines, but everything depends on them being taken up by enough people, globally. Many countries are distributing these vaccines successfully, but new strains are appearing and we have been warned by experts that such mutations may be an ongoing risk. Australia is currently lagging behind many nations in its vaccination program. We now wait and see.

According to the Johns Hopkins University Coronavirus Resource Centre, as of mid-June 2021 the total confirmed cases globally exceeded 176 million and deaths from the virus had just passed 3.8 million. In the US more than 600,000 people had died, in Brazil more than 490,000, in India more than 380,000, and Mexico more than 230,000. In Europe, Italy had recorded more than 127,000 deaths, France more than 110,000, and the UK more than 128,000 deaths. These numbers are still rising and sporadic lockdowns continue.[25]

In the developing world, we may not be seeing accurate figures but it is clear that numbers are still growing. This year, 2021, we have seen the virus move into poor and heavily populated regions and this will continue to be disastrous for some time. We watch and pray.

---

25 Johns Hopkins University, Coronavirus Resource Centre, https://coronavirus.jhu.edu/map.html

Australia

> *Australia is richly multicultural, and this diversity brings a vibrancy that is hard to match anywhere else in the world. [It is] an inclusive, democratic, pluralist society which seeks to provide opportunity for all who live here; a society in which our achievements may only be limited by the scale of our determination, and the scope of our imagination.*
> – **Dr Mehreen Faruqi**, Greens senator for New South Wales, in her maiden speech to Parliament

On returning to Australia from overseas one time, Neelo and I were chatting to the driver who brought us home from the airport.

'How long have you been here?' he asked.

'Thirty-plus years.'

'Are you happy?'

'Yes, we're really happy here. Why? Are you unhappy?'

He explained that he had come here from Egypt and said many of the same things I have heard from non-natives about Australia being a racist country; that, as a migrant, he is the focus of discrimination; that the Australian government is no good.

'I'm from Pakistan myself. How long have you been here?'

'Twelve years.'

'You've got family and children?'

'Yes.'

'Do you own your house?'

'Yes, with a mortgage.'

'Do you own your car?'

'Yes.'

'Do your children go to a good school?'

'Yes.'

'Do you feel safe here?'

'Yes.'

'Are you persecuted here?'

'No.'

'Do you ever fear for your life?'

'No.'

'Have you sponsored any family members to come here?'

'Yes, two.'

'Have they settled into good lives?'

'Yes.'

'So, do you feel that this is a better place for your children and yourself than Egypt?'

'Yes.'

'It sounds to me that there are many good aspects to your being here. I find it's healthier to focus on those, rather than on the little things that upset you each day.'

I do believe that contentment is a choice, that we can choose to recognise what a wonderful life we can have, regardless of our circumstances.

Most Australians view their country as a successful multicultural society. There is a widespread laissez-faire attitude that we shouldn't get uptight about racism, religious intolerance, bullying, gender inequality, and such. Australians have a tendency to just dust this sort of thing off with an 'It'll be OK, mate'. However, migrants will tell you that racism does indeed exist in Australian society.

> *The levels of racism amongst many white Australians seem to match the levels of denial about their being racist.*
> — **Sisonke Msimang**, author, Head, Storytelling & Training, Centre for Stories, Perth

> *The majority of Australians are not racist per se; however, passivity is a layer of racism, and that should always remain solid in everyone's thinking.*
> — **Gerry Georgatos**, human rights campaigner and investigative journalist

It's almost like our racial discrimination has been hidden under larrikinism.

– **Harry O'Brien**, Collingwood AFL player

Racist comments pass as jokes, but such casual racism hurts. It hurts the subject to whom it is directed. It also eats away at the humanity of the person who says it.

As a family we have always felt that if you do not deal with racism, if you are not part of the solution, then you become part of the problem. My way of dealing with this is to brush off such comments with humour and move on, because if I give them attention, I provide air to the situation and power to the person instigating it. I would rather remain in control and show the other person up for what they are. However, as an adult migrant in a new country, my experience has been quite different to that of my children who have grown up here. The bulk of their lives has been spent in Australia, and they actively call out racism when they see it.

I say these things about Australia, but I know from experience that these problems are not isolated to one country. In our small connected world, what occurs in one country is heard and has the potential to influence countless numbers of people across the globe. That is why it is important that those of us who can lend influence to improve people's lives in any way should do so.

I do worry that the generation who are now 18 or 20 years of age seem to feel quite entitled, more focused on themselves, when compared to previous generations. I see it in Pakistan, Timor-Leste, and Australia. *I deserve more, I deserve better.* Everybody arguably deserves better, but you need to *make* things better for yourself, and not expect everything to be handed to you. I worry that when something does go wrong in their lives, these young people may not possess the skills and tools to cope because they haven't learnt to focus outwards and work hard.

We tell our children that you can get whatever you want if you work hard enough to achieve it. But what if you don't know what you want, or who you wish to be, how can you achieve that? I believe that it is important, early in life, when children are still figuring out who they are, to encourage them to visualise what they want to be later in life. This is similar to the way athletes are trained to visualise hitting that perfect ball or striding past their competitors on the running track. If you visualise the life in front of you, you are more likely to achieve your desired outcome.

If you ask an Australian high school graduate what they want to do, they will more often than not say they'd like to travel, have a gap year, or go to Europe. In developing countries, there's no such thing as a gap year. Just as running water, electricity, health, education, and other amenities are taken for granted in Australia and other developed countries, these things are not always easily available everywhere in the world.

Interestingly, the first thing my brother commented on when he came to Australia from Pakistan was how amazed he was to have seen both the chief minister and the minister's driver shopping in the same supermarket. It was a shock to him that two people with such different positions in society and vastly different incomes could both afford to shop in the same place. This wonderful egalitarianism is a key ingredient of what I love about this country. Most people in Australia have sufficient income to live a decent life, but I am not sure they realise how fortunate they are.

Freedom breeds opportunity and allows the majority of people living in Australia to entertain a variety of different career ideas throughout their lives. Most of us have the luxury of being able to choose. If you are not successful in one career, you can go and do something different in which you may find success. The same goes for anyone, from any cultural or racial background. If you live in a country like Australia, you are, for the most part, the master of your own destiny.

The difference between thinking about who you are and what you want to do and achieving this involves not being afraid of failure and taking the step(s) necessary to effect it. I can say with certainty that I have never been afraid of failure. I have, at times, applied various levels of caution and been judicious in decisions, but I have always been brave enough to continue moving forward. Fortune favours the brave, as they say (although it does no good for my anxiety and stress levels).

On a broader level, there is something about the migrant experience that generates a greater tolerance to risk, and that is sometimes displayed in business. Those of us who have come from Pakistan remember the levels of competition and corruption. My Pakistan has been taken away by power-hungry corrupt politicians over decades; intolerance has grown and the country has gradually shut down. Disillusioned citizens have left, resulting in a major brain drain. Even prime minister Imran Khan regularly talks about the corruption in his country. For example, Pakistan has the least number of taxpayers in the world – fewer than one per cent of the adult population is registered to pay tax.

Many, many migrants come to Australia from difficult environments where opportunities are typically limited, corruption is rife, and safety is not guaranteed. When they come to a country like Australia, where there is almost no day-to-day petty corruption, they see that opportunities abound. They even find government training programs that pay their wages on behalf of their employer. These migrants can apply for assistance to start a business or buy a house, opportunities that do not exist in their own country.

It is up to all of us to find our own path to success, regardless of our religion, colour, or any other trait or circumstance. Some people get that 'light-bulb' moment, realise their place and potential in society, and go for it. Others procrastinate and complain. While it is never easy, we each need to discover how to believe in ourselves, and to declare, 'I will see this through!'

It is worth striving for.

It has taken many years for things to start to stabilise in Timor-Leste. For the 18 years I lived there, before moving to Sydney, I lived in the same house, drove the same car, and lived the same lifestyle as I had had in Australia. We have lived carefully, and Timor-Leste has treated us well. I am fortunate to have had the opportunity to develop our business in Timor-Leste and, in the process, to help develop the lives of the people who work with us, and to contribute to the economy, the country, and the social scene.

Neelo and I didn't have a son, but we are blessed with three girls. Long before Timor was on our radar, we had decided that if we ever had a son, we would name him *Temur*, after the Mughal Emperor, Temür Khan (1265-1307). While that never happened, we were introduced to Timor, where we have many sons and daughters. Timor has given us the capacity and the opportunity to contribute wonderful things, and in turn, we have lived a full and rewarding life.

I left a part of me in Timor-Leste and I am learning to cope with that. I still need to remind myself that I retired for a reason. I take medication for my anxiety and, all in all, I have been fine since retiring, although my doctors tell me to travel only to places where I know I can receive immediate heart surgery, if required, as I did in Pakistan and France recently. Sadly, Timor-Leste does not qualify – not yet.

In thinking back on my life now, filled with achievements and sprinkled with failures, the many things that I am eternally grateful for and those things I inevitably wish I could do over, my thoughts return to that pivotal moment in time, all those years ago – yesterday – when my father's wisdom irrevocably changed the direction of my life.

I was drifting and he made me a deal: a shiny, red, top-of-the-line motorcycle if I came to work for him. Only then did I glimpse where my talents lay. That motorcycle, that opportunity, sped me down a new path, one where all things seemed possible. That my father knew what would motivate me caused a trickle-down effect through my life. It gave me the right attitude to support my future wife and family, and to build a business that provides hundreds of people and their extended families with a better life.

Life is good.
Thank you, Abba Jee.

Appendices

Names – family and friends

Abba Jee	my father, Nabi Dad Khan Awan
Ahsan (Guddu) Awan	one of my brothers
Ammie	my mother, Ismat Jehan Awan
Hugh & Sue Bradley	Darwin friends
Ismat Jehan Awan	see Ammie
Ismat	my youngest daughter
José Ramos-Horta, H.E.	Nobel Laureate and former President and Prime Minister of Timor-Leste
Mari Alkatiri, H.E.	former Prime Minister of Timor-Leste
Mrs Mirza or *Nanoo*	my mother-in-law
Mrs Norma Grant	family friend from Darwin
Mujahid Hamid	my friend and mentor from Pakistan
Nabi Dad Khan Awan	see Abba Jee
Nazar (Shaan) Awan	one of my brothers
Neelofer (Neelo)	my wife
Peter Anderson	our business consultant in Darwin
Peter Berney	our first staffmember in Timor-Leste
Rayeed	my son-in-law; married to my daughter, Saba
Saba	my middle daughter
Sam	my son-in-law; married to my daughter, Zeenat, and CEO of East Timor Trading
Shane L. Stone	past Chief Minister of the Northern Territory
Tahir (*Bhai*) Memon	family friend
Taj Mirza, Dr	my father-in-law
Tim Hargreaves	family friend
Waris Awan	my elder brother
Xanana Gusmão, H.E.	former President and Prime Minister of Timor-Leste
Zeenat	my eldest daughter

A handful of staff with whom I worked closely at East Timor Trading Group

Ally Alianca	Front Office, Discovery Inn
Celena Soarez	Government Relations Coordinator
Eligio Pereira	Company Auditor
Elvis Pereira	Warehouse Manager
Jenna Poblete	Retail Area Manager
Lucio Alves	Delivery Driver
Marcea Exposto	Duty Manager, Discovery Inn
Marcelino (Lino) Sarmento	Sales and Marketing Manager
Maricel Deloso	General Manager, Supply Chain
Nina Poblete	General Manager of HR and Corporate Affairs
Norlyn Miso Ngo	Hospitality Division, Demand Planner
Pedro Gomes	Warehouse Coordinator
Reinato De Araujo	Regional Sales Manager
Ryan Ilham Saputra	Innkeeper, Discovery Inn

Staff Stories

Marcelino (Lino) Sarmento
Sales and marketing manager

I was born west of Díli in Same, in Manufahi district. I am 47 and have two boys, 12 and 14 years old.

I began working for Mr Awan on 1 July 2002. My manager originally was Peter Berney and I helped him on his rounds to shops and promoting products. I have had various roles at East Timor Trading Group, and am now sales & marketing manager. I learnt English on the job and have built relationships throughout the city and country.

I met Mr Awan when I was working for his sub-distributor, selling products like Benson & Hedges, Dunhill, and Winfield, when UNTAET was still here. Mr Awan said, 'If there's anyone looking for a job, come and follow me'. Since then, Mr Awan has done so much to help the Timorese learn skills and work honestly. I love working here because Mr Awan is very human and cares for everybody. I am very lucky to have him as a boss.

I have learnt many things about how to do my job by watching movies and reading magazines. When people say, 'This product is good,' I say back to them, 'Yes, it's very good'.

In the early days, I used to work in the districts, but now I focus completely on Díli. It wasn't really worth my while going there back then, because it took days due to the poor roads. Some district roads are still dangerous because of landslides, but they are improving. If I get stuck in the districts, it stops money coming in from my city accounts, so that's not good for business.

I am always focused on where I can sell the most and get the best income. I also know which shops don't pay their bills, and so I have to decide what we can sell to them. I tell them that if they don't pay their bills, the boss will be unhappy with me, so I have learnt to sell only to honest people. Some say they will pay in 10 or 12 days, and then they don't pay. That's not good for me. I want to be able to be honest with myself and with my boss, so I say to them that they have to pay their bills when they are due. I also want to have a good relationship of trust with my customers.

Mr Awan doesn't tell you what to do; he nurtures you and gives you good advice to help you learn on the job. I have had experience taking orders, doing sales, and with wide experience we can grow the company and employ more people, which is good for the country.

East Timor Trading Group has given me a wonderful career, and I feel that I know so much about what other parts of the world are like because of the products I sell.

Reinato de Araujo
Regional sales manager

I am 43 years old, was born in Díli on Christmas Eve, 1976.

In my early jobs, I was a taxi driver, and then, in 1999, I worked as one of the polling staff in the UN mission for the election. My life in those days was very difficult financially. I was looking for a good job, but it was hard.

The culture in Timor-Leste is that when people have a party, everyone in your family sits together, but because I had no job and no income, some of my family said, 'You have no money. You can't sit here, Reinato.' It was a very sad time for me.

I started working for Mr Awan in December 2006 as a driver delivering to shops in Díli and to 12 districts around the country. It was very hard work in those days, because the roads were terrible, but I saw that the work could change my life, which it did. After I started this job, my family began to say, 'Don't forget to invite Senhor Reinato'.

At first, I didn't know how to use a computer, so Mr Awan sent me on a course. With those skills I began working at Obrigado Barracks as a cashier in the canteen, followed by the Heliport shop [the Australian troops compound], and then at Gloria Jean's Timor Plaza, when it opened in 2012.

My life now is good. I have three boys and four girls. Four of them, 16, 14, and 10-year-old twins, are at school. The others are still small.

My favourite part of the job is visiting the shops. I love communicating with my customers. I feel like I get the same respect as the big boss, and that makes me very happy. Some of my friends ask why I don't go to Australia or somewhere, but if I can earn money living in Timor-Leste, then I'm much happier, because all of my family are here.

Ryan Ilham Saputra
Discovery Inn, innkeeper

I am originally from East Java. While living there I did a short course in hospitality and got a job as a marketing manager in Bali, and that's when I met Mr Awan. My first job at the Discovery Inn began on 17 February 2007. I was duty manager, and from there I became innkeeper.

I love meeting people from all over the world and also marketing the business. The staff in the hotel are wonderful but coordinating the shifts is the most challenging part of my role.

The task for the government is to work out how to bring more people here. Tourism is only one per cent of the economy at the moment, which is a test for me as innkeeper. Most people come for business and we're lucky to have contracts with NGOs and organisations like the World Bank. The government needs to develop tourism, along with the roads and airlines, to make access easier and air tickets cheaper.

There is a new national hotel association that will work with the government to promote tourism and encourage more traffic. To assist this promotion, we attend hospitality exhibitions in the region to introduce Timor-Leste to the world. Most people don't know anything about the country, so our objective is to improve awareness.

Marcea Exposto
Discovery Inn, duty manager

I began working for Mr Awan in 2005 at the UN's PX Obrigado, in early support services, making pizza and sandwiches in the café, and as a cashier, and then in the supermarket. When Discovery Inn opened in 2007, I moved there. Mr Ryan and I set up everything here at the hotel.

I began as supervisor, then became Diya Restaurant's manager, and now I am duty manager.

Originally, I wanted to study international relations, because I wanted to become an ambassador, but after working in hotels, I changed my mind and Mr Awan gave me time off to complete a bachelor of business degree in hotel management at the Díli Institute of Technology, which I completed in four years.

I'm so very happy here because Mr Awan is more like family than a boss to us all.

Before I joined East Timor Trading Group, I could only speak simple greetings in English, but Mr Awan wasn't worried about that; he said I would practise and learn on the job.

Because we are a small hotel, we are trained in all areas, so if a staff member cannot come to work, the rest of us can do their job – it is not like a rigid job, where you do only one thing.

I have four sisters and two brothers, and I work to help support all of my family in Timor-Leste. My eldest sister lives in Darwin and my mother is an optical nurse at the Díli hospital.

Ally Alianca
Discovery Inn, front office

I was born in Baucau [Timor-Leste] and moved to Díli in 2000 when I was studying biology at university, but I stopped after five semesters because I support my brother and sisters and needed to earn more. I can study again later.

I started working for Mr Awan first at PX Obrigado in 2006, and then at Discovery Inn from 2008. East Timor Trading Group looks after us all very well, and since I began at the hotel, I have worked in many different roles.

I most enjoy reception and the front office because I get to meet and look after guests from all over the world. I have learnt most of my English since working here.

What the country needs is more tourists, so when I meet foreign people, I always promote my country and ask them to send more people to see our traditional culture and our beautiful mountains, lakes, waterfalls, and areas that no one publicises much yet.

It's important that the government promote the country more and also teach staff at the airport and in taxis how to treat visitors. They say, 'This is good', 'That is good', but they need hotel training to better sell the activities and sites available here to visitors. I always tell young people to study overseas and promote our country to the people they meet.

The staff at the hotel are all very caring, and Mr Awan has taught us how to look after customers very well. Our regular customers say they like to stay here because it feels like home.

Pedro Gomes
Warehouse coordinator

Before working for East Timor Trading Group, I had casual employment at the Delta Café. As a father of three, to be given a job in a growing business was very important to me. I began working as a casual security person at Mr Awan's house in 2002, when the warehouse containers were in the back garden. When East Timor Trading Group moved to the new premises, I became a casual in the warehouse and became permanent, bonded warehouse help in 2007. I am now warehouse coordinator.

This is a much more varied job and complex to manage because of the large number of different items. I start work at 8am and finish at 6pm, and my main role is to check and sign the invoices and to organise the packing of the trucks ready to leave for the retailers and wholesalers.

Before I started, I couldn't speak English at all; now I have quite a bit more, and have learnt to use the computer system to create picking and packing slips, so we can get the stock from the warehouse. I like using the computers, and these skills allow me to improve my prospects for the future.

Lucio Alves
Delivery driver

I was originally from Maubisse [Timor-Leste] and moved to Díli in 2001. I now have two children, a girl who is four and a boy who is three.

I am one of the company's longest serving staff, having begun working for East Timor Trading Group in 2002 as a security guard at the Awans' house in Farol, when we had five containers in the garden. I was doing general things like washing cars, cleaning, and security, before I moved to Obrigado Barracks, and then to East Timor Trading Group as a delivery driver.

I help take orders around Díli with Lino in the mornings until 1pm, and then deliver the orders in my car for two to three hours each afternoon. I usually go home at 6pm, so it's a 10-hour day. (Of course, I get overtime.) I have developed relationships with all the shops I deliver to, so I look after them.

What I like most about East Timor Trading Group is that they look after us and it is a safe job. I don't like computers and prefer to remain as a driver, tending our relationships with the shops.

I'd like to thank Mr Awan, Madam Neelo, and Mr Sam, for helping us in this company, because there is a good future for us here. Mr Awan is like a father to me.

Elvis Pereira
Logistics manager

I began working for East Timor Trading Group in November 2004 as an assistant in the warehouse on the main site. I would take the stock to PX Maliana and help in the airport duty-free shop as a cashier. In the warehouse I learnt to use a forklift and, in 2012, was one of the first Timorese to become warehouse supervisor, looking after stock control and shipping.

What I love about working here is that it's like my second family. It's good because the company is growing. When I started there were only two international employees and half a dozen Timorese. Now, there are almost 300 people. What I like most about my job is the contact with the customers and speaking to people.

Timor-Leste feels good now. I have a good job, and can also focus on my accounting study, which I do in my free time.

When I started working here, I was often late to work, so Mr Awan gave me an alarm clock. I used it, and for a while I arrived on time, but three to six months later, I started to be late again. So, Mr Awan bought me a push bike, so I could get to work on time. Then, after that, he bought me a motorbike.

Because of my job here, my four brothers and six sisters can continue their education. One of my brothers, who was 11 when I began here, has now finished university because I was able to pay for his education. It means a lot to me that I can help my family.

Eligio Pereira
Auditor

I am from Lospalos in the east of the country, and have three brothers and two sisters.

I had worked as an auditor before starting at East Timor Trading Group as a cashier on 20 August 2007. I realised this company would have a good future for me and my family, because as the country grew, it would need more imports.

I became chief cashier in 2014 and remained there until 2017, when I moved to the audit department. Since then, I've trained in MYOB and am now the company-wide auditor. I learnt accounting at the Institute of Business in Díli, and East Timor Trading Group paid my study fees because it would help me do my job well. As an auditor, I got to see the profit and loss sheets, so I saw that the company was financially strong.

East Timor Trading Group has given me and all the staff such a good future, not only because of the money but also through the experience and the education we've received.

Mr Awan supported me when my father died and helped with my brother's children's school fees - he said that as long as my brother sent the receipt, they would not ask the money to be repaid. My job here has also meant that I can pay for my brother to study IT in Indonesia, and for my younger sister to study at university.

So, the benefits of working here pass on to my family and I always try to be hard working because Mr Awan treats us so well. It is a tradition in Timor-Leste to support your brothers and sisters for life, and friends. This makes us a very strong community - we have very human-based thinking. Mr Awan is the same - he always asks how you and your family are. Most bosses never ask how your family is. In the future, I would like to become one of the local senior managers.

Nina Poblete
General manager, HR and corporate affairs

In 2006, my aunt was working as a hotel manager in Díli when she met Mr Awan and mentioned that I was looking for a job in auditing if he had any positions available. I was working as an internal auditor in the Philippines at the time but was keen to work overseas somewhere. I was lucky because a position was available in the audit department, so I moved to Timor-Leste in August 2006. Not long after that, in September 2006, my best friend, Norlyn Ngo, moved to Timor-Leste also.

Mr Sakib first gave me a job in auditing because of my experience, and from there he offered me the job of running PX Obrigado with its supermarket and café, which I did until March 2007. Late in 2007, Mr Awan opened the Discovery Inn and gave me the job of assistant innkeeper, which was a complete change of role for me. Now, I am the general manager of HR and corporate affairs.

The main thing I like about East Timor Trading Group is that it is a family. I feel connected, and that I belong here. Mr Awan believed in me and trusted that I could do the jobs he gave me, even when I felt I couldn't.

Now, Timor-Leste is a safe country, and at East Timor Trading Group there are always good opportunities for employees to move through the business and be promoted to new roles.

Jenna Poblete
General manager, retail and hospitality

I started working at East Timor Trading Group in January 2011. Nina Poblete, the general manager of HR and corporate affairs, is my aunt, and I asked her if she could introduce me to Mr Awan in case any jobs were available. The job of staff controller at PX Obrigado was available, so Mr Awan interviewed me and I got the job. When Mr Awan decided to open Gloria Jean's in 2012, he moved me there as a supervisor, and eventually I became the manager of Gloria Jean's. I have been area manager for all retail outlets, which includes Cheers, Il Gelato, and Gloria Jean's. Then in late 2019, I was promoted to general manager, retail and hospitality, which added Discovery Inn, Burger King, and other retail outlets to my responsibilities.

What I like most in my role is that the work provides challenges every day, because in operations it's not simple; there are always HR challenges, particularly because we are training Timorese staff to move into management positions. We now have one outlet run and managed 100 per cent by Timorese staff. We are also in a period of strategic change to ensure we remain profitable and grow our businesses. One of the biggest challenges is keeping track of the costs and making my budget targets, while maintaining high standards.

Timor-Leste has changed my life because when I arrived, it was totally undeveloped, but now it is a growing country. I love the work because I enjoy all the people around me – we are all family. We really miss Mr and Mrs Awan so much now that they have left Timor-Leste.

Celena Soarez
Government relations coordinator

I was born in Díli, but my father is from Atauro Island and mother from Baucau. I have four children, all boys. It was my husband who introduced me to East Timor Trading Group when he worked as a Tetum language teacher for Madam Neelo. I asked my husband to give her my CV because I had experience working as a waitress at a restaurant in Díli called Restora.

On 27 September 2010, I had an interview with Mr Awan and was given a job as a cashier in the Obrigado Barracks. I had studied before starting work here, and even though I didn't have the right experience, Mr Awan said that if I worked with my heart and my mind and with passion, then I would learn. I soon moved to the airport duty-free shop as cashier. A year later, my manager resigned and Mr Awan came to see me on his way to Darwin and said, 'Congratulations! You will be the new duty-free shop supervisor.'

It was a big surprise, and it was very unexpected to receive this news from the big boss, rather than from my direct manager. Mr Awan is like a father to me and treats us all with great respect.

I am now government relations coordinator in the HR department. Every day is a challenge and I often meet with high-level people in the government, so it is a huge transformation for me, after starting in the duty-free shop. I am also studying electrical engineering at the National University of Timor-Leste. I hope the company continues to grow because the company family is like a model for us.

Norlyn Miso Ngo
Demand planner, hospitality

I am Filipino by birth and came to East Timor in September 2006 because a friend of mine, Nina Poblete, was working for Mr Awan. She was initially very unhappy alone in the country, so Mr Awan asked her what would make her happy. She told him that if she had a friend here, it would be better. She contacted me, I spoke to Mr Awan, and he offered me a job.

My first job was in the purchasing department. Then I moved to the PX Obrigado, and later to the heliport. I held a couple of other roles, and then, when Gloria Jean's at Timor Plaza was opening, Mr Awan asked me to recommend staff. I worked there for a while, until after a few months we opened Il Gelato, and then Makanan.

The following year Mr Awan surprised us with the Burger King franchise. I was sent to the Philippines for training while Mr Sam trained in Sydney, and in December 2013 I started at the new franchise.

I am now demand planner for the hospitality division in the company's head office, which means I operate across the whole hospitality division – Gloria Jean's, Burger King, Makanan, and Discovery Inn.

When I came here, I hoped to find well-paying work so I could support my mum and pay for her dialysis treatment, which I have done. Because we are far away from our families, Mr Awan looks after us. A few of us were invited to the wedding of his first daughter, in Australia. Mr Awan gives you big responsibilities, but he is 100 per cent there to support you.

Many of us call Mr Awan 'Daddy Boss' because he and Madam Neelo treat us like a family, with the personal touch. Because of that, I treat his company like mine, because we want the best for us all.

www.ingramcontent.com/pod-product-compliance
Lightning Source LLC
Chambersburg PA
CBHW070249010526
44107CB00056B/2398